VISIONS OF ROSES

VISIONS OF ROSES

Text by
PETER BEALES
photographs by
VIVIAN RUSSELL

A BULFINCH PRESS BOOK
LITTLE, BROWN AND COMPANY
Boston   New York   Toronto   London

First Edition

ISBN 0-8212-2318-6
Library of Congress Catalog Card Number 95-82124
A CIP catalogue for this book is available from the British Library

Designed by David Fordham

Published simultaneously in the United States of America
by Bulfinch Press, an imprint and trademark of
Little, Brown and Company (Inc.),
in Great Britain by Little, Brown and Company (UK)
and in Canada by Little, Brown & Company (Canada) Limited

PRINTED AND BOUND IN ITALY

Acknowledgements

The Author

I am indebted to all the owners and administrators of the gardens featured in this book and wish to express heartfelt thanks to each of them. I hope it is not presumptuous to feel that I have also widened my circle of friends. My knowledge of roses and rose gardening is considerably enhanced as a result of visiting their gardens. Speaking of friends, warmest thanks are due to Bill Grant for giving me the freedom of his home and without whom it would have been impossible to visit the gardens of California in the time available, and to Elena and Ezio Pizzi for not only putting me up but whisking me around Italy. Thanks to David Howard of Howard and Kooij's Nurseries for his help in identifying some of the herbaceous plants. The chart on pages 18–19 is based on one originally designed by Amanda Beales.

Travelling and writing are time-consuming and could not happen without the understanding of a supportive family: my wife Joan whose generous hours on the word processor I dare not add up and who so unselfishly allowed me to take the credit; my daughter Amanda and grandchildren who allowed me uninterrupted space; and Richard, my son, who broke both distance and speed records in driving me around France. Thanks to my fellow directors and staff for carrying on without me, especially Ian Limmer, for running the nursery through the worst drought in its history, and Jan Kemp, office manager and PA, for proving that my presence is not really needed for the place to run smoothly. Then there are those at Little, Brown: in particular Vivien Bowler, for patiently supporting and nursing me through a bad patch, Mari Roberts and Penny David for their sensitivity of interpretation, and David Fordham for his superb design. Finally, Vivian Russell – thank you, Vivian; without your camera artistry this would be a very dull book indeed.

The Photographer

In addition to all the gardeners who gave me permission to photograph their gardens, I would like to thank most particularly three people whose gardens aren't in this book: Bill Grant, Elena Pizzi and Ngaere Macray.

Bill Grant, the Master Networker, took me personally to all the California gardens as well as introducing me to his friends Elena and Ezio Pizzi in Rome, and Suzanne Verrier in Maine. Suzanne took me to the two other Maine gardens. Thanks to Elena's hospitality and her command of the Italian language and road, we not only managed to find the gardens, but survived to tell the tale. My thanks to Maria Giulia Cimarelli for suggesting the Cetinale garden, then unknown to me. I would also like to thank Erica Hunningher for putting me in touch with Ngaere Macray from Saga Press who very generously gave me all the contacts for the Long Island gardens. A book like this owes its life to people like these and I am most grateful to them.

The rose portraits on pages 24, 33, 36, 38, 42, 47, 53, 56, 59, 62, 68, 70, 75, 82, 87, 89, 94, 98, 100, 102, 109, 116, 117, 122, 134, 136, 140, 143, 147, 148, 150, 154, 158, 159, 166, 171, 175, 176, 181, 182, 190, 192, 196 and 204 were supplied by Peter Beales. Peter and Joan Beales have done more than anyone else to spread the love of old roses and make them available to everyone. Without them, this book would not exist.

USEFUL ADDRESSES

WORLD FEDERATION OF ROSE SOCIETIES

These associations may be approached directly for details of local rose gardens open to the public. The World Federation of Rose Societies is at 46 Alexandra Road, St Albans, Hertfordshire AL1 3AZ, United Kingdom.

BERMUDA
Bermuda Rose Society
PO Box 162
Paget PG BX

CANADA
Canadian Rose Society
10 Fairfax Crescent
Scarborough
Ontario MIL 1Z8

DENMARK
Det Danske Rosenselskab
c/o Peter Jordt, President
Kirkedalsvej 63
Rárup
DK 7130 Juelsminde

FRANCE
Société Française des Roses
6 rue J.B Couty
69009 Lyon

GERMANY
Verein Deutscher Rosenfreunde
Waldseestrasse 14
D-76530 Baden-Baden

GREAT BRITAIN
Royal National Rose Society
Chiswell Green
St Albans
Hertfordshire
AL2 3NR

INDIA
Indian Rose Federation
852 Napier Town
Jabalpur 482 001 (MP)

ISRAEL
Wohl Rose Park
PO Box 10185
91101 Jerusalem

ITALY
Associazione Italiana della Rosa
Roseto Niso Fumagalli
Villa Reale
20052 Monza (MI)

JAPAN
Japan Rose Society
3-9-5 Oyamadai
Setagaya-ku
Tokyo 158

LUXEMBOURG
Letzeburger Rousefrenn
51 Avenue du 10 Septembre
L–2551

NETHERLANDS
Nederlandse Rozenvereniging
Stadskwekerij Den Haag
Kwekerijweg 8A
2597 JK Den Haag

NEW ZEALAND
National Rose Society of
New Zealand
PO Box 66
Bunnythorpe

NORTHERN IRELAND
Rose Society of Northern Ireland
c/o Mr R Brooks
10 Eastleigh Drive
Belfast BT4 3DX

NORWAY
Norwegian Rose Society
Smiuvn 8
N–0982 Oslo

PAKISTAN
Pakistan National Rose Society
36 Nazimddin Road F–7/1
Islamabad

POLAND
Polish Society of Rose Fanciers
ul. Broniewskiego 19/7
01–780 Warszawa

ROMANIA
Asociatia Amicii Rozelor
din Romana
c/o Adriana Florincescu
Univ. Stiinte Agricole (University of
   Agricultural Sciences)
Manastur Str 3
RO–3400 Cluj–Napoca

SOUTH AFRICA
Federation of Rose Societies
of South Africa
c/o Ludwig Taschner, President
PO Box 28188
Sunnyside 0132, RSA

SPAIN
Asociacion Espanola de la Rose
Rosaleda Ramon Ortiz
Parque del Oeste
28008 Madrid

SWEDEN
Svenska Rosensällskapet/Swedish
   Rose Society
c/o Gunnar Ståhl, President
Martinvägen 33
S–161 55 Bromma

SWITZERLAND
Gesellschaft Schweizerischer
Rosenfreunde
c/o Hans Rathgeb
PO Box 1274
CH–8640 Rapperswil

URUGUAY
Asociación Uruguaya de la Rosa
Cavia 3099
11300 Montevideo

USA
American Rose Society
PO Box 30000
Shreveport
LA 71130–0030

ZIMBABWE
Rose Society of Zimbabwe
PO Box 366
Highlands
Harare

A CELEBRATION OF OLD ROSES

A video, written, narrated and presented by Peter Beales and directed by Vivian Russell, is available from the address below.
Please enquire about cost including postage and packing.
Vivian Russell Inc. Ltd, Coombe Cottage, Borrowdale, Keswick, Cumbria CA12 5UY

PETER BEALES ROSES

Peter Beales's roses catalogue is available from: Peter Beales Roses, London Road, Attleborough, Norfolk NR17 1AY

Photograph on the previous two pages: *the Rose Garden at Nymans with its early twentieth-century ramblers and scramblers over arches and pillars;* photograph on the following two pages: *grapevines and roses in the gardens of Villa Cetinale.*

CONTENTS

FOREWORD

The distinctive blooms of the beautiful early-flowering climbing Hybrid Tea 'Mme Grégoire Staechelin'. This rose is also known as 'Spanish Beauty'.

The delicate ivory shell-like petals of the modern shrub rose 'Jacqueline du Pré' unfold in characteristic fashion.

ET'S DO A BOOK ABOUT ROSE GARDENS,' ONE OF US SAID. 'Not just a list of those open to the public with scant detail, but a fairly in-depth appraisal of a selected few. A book that gives an appreciation of their setting and content, some background on their creators or custodians and any other perspective which might be appropriate as seen by a rosegrower.' It seemed like a good idea at the time, but none of us – Vivian, myself or our publishers – knew quite what we were letting ourselves in for.

Why should this book have different problems from any other book covering thirty-three gardens? In the first place, gardens as a whole usually have something happening in them at any time of year, whereas roses – whatever the role they play in the landscape – are best photographed during their peak flowering season, which usually lasts only about three weeks, at the most, each year. Secondly, some of the gardens in this book are thousands of miles apart. Then there is that everyday enemy of photographers, the weather, which is not only unpredictable but, more often than not, downright uncooperative. Such problems were mostly Vivian's for she went on ahead of me and, by so doing, was free to interpret the gardens with a photographer's eye; in fact, none of the gardens was visited by us together. As for me, well, I confess that several of my visits were out of season, for there was no other way. Peak rose season is my busiest time of year. However, with a few years of experience behind me, I need not necessarily see a rose garden in full bloom to know what it can be like at its best.

We started with a list and a plan, of course, but, like all good lists and plans, these soon had to be amended. Some gardens we had meant to include were simply not geographically possible within the given time, so others, equally interesting, were added as we went along. As it was, the photographs were taken over a period of two seasons.

It was never our intention to include gardens already well documented. Rather we sought a mix of the better-known but unsung, and the unknown deserving of acclamation. Without exception we chose the sort of gardens that Vivian and myself enjoy – not too many serried ranks or formal beds of bright Hybrid Teas or Floribundas. Not that we have anything against these; simply, they do not fit easily into our sort of landscape.

Much as it would have been desirable, it was not possible to venture into the Southern Hemisphere or to the Far East, even though we knew of good gardens in those regions. Instead, we concentrated on Great Britain, France, Italy and America. We originally hoped to cover thirty gardens but lost count and have ended up with thirty-three.

Having consciously decided not to include the famous, we also felt that we could not do justice in a book such as this to major collections. Our definition of 'a collection' is where this is the main purpose of a garden's existence – as opposed to gardens created for their intrinsic pleasure (which may be for the benefit of their creators only, or for rose-lovers generally). In fact, some of the gardens we cover *contain* a collection; these are included because they fall naturally into the latter category – their collections are organized to give pleasure rather than simply as documentation. Rose devotees who own collections will perhaps consider our criteria a little harsh and, as a committed rose collector myself, I understand that point of view. I also appreciate that the line between a rose collection and a landscaped garden with roses is a vague one. However, we had to draw that line somewhere, and the thirty-three gardens included in the book are selected according to personal, subjective criteria. I would, however, like to mention here some of those gardens which we have not included – because they fall into the 'collection' category, because they are already well known and well documented, or because time, distance and the limited space available did not allow us to fit them in.

The brightly coloured, fully open flower of the modern shrub 'Cerise Bouquet' shows clearly its beautiful, old-fashioned form.

OTHER GARDENS TO VISIT

 N GREAT BRITAIN THESE INCLUDE THE GARDENS OF THE Rose at Chiswell Green, St Albans, the headquarters of the Royal National Rose Society. This is one of the world's most important gardens and plans are advanced to enlarge it over the next few years. The National Trust has a number of very good rose gardens in its care, one of which, Nymans in Sussex, is included. Besides this there are also the famous garden of the late Vita Sackville-West at Sissinghurst Castle, Kent, the wonderful one designed by Graham Thomas at Mottisfont Abbey in Hampshire, in the care of Head Gardener David Stone, and a fine one at Hidcote Manor, Gloucestershire. Also in Gloucestershire, very near Hidcote in fact, is Mrs Binney's Kiftsgate Court, famous for its massive *R. filipes* hybrid of the same name. At Wells, Somerset, is the fairly new but fascinating 'Time Trail of Roses', half an acre of rose history put together by Susan Lee. Roses also play a prominent part in the two gardens of the Royal Horticultural Society, one at Wisley, Surrey, and the other at Rosemoor, Great Torrington, Devon. In the north of England, too, there is a number of good rose gardens, the two most famous being those at Castle Howard, Yorkshire, built up under the direction of James Russell during the late 1970s and '80s, and those at Harlow Carr, Harrogate (also in Yorkshire), the Headquarters of the North of England Horticultural Society. Within the rose trade both David Austin's gardens at Wolverhampton and mine at Attleborough, Norfolk, are well worth a visit. Across

Mimicking a weeping willow is Rosa filipes 'Kiftsgate', drooping gracefully towards the waters of the moat. The hips of this very vigorous rose provide colour here in Plumpton Place gardens well into winter (following pages).

Several Hybrid Perpetuals, the predecessors of the modern Hybrid Teas, have come down to us today from their heyday, the Victorian era. This red is one of the most famous of them all: 'Général Jacqueminot'.

the Irish Sea the Emerald Isle is blessed with several good rose gardens, including St Anne's Park, Dublin, Lady Dixon Park, Belfast and Rowallane Gardens, County Down. Scotland has its own National Trust and several fine rose gardens are under its auspices – Drum Castle in Banchory, Culzean Castle, Ayr, and Mallerney House in Edinburgh among them. There is also a good rose collection in Edinburgh Botanic Gardens.

Four of the lovely rose gardens of France are included, but no book on this subject would be complete without acclamation of four others – Roseraie de l'Hay and Bagatelle in Paris, the Tête d'Or at Lyons and Floral de la Source in Orléans. The fact that there are no German gardens in this book is a matter of personal regret, but circumstances conspired against them, with two consecutive early-flowering seasons rendering them difficult to photograph. Sangerhausen, for example, which has the world's largest (and one of the oldest) collection of roses is vital for the conservation of many historic varieties. There are also fine rosariums in some of Germany's parks, including those at Karlsruhe, Uetersen, Dortmund and Kassel, not to mention the lifetime's work of the private collection of Dr Grimm, also at Kassel. In Italy there is an ever-increasing interest in classic roses, and rose gardens flourish in lots of public parks. Near Rome, at Cavriglia D'Arezzo, is the impressive lifetime's work of the famous Professor Fineschi, and Maria Giulia Cimarelli is just starting an important garden at Florence. In Belgium, among others is the lovely Rose Garden of the Comtesse D'Ursel at the Château de Hex and a fine Rosarium at Genk. In fact, all over Europe – from Gothenburg in Sweden to the Parc de la Grange in Geneva, Switzerland, from the Westbroekpark Rosarium, The Hague, Holland to the Parque del Oeste, Madrid, Spain – public rose gardens abound. There is also a beautiful rose garden in Israel, called the Wohl Rose Park, in front of the Knesset in Jerusalem.

In the United States of America the awareness of Heritage Roses is, nowadays, reflected in the many rose gardens devoted to them around the country. Eight in particular I must mention briefly, for each is significant in its own way. In New York the Cranford Rose Garden, part of Brooklyn Botanic Gardens, is an oasis of roses in the centre of Brooklyn, sociologically important in that many of its ethnic groups rub shoulders while enjoying the roses. The design of this garden has not been changed since it was first laid out in the mid-1920s and has one of the few remaining collections of roses from between the wars. It is admirably looked after by resident Rosarian Stephen Scanniello. Also in the north-east is Nashua, New Hampshire, where Mike Lowe has a garden full of old roses. These are important not just for being a fine collection but for the fact that many of the plants are growing on their own roots, a means of propagation in which Mike specializes. Over on the West Coast at Pasadena, California, is the Huntingdon Botanic Gardens, where Rosarian Clair Martin III has built up a large collection of Teas and Chinas – roses that really enjoy the temperate climate there, and well worth seeing. A little way north of Pasadena are the gardens of 'Roses of Yesterday and Today' – among the pioneers, it is sometimes forgotten, in the import and distribution of old roses from Europe in America. Yet farther North, in Oregon, John and Louise Clemments of Heirloom Roses have developed a magnificent display garden around their flourishing rose nursery; like Mike Lowe, they too produce all their roses on their own roots, budded roses being prone to viruses in America. Over in Texas is a large and interesting display garden at the 'Antique Rose Emporium' near Brenham, again alongside an 'own-root' rose nursery run by Mike and Jean Shoup. East from Texas is the Heritage Rose Garden of Malcolm Manners at the Citrus Institute, Lakeland, Florida. Over recent years, Malcolm has been specializing in the identification and eradication of rose viruses, so this too is an important collection. The American Rose Society has its Headquarters at Shreveport, Louisiana, where they have an extensive and interesting garden of both old and modern varieties. Offshore, in the Atlantic, the island of Bermuda has several excellent private rose gardens owned by members of the Bermuda Rose Society. This society also maintains a delightful rose garden which includes all the special 'Bermuda' roses at Camden House near Hamilton.

Then, of course, there are the Antipodean gardens. Whenever I have visited Australia and New Zealand the many rose devotees of those two countries have always made me feel very welcome. In Adelaide, South Australia, is the extensive display garden of 'Ross Roses', built up by the late Dean Ross and his wife Maureen, who now runs the business. Two hundred miles or so north of Adelaide on the banks of the Murray river, just outside the town of Renmark, is David Ruston's famous Rose Garden, which is not only a valuable source of propagation material for rare and unusual roses, but also beautifully laid out and maintained. I visited the garden in 1985 and the somewhat stressful twenty-four-hour bus ride afterwards to Sydney, *en route* to New Zealand, did nothing to dispel the pleasant memories of that place. There are many other good rose gardens, both private and public, in Australia.

The New Zealand climate is ideal for roses and as a result there are probably more rose lovers in that country per head of population than anywhere in the world, and certainly more rose gardens per square mile in the populated areas than anywhere else I know. One, overlooking the views of Canterbury Plain, is that of Sally Allison, an active member of the New Zealand Heritage Rose Group. Sally has a particularly fine lot of climbers and ramblers. Trevor Griffiths has another at his nursery at Timaru, full of rarities and species. Trevor is one of the pioneers in the renaissance of old roses in the world, with several excellent books on the subject to his credit. Another nursery specializing in Heritage Roses a little farther north on South Island at Nelson is 'Tasman Bay Roses', which belongs to Nigel and Judy Pratt, whose son Ben spent some time working with us at our nursery here in England. They, too, have a superb collection in a well-laid-out display garden. In the North Island at Auckland are the public Parnell Rose Gardens, the gardens of 'Bells Roses' and the delightful private garden of Toni Sylvester, a past president of Historic Roses, New Zealand; as well as a wealth of others.

The thirty-three gardens in this book, diverse as they are in style and content, represent the hundreds of rose gardens in the world and the thousands more where roses play an important part in the landscape. The one thing that has come through to me most of all in writing this book is the incredible versatility of the genus *Rosa*.

An unusual study of Bourbon rose 'Mme Alfred Carrière'. This is one of the most useful roses to have been raised during the Victorian era and, indeed, the most popular, for it tolerates the rigours of a north-wall position better than most

THE ROSE IN THE LANDSCAPE

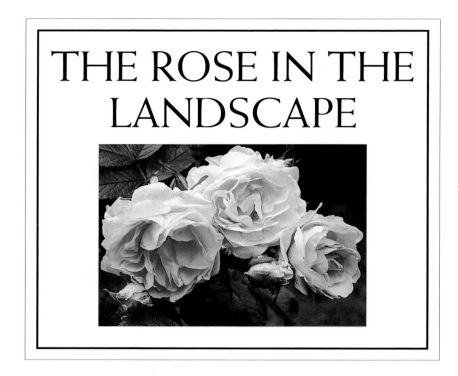

*T*he varying shades of the old rambler 'Albertine', together with its freedom of flower, make it one of the most common and best-loved roses in today's garden landscape.

*A*ny garden can be enhanced by roses but especially by species roses for in most cases they survive without too much attention. Their ranks include both plants that behave formally and those of informal habit. This one, Rosa dupontii, makes a handsome, tall-growing shrub.

ISTORY, ART AND LITERATURE FROM DIVERSE PARTS OF THE globe relate how the rose has been regarded as a symbol of beauty and affection for a very long time. It has been valued for its wide-ranging application in the landscape since the time when man first started cultivating gardens. The old Chinese civilizations and those of Persia, Greece and Rome revered the rose for its fragrance and eloquence of display. More recently, as witnessed in the thirty-three gardens described in this book, its great versatility has been utilized to great effect in gardens of all sizes and types and in many different soils and climates.

The range of roses to choose from these days is far more extensive than it has ever been before. As well as multifarious new varieties being introduced each year, there are many more types than could possibly have been envisaged when roses started to come into vogue at the beginning of the nineteenth century; a fashion started by the Empress Josephine with her collection at the Château de la Malmaison near Paris. In those days it was her patronage of nurseries that inspired breeders to explore the wider possibilities of roses as garden plants, an exploration that continued through the Victorian era and still goes on to this day. At first roses were segregated into their own space. Although this still happens today, influential landscapers such as Gertrude Jekyll recognized the fuller potential of many roses and used them more in supporting roles, combining them with other plants and giving them architectural roles on buildings and garden structures. Nowadays where there is a space to be filled anywhere in the garden, for whatever purpose, there is usually a rose which can be found to fill it.

Since Jekyll's day a new factor has become important – 'cost effectiveness'. Breeders have been busy satisfying this need by developing such new families of roses as 'patio' roses and 'ground-coverers', as well as vastly improving the floriferousness and colourfulness of other types, in particular the floribundas and climbers. Not all modern developments, though, are to everyone's liking. Some believe that the

quest for roses with ever bigger blooms of brighter, stronger colouring has taken the rose, as a landscape plant, in the wrong direction; others feel that the older roses have little or no role to play in present-day schemes. These are all matters of taste – but more often than not these days roses are ignored altogether by modern designers. Many a landscape scheme that I have seen consisting of so-called cost effective plants could be considerably enhanced, at no greater expense, by the use of 'classic' roses.

What is a 'classic' rose? There is no straightforward answer. I always find it onerous to make comparisons between roses and have an intense dislike of putting them into league tables. The nearest I can come to a definition is to summarize classic roses as those which, no matter what their age or origin, will fit comfortably into any space in the garden without screaming; and will harmonize with both the buildings they serve and their wider surroundings. Many of the roses that appear again and again in the gardens featured in this book, demonstrating their versatility in all sorts of situations, are examples of such classics.

Anyone choosing roses could be put off by the sheer magnitude of choice. The chart on pages 18–19 will help you choose roses of your desired colour that are appropriate to the garden circumstances and the role you want the roses to play. As a designer I treat each garden as unique, getting to know both the requirements of the site and the vision of the owner, and marrying these together into a solution that has roses growing happily and attractively in place. Here, to help and to inspire you,

Few gardens use ramblers more dramatically than Ninfa, just south of Rome. This ancient wooden bridge features a huge plant of 'American Pillar' on the far side and a sprawling yellow 'Easlea's Golden Rambler' on the near side.

'*Seafoam*', *a semi-procumbent modern rose, proves how valuable roses are in the landscape as it flourishes among a wealth of shrubs at Plumpton Place.*

are some of the considerations I bear in mind during this process, with particular reference to the gardens in this book.

COMPLETE ROSE GARDENS

 HERE NO EXACT RULES IN DESIGNING A COMPLETE ROSE garden or a rose garden within a garden, but there are some basic principles to observe. In the larger schemes, paths should go in as many directions as possible, to lead into and amongst the roses. There should also be changes in the topography of the shrubs. Planting together groups of three at least of each type achieves a good effect. Colour can either blend or contrast in the same region, but never both. No bed or border should be too wide and all should be in proportion, one to the other. If arches and pillars are to be included, they must be proportionate in height and of equal distance apart. Standard or tree roses can be brought into play in such schemes but, again, ultimate height and shape should be considered in the context of the overall size of the garden. On a flat site a rose garden is considerably improved by having clearly defined boundaries such as hedges, walls or trellising. Paths, such as paving, shingle or grass ones, are very important. Grassy paths should be wide enough to take a mower without damage to the roses. This brings me to another personal preference: roses overhanging the paths to be 'brushed against'. I also like to place little stepping stones among the roses so as to be able to get in the midst of them here and there. Always, to get the best effect, use a mixture of summer-flowering and repeat-flowering varieties, especially in the larger schemes. Places to sit and relax among the roses are also important.

GROUND COVER WITH ROSES

 ROUND COVER IS ALWAYS AN IMPORTANT FEATURE OF ROSE gardens but any rose variety selected for this purpose should be dense in growth, for partial ground cover causes more problems than it solves. Roses that grow broader than they are tall are often described as 'ground-cover roses'. They include some quite old varieties and many more modern ones. I never use spreading roses amongst shrub ones; such roses are best used on their own to serve specific ground-cover requirements. There are also many alternative ground-cover plants suitable for planting with shrub roses. At Nymans, for instance, blue and white perennial geraniums are used most effectively and agreeably, and at Helmingham London Pride works marvellously, to mention just two examples. I always find it better to plant ground cover in the year following rose planting, once the roses have become established. Spring-flowering bulbs are always an asset among roses and can be planted profusely. Defining beds and borders with some form of edging is also is very important. This can be done with hard materials such as flint stones or bricks, or with plants like box and lavender.

ROSES IN SUPPORTING ROLES

 HILE BY NO MEANS EVERYONE HAS THE SPACE TO SPARE to plant a full rose garden, most people can find room for a rose or two among other plants, perhaps in a herbaceous border or shrubbery or even in the vegetable garden. As a matter of personal taste I do not find that roses of any type associate easily with conifers or heathers. In my travels I have found some marvellous gardens where owners and designers have combined roses with all sorts of varied flora most effectively. Several of these special combinations have been highlighted or singled out for mention in the essays about the gardens, and will serve as inspiration for readers. Mixing and matching with such wide-ranging options is very difficult to teach; in fact all the best combinations are usually achieved by trial and error over a number of years.

Rugosas can be kept within bounds by judicious pruning. 'Monte Cassino' shares space alongside an old urn with shrub rose 'William Baffin' in the gardens of Suzy Verrier at Atlantic Street, Portland, Maine.

THE USE OF RAMBLERS, SCRAMBLERS AND CLIMBERS

 THESE ROSES ADD AN EXTRA DIMENSION TO ANY garden and all manner of structures can be brought into play to display them to best effect, including allowing them to grow up into the branches of trees. The best roses for this purpose are the scrambler-type ramblers; for obvious reasons of visibility whites, creams and yellows are better than the darker colours of deep pink and red. It is usually a mistake to use repeat-flowering varieties for tree climbing; the stress they have to endure in climbing into the shade of trees in poor soil renders them quite inadequate for this purpose. Arches of roses spanning pathways can be very attractive and most garden centres now stock a wide selection. A good sturdy structure is essential, since the arch will need to last, and to support the weight of the roses, for several years. Again, most climbers and ramblers are suitable for archways, but remember: the more prolonged their flowering season, the longer they will take to grow to full effect. Arbours or pergolas can look superb adorned with roses of any type but, again, generally speaking, continuity of flower is not easy to achieve. As a rule any climber or rambler will enjoy growing on walls but it is here that the continuous-flowering varieties really flourish. Westerly or easterly aspects are best. South-facing walls are hot and consequently the roses will bloom early and fade quickly. Few roses will tolerate a north-wall position so it is best to seek advice before making a choice.

ROSES AS HEDGES

 ROSE HEDGE IN FULL FLUSH CAN BE A MOST BEAUTIFUL sight and almost any type of rose can be adapted for this purpose but its effectiveness will be determined by the vigour of the chosen variety. If density is important in, say, a boundary hedge, then no better choice can be made than one of the several varieties of Rugosas. If the purpose of the hedge is purely ornamental then the Hybrid Musks and some of the more modern shrub varieties are probably best. Some species roses also make good hedges.

CHOOSING ROSES

 HE ROSE, WE NOW KNOW, IS A MOST VERSATILE GARDEN plant. It can be grown in windowboxes and in pots or up into the branches of very tall trees. It can cover the ground and will grow on walls. It looks superb on its own as a specimen shrub or will associate happily with others of its kind to perform the duties of bedding plants. Many are highly fragrant and several bear ornamental hips and have attractive thorns or autumn foliage. While all prefer a heavy clay soil, many grow happily in impoverished ground. A few tolerate shade and almost all enjoy the sun. None is perfect but all respond to loving care. It is no wonder that the rose enjoys the distinction of being the world's favourite flower and the most widely grown garden plant.

CHOOSING THE RIGHT ROSE

This chart pays special attention to roses featured in the book. There are, of course, many other equally suitable varieties available from specialist rose growers worldwide.

	COLOUR	SMALL SHRUBS FOR LIMITED SPACE; ALSO GOOD FOR CONTAINERS. GROW TO A MAXIMUM OF 1.2 M (4 FT).	HEDGING VARIETIES; THE MOST SUITABLE CHOICES	DENSE, THORNY BARRIERS; GOOD FOR PROTECTION FROM INTRUDERS – ANIMAL OR HUMAN
	White to cream	Horstmanns Rosenresli White Pet Yvonne Rabier	Alba Maxima Alba Semi-plena Mme Hardy Schneezwerg	Blanc Double de Coubert R. rugosa alba Nyveldt's White Schneezwerg
	Cream to lemon	Gruss an Aachen Jacqueline du Pré	Nevada R. pimpinellifolia	R. altaica R. pimpinellifolia
	Soft yellow/primrose	Windrush Moonlight	Moonlight	
	Bright yellow	Golden Wings Lichtkönigin Lucia Chinatown	Agnes Frühlingsgold Golden Wings	Agnes
	Golden/orange yellow	Perle d'Or Graham Thomas Soleil d'Or	R. foetida persiana	R. × harisonii Canary Bird
	Apricot/flame	Abraham Darby	Cornelia	Maigold
	Peach/buff/copper	Comtesse du Cayla Mrs Oakley Fisher Général Schablikine	Buff Beauty	Lady Penzance
	Scarlet	Belinda Robin Hood Precious Platinum	Belinda Robin Hood	R. moyesii Geranium Scharlachglut
	Crimson/deep red	Rose de Rescht James Mason	F. J. Grootendorst Mrs Anthony Waterer Rose de Rescht	Meg Merilees
	Purple/red	Charles de Mills Tuscany Superb	Tuscany Superb	Parfum de l'Hay
	Purple/violet	Belle de Crécy Yesterday The Prince	Reine des Violettes The Prince	William Lobb
	Blush	Anna Pavlova Alfred de Dalmas Cécile Brünner Heritage	Souvenir de la Malmaison	Stanwell Perpetual
	Soft pink	Souvenir de St Anne's Jacques Cartier Fantin-Latour	Baroness Rothschild Felicia Maiden's Blush	Belle Amour
	Bright/mid-pinks	Ballerina Bonica Comte de Chambord The Fairy	Comte de Chambord Empress Josephine Ballerina	Sarah Van Fleet
	Deep pink/cerise	Duchess of Portland R. gallica officinalis	R. californica plena	Cerise Bouquet Roseraie de l'hay
	Striped varieties and bicolours	Mutabilis Camaïeux Rosa Mundi Sadler's Wells	Ferdinand Pichard Sadler's Wells	

SHADE-TOLERANT VARIETIES; THE BEST CHOICES. FOR CLIMBERS, SEE NORTH-WALL VARIETIES	CLIMBERS FOR NORTH WALLS; WILL ALSO DO WELL ON OTHER WALLS	FREE-FLOWING PILLAR ROSES; ALSO SUITABLE FOR ARCHES AND PERGOLAS	CLIMBERS AND RAMBLERS FOR ARCHES, PILLARS, WALLS, OR WHEREVER A ROSE IS REQUIRED TO REACH 4 M (OVER 12FT).	RAMPANT VARIETIES; SUITABLE FOR TREE CLIMBING OR COVERING EYESORES
Mme Hardy Mme Plantier Prosperity Mme Legras de St Germain	Astra Desmond City of York Mme Alfred Carrière	Sombreuil Long John Silver White Cockade	Iceberg climbing Mme Alfred Carrière Sanders' White Long John Silver	Bobbie James Kiftsgate Rambling Rector R. mulliganii
Moonlight R. pimpinellifolia Sally Holmes	Albéric Barbier Paul's Lemon Pillar	Céline Forestier	Paul's Lemon Pillar	Treasure Trove Wedding Day
R. primula Dunwich Rose	Mermaid	Casino	Mermaid Primevère	Le Rêve
Frühlingsgold Lichtkönigin Lucia	Emily Gray Leverkusen	Rêve d'Or Golden Showers Goldbusch	Leverkusen	Emily Gray
	Claire Jacquier	Ghislaine de Féligonde Crépuscule	Alchymist Lady Hillingdon climbing	Easlea's Golden Rambler
Cornelia	Maigold	Schoolgirl	Desprez à Fleurs Jaunes Maigold	Desprez à Fleurs Jaunes
Buff Beauty	Gloire de Dijon	Compassion Meg	Mrs Sam McGredy Bouquet d'Or Souvenir de Mme Léonie Viennot	Alister Stella Gray
R. moyesii Geranium Scharlachglut	Cramoisi Supérieur climbing Paul's Scarlet	Cramoisi Supérieur climbing Paul's Scarlet	Souvenir de Claudius Denoyel	Scharlachglut
Gruss an Teplitz Henry Kelsey Mrs Anthony Waterer	Parkdirektor Riggers Cadenza	Cadenza	Ena Harkness climbing Guinée	
Tuscany Superb				
Tour de Malakoff Reine des Violettes	Veilchenblau		Veilchenblau	Veilchenblau
Ispahan R. pomifera	Dr W. Van Fleet Debutante	Blush Noisette New Dawn	Dr W. Van Fleet The Garland	Francis E. Lester Cécile Brünner climbing
Félicité Parmentier Felicia Complicata	Kathleen Harrop	Kathleen Harrop Narrow Water	Albertine	Paul's Himalayan Musk
Bourbon Queen Louise Odier Vanity	François Juranville Mme Caroline Testout Mme Grégoire Staechelin	Aloha Pink Perpétue Rosy Mantle	Dorothy Perkins Mme Grégoire Staechelin Mme Caroline Testout	American Pillar François Juranville
Cerise Bouquet Mme Isaac Pereire	Zéphirine Drouhin	Parade Zéphirine Drouhin	Viking Queen	Sénateur La Follette
Variegata di Bologna Honorine de Brabant	Phyllis Bide	Phyllis Bide	René André	

ROYAL LODGE
WINDSOR, BERKSHIRE, ENGLAND

 HE GARDENS AT ROYAL LODGE, WINDSOR, ARE ABLAZE WITH colour in late spring each year when the rhododendrons and azaleas are in full flush in the acid, sandy soil of the Berkshire-Surrey borders. By comparison, when the roses come into flower a little later on in June and July, they are subdued and quiet. I am rather biased, of course, but roses are so much more intimate and personal, and they have no need to try to imitate the colourful exuberance of spring – especially in this garden, which belongs to Her Majesty Queen Elizabeth the Queen Mother. The Queen Mother loves her roses and, as well as these here at Royal Lodge, has many more in other gardens, especially at the Castle of Mey, her home in Scotland.

As well as being a regular visitor to flower shows such as Chelsea, Her Majesty is Patron of the Royal National Rose Society and has always taken a keen interest in its affairs. Her visits to shows are always appreciated by the exhibitors not only because her knowledge of gardening, roses especially, is so extensive, but also for her wonderful gift of putting people at ease. Over the years two roses have been named after her. The first and most famous, 'Elizabeth of Glamis' (1963), was bred by Sam McGredy of Northern Ireland, who now lives in New Zealand and continues to be one of the world's leading rose breeders. 'Elizabeth of Glamis' is a lovely fragrant, bright salmon-pink Floribunda. More recently, to celebrate Her Majesty's ninetieth birthday in 1990, a pretty little pink 'patio' rose (or compact Floribunda variety) named 'Queen Mother' was presented to her at Chelsea Flower Show by Charles Notcutt of Mattocks Nurseries. This rose was bred in Germany by Wilhelm Kordes.

The Queen Mother's favourite flower show must be the one held on the last Wednesday in July each year on the Royal Estate at Sandringham in West Norfolk. This event is for charity, and is a happy and relaxed affair centred around the staff of the Estate. Nowadays it is as much a country fair as a flower show. Her Majesty, in recent years accompanied by her grandson the Prince of Wales, has not missed this

Well-proportioned and elegant, Royal Lodge is, by comparison with most of the other royal houses, modest in size. The south front overlooks the sunken rose garden which has been planted with one hundred of the Queen Mother's favourite shrub and old-fashioned roses.

This enchanting small-scale replica of a Welsh cottage complete with furniture was presented by the people of Wales to the Queen, then Princess Elizabeth, on her sixth birthday. The formal front garden now features ninety plants of the rose 'Queen Mother', a gift from its raiser on the Queen Mother's ninetieth birthday (facing page).

21

'Scabrosa' is one of several Rugosas in the Rose Garden at Royal Lodge. This variety was planted not just for the beauty of its single fragrant flowers but for the enhancement its large hips give to the garden in winter.

event since 1954. My firm has exhibited there for the last quarter-century, and it has become one of the highlights of our show calendar. Escorted by Fred Waite, the Head Gardener at Sandringham House, and accompanied by her guests, Her Majesty always visits the displays and chats informally to each exhibitor. It was on one such occasion, on our stand, when she and one of her guests, the late Sir Frederick Ashton of ballet fame, were admiring the rose 'Anna Pavlova' that she said, 'Wouldn't it be lovely if Fred could have his own rose?' As if by command, and to my great delight, the very next summer a bush of the rose 'Anna Pavlova' threw a white sport which we named after Sir Frederick. I presented the blooms to a smiling Queen Mother and a thrilled Sir Frederick Ashton at the next Show.

Always in the Royal Party at Sandringham Show are the Duke and Duchess of Grafton. It was they, jointly with the Prince of Wales, who gave me the opportunity to become involved with the roses at Royal Lodge by commissioning me to re-plan the Rose Garden there for Her Majesty's eighty-fifth birthday.

Royal Lodge is well loved by the Queen Mother and she spends as much time there as possible. It stands secluded among trees on the southern edge of Windsor Park. Anyone passing by would hardly know it was there. Quite unaware that they would soon be called upon to become King and Queen, the Duke and Duchess of York, as they were then, first moved to Royal Lodge in the early 1930s. Prior to their coming it had been unoccupied for many years and had become neglected and overgrown. However, the Duke and Duchess had fallen for the essential character of the place, and undaunted by the effect of years of abandonment, quickly, often with their own hands, applied their shared love for gardening to fashioning the grounds into the quiet, cared-for, informal woodland-style gardens they are today. Sometimes, especially after becoming King and Queen, the royal couple took advice from that great gardener Sir Eric Savill, who, in his capacity of Director to the Estate's Parks and Gardens, lived near by.

All along the south facade of the house is a York stone terrace with borders each side and a long central bed edged with lavender. John Bond, the keeper of the gardens at Windsor, told me that it has now become traditional each spring for these

---

ALTHOUGH NOT entirely typical of a rose of that group, this very beautiful variety is a Hybrid Perpetual. It was raised in France in 1860. Its shape and the way the blooms present themselves among the foliage is very reminiscent of the Damasks, as is its delicious perfume. Unlike most of the Damasks, though, 'Reine des Violettes' goes on flowering right through the summer and well into autumn.

The flowers unfold from plump round buds into large, flat rosette shapes and are borne in tight clusters. Their colour is the most lovely mixture of purples and greys. A minor fault, I

HYBRID PERPETUAL

'REINE DES VIOLETTES'

suppose, is that the many-petalled flowers easily shatter if cut and taken indoors.

A very special feature is its smooth greyish-green leaves, which are large and produced very freely in good soil. The stems are also greyish-green, upright-growing and practically thornless. This variety hates to be starved by being planted in poor soil; it appears not to mind at first, but quickly degenerates into an impoverished state. It should, however, be grown in every garden where the condition of the soil is good and it can be given a little bit of extra loving care.

beds and borders to be filled with the lovely combination of soft pink 'Clara Butt' tulips and blue forget-me-nots and, following these in summer, a mass of salmon-coloured 'Irene of Denmark' pelargoniums. There are no plants on the walls of the house, but over the doorway in the west-facing wall of the east end of the terrace is a splendid entanglement of *Wisteria sinensis* and *Rosa banksiae lutea*. A row of the Queen Mother's very own 'Elizabeth of Glamis' is growing all along the front of the little two-foot-high wall that defines the southern edge of the terrace. Down below this, seven steps down in fact, is the small sunken Rose Garden which has been here for a very long time.

There was an east wind blowing on the day of my visit to Royal Lodge in December 1984, a bitterly cold wind to which Her Majesty seemed totally oblivious. My brief was to suggest a planting plan and advise on cultivation matters. Many of the old roses looked tired and several were struggling in soil which had grown roses for many years, so it soon became clear that before any new roses could be planted, the soil had to be removed and replaced with new topsoil in which roses had not previously grown.

The basic design is simple and remains unchanged from the original. Two long paths paved with York stone lead from end to end, with lateral paths dividing the area into four equal-sized beds, each holding about twenty roses. A tall beech hedge with two little seating alcoves protects the garden from the east and an equally tall

*R*ugosas are among the most healthy of shrub roses. Here the clove-scented, reddish-purple flowers of *'Roseraie de l'Hay'* and those of the white *'Blanc Double de Coubert'* show off to effect in the east border of the sunken rose garden at Royal Lodge.

HYBRID TEA

'ANNA PAVLOVA'

FOR SOME years this rose was a treasured seedling in our trial beds. I loved it but could not decide whether or not it should be introduced, for I always felt it to be a little too shy in producing its flowers.

It was a friend, Keith Money, who in 1981, after having written a definitive work on Anna Pavlova, insisted that it should be named after the great ballerina and eventually persuaded me to introduce it. He was right. It deserved to be sent out into the world and, since then, has gone on to become one of the best loved of my roses, especially in warmer parts of the world where its flowers are produced so much more freely than they are in England.

In good soil this variety takes on an upright stance to a height of about four feet. Its foliage is large, semi-glossy, rounded in shape and dark green in colour. Its flowers are very large and held on strong firm necks; their colour is the most delicate shade of pink. They have a stronger scent than any other rose I know.

On the negative side, it is not happy in light, less fertile soils, and its flowers do not open cleanly in wet or humid conditions.

evergreen hedge of *Chamaecyparis lawsoniana* forms the western boundary. Beneath this hedge a narrow border is now planted with a mixture of species roses and Rugosas to add the extra interest of hips and coloured foliage to the garden each autumn. Among these I used *Rosa woodsii fendleri*, which has lovely pink flowers in June and waxy red fruit in September, and *R. rugosa alba* for the continuity of its pure white single flowers and the huge, tomato-like hips which last well into winter.

Because this garden can be viewed from above and is totally enclosed, I tried to create the effect of a huge bowl of pot-pourri, not only as an image to look down on to, but as a temptation to walk into. To achieve this some of the roses are planted closer together than would normally be the case, and fragrance was an essential factor when selecting varieties. In all, about one hundred are here. Of the older classics, the lovely purple Hybrid Perpetual 'Reine des Violettes' just had to be included; likewise the sumptuous soft pink Bourbon 'Souvenir de la Malmaison' and the Portland 'Jacques Cartier' for its refinement and continuity of flower. Among the more modern varieties are two ever-flowering pink Floribundas, 'Nathalie Nypels' and 'Centenaire de Lourdes', and a little-known but very lovely white fragrant Floribunda, 'Horstmanns Rosenresli'. Other well-known roses which just could not be omitted for reasons of celebration or sentiment – or because they were given to Her Majesty as presents – are, for example, the soft yellow and pink 'Peace', commemorating the end of the First World War; 'Silver Jubilee', a lovely bright

pink from the late James Cocker of Aberdeen, celebrating Her Majesty Queen Elizabeth II's twenty-fifth year on the throne, and 'Sandringham Centenary', an orangey-pink Hybrid Tea bred by the late Bill Tysterman to mark the hundredth anniversary of Sandringham Flower Show. Then, as an acknowledgement of the Queen Mother's interest in the ballet, mostly for their perfume but also, I suspect, partly from vanity, I included two of my own varieties, the already-mentioned 'Anna Pavlova', and 'Sir Frederick Ashton'. The latter was planted here well in advance of its introduction.

A few steps from the sunken Rose Garden just to the east of the house is another part of the garden devoted to roses. This, too, has been here for some time. It is known as 'The Princesses' Garden', for it was here that Princess Elizabeth, now the Queen, and Princess Margaret did their gardening when, as little children, they stayed here at Royal Lodge away from the public eye. The roses here are mainly Hybrid Musks, among them 'Buff Beauty', 'Felicia', 'Cornelia' and 'Moonlight', along with two China roses, the lovely little bronzy-yellow 'Perle d'Or' and the ever-delightful multicoloured 'Mutabilis'.

Royal Lodge is one of Queen Elizabeth the Queen Mother's private homes. I am privileged that Her Majesty's enthusiasm for roses has given me the opportunity of a small involvement in her garden, and deeply honoured to have been given permission to write about it in the pages of this book.

The rose 'Queen Mother' is a delightful, low-growing, semi- procumbent compact Floribunda, with a healthy, glossy foliage and a slight but distinct perfume. It is ideally suited to mass planting.

As you would expect, several of the Queen Mother's own rose 'Elizabeth of Glamis' have pride of place in the gardens. Here it is seen among the lavender that edges the beds and borders along the south terrace (facing page).

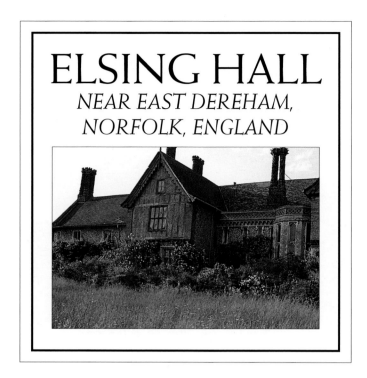

ELSING HALL
NEAR EAST DEREHAM, NORFOLK, ENGLAND

Edward the Black Prince had an association with Elsing Hall and history oozes out of every nook and cranny here, accentuated by the wonderful collection of old roses growing in the gardens.

ELSING HALL NESTLES IN COMPLETE HARMONY WITH ITS location in a modest tree-strewn valley in central Norfolk. From the higher ground of sheep-grazed parkland, the impressive, moated fifteenth-century house is first glimpsed through the well-clothed limbs of two huge and ancient copper beeches. Dominating this first sighting are six pairs of tall red-brick ornamental chimneys which, as one draws nearer, gradually seem to diminish to become proportionate to the high-roofed edifice. Elsing stands in thirty acres of good fertile soil on the site of an early twelfth-century castle, some parts of which are still visible; here and there bits of its ancient foundations have been cleverly utilized as features by the present owners, David and Shirley Cargill. Many years ago, soon after I started my own collection of old roses, I was privileged to see an earlier rose garden created by the Cargills in a different part of the county, so I knew that a visit to Elsing Hall would be a delightful experience.

As you approach through the shade of the copper beeches, it becomes clear that this is not just an ordinary garden but one created by sensitive artists with a love for things natural and a flair for harmonizing that which was not there before with that which was. The first evidence of this is in the form of two strange, bell-like objects on either side of the one and only entrance. They really have no business to be there and yet look as though they belong, for, each clothed in that lovely but durable white and soft pink rambler 'Francis E. Lester', they have become absorbed into the general ambience of the place. This rose, often used as a tree climber, is an admirable choice; it is capable of draping itself and partially covering – yet not totally obscuring – objects such as these. It flowers profusely for about three weeks in June and then later in the autumn produces a glorious display of tiny orange-red hips.

At this point there is a strong temptation to cross over the inviting rose-clad humpback bridge leading to the island on which the house stands, but this should be resisted until later, since much of the garden is spread randomly outside the moat.

A copy of Canova's 'Paulina Borghese' is seen here through the arch in the east wall of the orchard at Elsing Hall. The roses cascading from above the archway are a mixture of climbers and ramblers including 'Phyllis Bide' and 'Adélaide d'Orléans' (facing page).

GALLICA ROSE

'CHARLES DE MILLS'

Although it is one of the more popular members of the Gallica family, this rose remains an enigma, for exhaustive researches have failed to trace its origins. It is most certainly an old variety, dating back probably to at least the middle of the nineteenth century. Efforts to identify Charles de Mills or Charles Mills have found only an Englishman who was a director of the East India Company in Victorian times, and it is thought unlikely that he ever had a rose named after him.

Its colour is a distinctive mixture of crimson, dark red and purple. In the clear light of early morning or of a summer evening it glows with a jewel-like luminosity, the reflections of the many folds of its petals intensifying its rich colour. The flowers are produced in profusion for two or three weeks from late June onwards and have a strong fragrance. Its growth is a little informal, but it never gets awkward or out of hand, attaining a maximum height of about four feet in good soils. Its foliage is dark green and healthy.

An ideal rose to grow among mixed herbaceous plants, 'Charles de Mills' looks especially good with white and creamy-yellow companions.

Instead, turn to the right and follow its grassy banks to the sensitively restored old stables – not a rose in sight at this point. Soon you will come upon masses of rambler roses on ten-foot-high walls. Barely visible through these is an open doorway hung with yet more roses. Having risked the prickles to force your way through, you will be rewarded by the discovery of a secret rose garden within a rose garden. At one time this was the kitchen garden which, in later years, also doubled as an orchard. The walls are festooned with ramblers and scramblers, mostly whites and creams, but here and there with various shades of pink, lavender and purple blended together.

Predominant is that famous old Moschata hybrid, 'Rambling Rector' – a rose of obscure origin probably dating back to Shakespeare's time and before; it flowers in huge creamy-white clusters from mid-June to early July. Later in the year bright yellowish-orange hips will follow. It is quite capable of climbing to twenty feet or more. In one spot on the south-facing wall is the equally conspicuous but less vigorous rambler 'Veilchenblau' with semi-double violet-purple flowers appearing at the same time as, and combining beautifully with, the creamy-white blooms of 'Rambling Rector'. A little farther along, emerging from the middle of the densely packed flowers of the ramblers, is the more recent 'Constance Spry' with its full-bodied, cabbage-like, myrrh-scented pink blooms. Nearer to the ground amid blankets of feverfew (*Tanacetum parthenium*) are some interesting shrub roses. Particularly noticeable is the rich purple ancient Gallica 'Charles de Mills'.

Nowhere in the gardens at Elsing is it possible to forget that water is an essential part of the scheme of things. Here the boundaries consist of walls on three sides with the ancient 'fish stew' of the moat on the fourth, south side. Along this the Cargills have planted a mixed border mainly of Moss roses such as the lovely soft pink 'Général Kléber' and the reddish, fully double 'Maréchal Davoust'. The fragrant pink Gallica 'Empress Josephine' (*Rosa × francofurtana*) and the lovely Damask 'Ispahan' are also in evidence among cream and white foxgloves and numerous other herbaceous plants. Foxgloves that dare to flower in any other colour are treated as rogues and instantly banished to the compost heap.

Here and there roses are planted to grow up into the apple trees; one happy combination encouraged to do this is the blush-white rambler 'Brenda Colvin' with *Clematis spooneri* (*C. montana sericea*). Scattered to good effect away from the edges and among the trees are clumps of more brightly coloured roses, the vigorous bright red Gallica 'Scharlachglut' making a vivid splash of colour in the centre. Another effective clump is the Rugosa 'Roseraie de l'Hay'. Where space permits, as it does here, 'clumping' – closely packed plantings of three or five of one variety – can be most rewarding. Stealing a glance at the copy of the reclined figure of Paulina Borghese by Canova, you leave this garden by passing through a low archway with yet more cascading 'Rambling Rector', this time beautifully blended with honeysuckle and clematis.

As you go south you come across a huge specimen of 'Sir Cedric Morris', a 'foundling' rose introduced by me in the late 1970s. It has greyish-purple foliage similar to that of *Rosa glauca* (*R. rubrifolia*) and masses of single white highly scented flowers followed by small rounded orange hips every autumn. This rose is covering an old dead tree. I recall vividly my first ever meeting with this rose in the gardens of the late Sir Cedric at Hadleigh in Suffolk. It was the biggest rose I had ever seen, at least thirty feet wide and high. Sir Cedric had found it some years earlier as a seedling – probably from *R. glauca* – alone in a cabbage patch.

The beautiful old Gallica rose 'Empress Josephine' mingles with a wild pink phlox in one of the borders at Elsing Hall. An observant local farmer was once overheard saying that the Cargills had never heard of a straight line!

Continuing now in a south-westerly direction, you will see on your right at least half an acre of a relatively new topiary garden, very interesting but not part of our current quest for roses. To the left the southern aspect of the Hall is now visible across lily pads at the widest part of the moat. Eye-catching on the southern bank is a lone weeping ash, its base garlanded with the soft pink 'Paul's Himalayan Musk'. The Cargills undoubtedly planted this rose here to climb to the top of the tree, the best part of thirty feet, but at present it is teasingly content to tumble gleefully into the shallow water.

Meandering alongside the moat you will come across a variety of different shrub roses too numerous to mention by name, but the distinctive *Rosa webbiana* with its small, star-like, soft pink flowers and greyish foliage is particularly memorable. The east side of the garden is more thickly wooded than the rest, providing protection for the Hall from the Siberian blasts of Norfolk winters. Here you will encounter evidence of the more flamboyant side of the Cargills in the form of a modern sculpture in stainless steel. Through the trees, heading back west beside the moat, you will see large clumps of mixed species roses. These are placed effectively to provide colour in this predominantly green area.

Having come full circle, you may now cross the moat towards the house over the humpback bridge. Its low walls, a pleasing mixture of brick and flint, are partially covered by a pretty creamy-white unnamed Multiflora seedling rose which I have

The Moss rose 'Général Kléber' is here captured in early evening light with globe artichoke in one of the borders of the secret rose garden. Above all other old varieties it is the Moss roses that evoke feelings of history in a garden, and especially so here at Elsing.

seen nowhere else. If there were not so many of these seedlings nowadays it would be well worth introducing, but there is also something to be said for Elsing having its own unique rose. A pause on the bridge is worthwhile both to take in the perfume of the seedling rose and to view the house and surrounding gardens from a good vantage point. From here you crunch along a gravel drive which leads to the inviting entrance to the Hall itself. There is nothing formal anywhere in the Cargills' design of things – in fact a visiting local farmer was heard to say, 'They've never heard of a straight line.' This informality is accentuated by allowing giant hogweed (*Heracleum mantegazzianum*) to grow at random along the drive and in the vicinity of the front door.

If it was a temptation to cross the humpback bridge earlier, it is now even more tempting to cross the threshold into the Hall, and if you were privileged to do so you would discover inside an extension of the informality and feelings of history evoked by the gardens. As the house is not open to the public, not everyone will have the opportunity to experience this; instead, you should strike back towards the east along the inner edge of the moat and past the grey flint chapel which adjoins the house. The winding path will then lead you through a thicket of shrubs on to a long, two-tiered terrace stretching the length of the side of the house. At first it will not seem like a terrace because it is so densely packed with a wide variety of herbs and perennials and roses, almost all of ancient origin. Here, all mixed up together, you will find such treasures as the red *Rosa gallica officinalis* (the Apothecary Rose or Red Rose of Lancaster) of ancient origin and its striped red-and-white sport, 'Rosa Mundi' (*R. gallica versicolor*), Albas such as *R.* 'Alba Maxima' (the White Rose of York), the beautifully formed blush-pink 'Great Maiden's Blush' and the silvery-pink, semi-double 'Celestial', the deep pink Provence Rose or Cabbage Rose (*R. centifolia*) and its relative, the pure white Moss rose 'Blanche Moreau'. I have mentioned only a few of the varieties here. The overall effect of this terrace is staggering, but nowhere is there anything that jars – harmony being the trade mark of the Cargills.

At the far end of the terrace the land falls gently towards the moat and here, beneath an expansive weeping willow, you will find a tangled mass of several types of old roses in a variety of pastel shades. Here, too, partially supported by the remnants of an old tree, is yet another specimen of 'Rambling Rector' cascading into the water. While this group of roses is a pleasure to mingle with, they are visually at their most attractive when viewed with their reflections from the opposite bank.

At roughly the middle of the terrace are some stone steps which descend to a marshy area of naturalized wildflowers and grasses. Although this has absolutely nothing to do with roses, it is a singular pleasure to walk on the soft, peaty soil among them. From here, looking back at the house, you will see that the south wall is well furnished with climbing roses. A huge plant of 'Mme Grégoire Staechelin' ('Spanish Beauty') fills the central aspect of the house over the door. This is a large, loosely formed rose made up of various shades of pink which thoroughly enjoys the warm, sunny position afforded it here. Another rose doing well on this wall is 'Mme Alfred Carrière', a repeat-flowering, well-foliated, white to blush-pink fragrant variety proving its versatility in this situation, for it is more often grown on a colder north wall. Two other noteworthy varieties basking in this sunny spot are the soft pink Centifolia 'Fantin-Latour' and the deeper pink Alba 'Königin von Dänemark'. These would normally be grown as shrubs, but with the benefit of the warm walls behind them, each here attains a height in excess of ten feet and wafts its perfume for many yards around.

Clearly these gardens are the joint creation of both David and Shirley Cargill, but I am sure that David would agree that Shirley has an affinity with roses and plants beyond that of the normal gardener. As far as I can tell, her philosophy is 'let it all hang out until it needs attention, then cut it off or pull it up'. Working with soil hundreds of years old means that pernicious weeds of perennial varieties are a constant irritant, but no weedkillers are ever used and, for that matter, very little fertilizer.

In all, the gardens contain some four to five hundred roses and it is difficult to know where to stop in describing them. Those who love roses should make a point of coming here when the gardens are open during June and July each year. Parties or groups should make an appointment.

DAMASK ROSE

'ISPAHAN'

THE DAMASK roses as a group are among our oldest. Their ancestry is complex and some of them are not easy to classify; 'Ispahan', for instance, may well have a good many Alba genes in its makeup. The first Damasks were brought back to Western Europe by the homecoming crusaders. This one, however, arrived much later: it was found growing in the area of Ispahan in Persia – now Iran – in 1832. Despite this late discovery and introduction, it probably dates back to ancient times.

As Damasks go, 'Ispahan' is one of the most garden-worthy, never outgrowing its welcome in any situation. Upright in habit, it has greyish-green foliage. Its blooms are about two and a half inches in diameter when fully open and are produced in profusion from mid-June to mid-July. Their colour, a clear candyfloss-pink, remains constant from bud stage until petal fall. They are fully double and, as with all Damasks, deliciously fragrant; the petals make excellent pot-pourri. This rose is tolerant of even the poorest soil, but in fertile ground will reach a height of four feet as a free-growing plant. It is best grown in groups of three, either among other roses or in mixed borders. This variety also does well in tubs or urns.

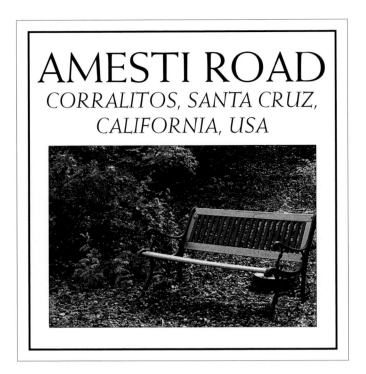

AMESTI ROAD
CORRALITOS, SANTA CRUZ, CALIFORNIA, USA

The delightful unnamed seedling from 'Mutabilis' grows beside one of the many places to sit and relax in this fascinating garden in California. 'A garden is for people, plants, animals and insects to enjoy,' says its creator Kleine Lettunich.

ECORDS PROVE THAT IN THE 1930S THE LAND ON WHICH this garden stands was very fertile. In those days it was an apricot orchard. But constant mismanagement by cultivating between the trees and a succession of extra-heavy rainy seasons in the 1940s and '50s meant that by the time Kleine Lettunich arrived in 1959, most of the topsoil had disappeared into the valley below, leaving just clay subsoil from which to fashion a garden. Bearing this in mind, what has come about in thirty years is truly remarkable, for now it is a beautiful garden of nine or so acres which functions very much in tune with nature. 'A garden is for people, plants, animals and insects to enjoy,' says Kleine, and the house 'a comfortable place to come into from the garden.'

This 'comfortable place' nestles into the south-western slopes of a hillside overlooking the Corralitos Valley. It was severely damaged during the earthquake of 1989, whose epicentre was just four and a half miles away. The swimming pool was irreparable and had to be turned into a fishpond. Nowadays the fish are never seen. Two predators – a kingfisher and a heron – lurk near by.

A daily ceremony is the feeding of the skunks on the terrace by the kitchen door. Dozens of these delightful animals (they smell only if they are threatened) come from all directions to enjoy their dinner of catfood pellets in the company of birds and any other creature who wishes to join in. However, more of these things later – I should be writing about roses. Although I must just mention the handsome, eight-foot-long boa constrictor who lives indoors next to the incubator that hatches desert tortoise eggs, and the two parrots who live the life of Riley and tell one so in no uncertain fashion.

The Corralitos Valley is one of the most fertile in California, producing a wide variety of fruit from apples to raspberries of a quality and flavour that is mouth-wateringly more-ish. There are superb views across the valley to both the south and west from several vantage points in these gardens.

The Hybrid Musk 'Buff Beauty' is set off by the dark green background of a Monterey pine (Pinus radiata) in a garden which is also a nature reserve and has beautiful views of the Corralitos valley to the south-east (facing page).

NOISETTE ROSE

'MARÉCHAL NIEL'

I HAVE A ten-year-old plant of this rose in our old greenhouse here in Norfolk. Each year when it comes into flower – as it does before any other rose except the Banksias – I consider its large, scented, sulphur-yellow bloom the most beautiful rose I have ever seen. Not true, of course, for later in the summer I will think this of others, but the flowers of 'Maréchal Niel' are particularly sumptuous and evocative of times past.

This rose was raised in France in 1864 as a seedling from 'Cloth of Gold'. In California, the South of France and other warmer climates it does far better out of doors than we can ever expect of it in England. Given protection from our worst weather, it is worth trying it in the south of England: Graham Thomas reports a plant ten feet high in a protected position at Mottisfont, blooming well in warm summers.

A criticism often levelled at this rose is its weak neck. Since it is a climber, this seems to me to be an advantage, for when I look up at its flowers they are hanging down to look at me.

At first Kleine planted alpines, thinking that they would tolerate the stressful conditions. After several years of just watching things die, she started to grow deeper-rooted subjects, constantly mulching them with all kinds of organic material such as seaweed, vineyard pulp and wood chippings to build up the depth of soil. She is totally devoted to the good things we have on this planet and believes passionately that we hold it in trust for future generations; consequently no sprays or chemicals are ever used – 'The garden is the last place to wage war.' In her efforts to find things that would prosper here she came upon roses, which most certainly enjoy growing for her – proving, I think, that there is no need to keep throwing chemicals about for them to flourish. Only small parts of this garden are irrigated and, unusually for California, nothing is ever watered until it is seen to need it.

The house sits roughly in the middle of the garden and the area around it is the only level part of the entire grounds. A sweeping metalled drive comes in from the east, and a retaining wall has been built to hold in the narrow, flattish border between the upward-sloping northern side of the gardens and the roadway. In this border are planted several roses and a wide variety of other plants, including a large clump of a native fleabane (*Erigeron*), its mass of small flowers looking like pale pink clouds against the hillside. Among the roses in this area is a delightful little variety called 'Happenstance' which, although I doubt its hardiness in England, I have added to my list of 'I wants'. A Hybrid Bracteata, it is a bush form of 'Mermaid'; I know not

Another of Kleine Lettunich's many unnamed seedling roses. This one deserves recognition – not to mention eventual naming – for its sheer floriferousness each spring.

whence it came. Also here, as well as in almost every other part of the garden, are Kleine's seedlings. She collects hips from lots of different roses and grows the seeds, selecting the best for growing on. Several of these are very interesting, including one in another part of the garden, a remontant form of 'Francis E. Lester' called 'Lyda Rose' after Kleine's daughter. This rose is also on my list of 'I wants'; another is one called 'Happy Face', a continuous-flowering shrub in bright pink bred by John Clements of Heirloom Roses, Oregon.

All sorts of other genera are raised from seed by this resourceful lady, inspired by the motive of attracting and feeding the wildlife, especially birds and small mammals such as chipmunks and squirrels. Pistachios, wild cherries, plums and crab-apples are thus the most common plants, other than roses, scattered on this hillside rising up above the north side of the house. Even the gophers benefit, in that potatoes are planted here and there about the garden on the 'fair shares for all' principle – the gophers get half, Kleine gets half. If they were planted all together, the gophers would get them all!

Considering that they never get watered except when it rains, which in summer is seldom, the roses here are in fine condition. A magnificent plant of the orange climber 'Compassion' grown as a shrub attracted me, as did a splendid specimen of a modern bright red rose called 'Precious Platinum', which Kleine enjoyed telling me was given to her by her good friend Bill Grant, who lives near by, 'because it was too

bright for his garden'. She carries secateurs whenever she goes around the garden and was busily dead-heading as we talked. Next to 'Precious Platinum' is an unknown Portland rose which has been found by local rosarian Fred Boutine in the Motherlode county; many old roses are to be found growing there, having been planted by the settlers at the time of the gold rush. One or two other of Fred's discoveries can also be found growing in this garden. To my delight I came upon a splendidly healthy plant of my own introduction, 'Sadler's Wells'. Kleine frequently cuts this rose for the house since it lasts so long in water.

Next, we came to what is called the 'fertilizer factory', a range of rabbit hutches populated by rescued 'Easter bunnies'. Also residing near by are bantams and goats. Here, sheltered by a grove of redwood trees growing in a neighbour's garden, is an enclosure for several families of tortoise, the oldest and largest member of which is well over fifty years old and the smallest, a few weeks. On the fence behind this area, which is actually a gully on the same level as – and to the west of – the house, is a huge and expansive *Rosa banksiae normalis*, the single white Banksian rose.

To the south of the house the land falls away quite steeply and at times I lost my footing on the thick mulching of wood chippings which serve to suppress the weeds and yet keep in the moisture. It was a hot day, 90° Fahrenheit at least, but average daytime temperatures are around the mid-seventies here in summer and around 45°F at night. In winter it can get cold, occasionally freezing with some snow. Just

The massed flowers of this unnamed seedling look superb among many other roses of similar type in the gardens of Amesti Road. Like all the other ones here this variety has to survive without irrigation.

35

MODERN SHRUB ROSE

'SADLER'S WELLS'

IN THE late 1970s I crossed the free-flowering shrub rose 'Ballerina' with 'Rose Gaujard', one of the most healthy Hybrid Teas, to bring forth a number of seedlings combining the attributes of both parents. The best of these was introduced in 1984 as 'Sadler's Wells', named in honour of the famous ballet company.

This is now one of my favourites among the roses I have raised. It produces huge clusters of well-spaced, semi-single flowers on an extremely healthy bush which grows to a height of about four feet. Its foliage is glossy. Each flower has a silvery-pink background laced with cherry-red, a colour which is even more enhanced in the autumn. These flowers seem impervious to wet weather. They make up for having only a slight perfume by lasting well in water when cut and taken indoors.

As a specimen shrub or as a hedge, this rose is always in flower. It is also good among herbaceous plants and it never requires too much attention.

as on the north side, there is much of interest in a dense planting with a wide variety of trees and shrubs. The first rose I found here was the lovely shapely pink Hybrid Tea 'Picture', which I would never have planted here myself, thinking it too temperamental. I would have been wrong; it is thriving and sporting several good-quality blooms. Close to 'Picture' is a group of the pink Floribunda 'Nathalie Nypels', the colourful Floribunda from Ralph Moore called 'Playtime', and the burgundy-coloured Hybrid Tea 'Smokey' from Jackson and Perkins. Disappointing, although not surprisingly so, was a plant of my fragrant pink 'Anna Pavlova' struggling to stay alive; this rose can be difficult even in better soils than this. By way of compensation for the sickly 'Anna', I found, a little farther on, a huge and healthy plant of my red 'James Mason' next to a tall shrub of Kordes' yellow 'Frühlingsgold'. I imagine they must be quite a sight in April and May.

Posts and wires have been put up in part of this area to support some climbers and ramblers. 'Constance Spry', although not in flower when I was there in July, was doing well; likewise 'Félicité Perpétue' and another very early flowerer, the pink 'Mme Grégoire Staechelin'. Here and there lower down the slope are plants of 'Double White Burnet' showing off one or two late flowers among a multitude of green hips which will later turn to mahogany. Close by is a young walnut tree planted, Kleine said, 'for the squirrels'.

On the eastern boundary which conceals the garden from the road is an assortment of shrubs and roses, among them several seedlings of *Rosa chinensis* 'Mutabilis', all the product of Kleine's seed-saving operation over the years. One that has already made its mark is a cross between 'Mutabilis' and 'Francis E. Lester', a delightful silvery-pink, continuous-flowerer aptly named 'Mateo's Silk Butterflies'. Here I found what I had expected to find in this part of the world, *R. californica* – not as big as I had thought it would be, but its profusion of hips evidence of a successful flowering earlier. Here too I found a cross between *R. californica* and *R. eglanteria*, a shortish plant with one flower still braving the heat for me, its colour that of *R. californica* and its fragrance 'Eglantine'. In growth habit it looks like a short form of the latter and very, very thorny. It was near this rose that I spotted another unique object, a pyramid of dead brushwood and twigs about three feet high partly concealed by honeysuckle. Kleine explained that it was a home for chipmunks; 'beneath the twigs are a few land drains in which they live at certain times of the year and, at others, store their winter food'. I should have known this was not just a heap of twigs waiting for a suitable day for a bonfire. In fact, as I discovered later, many of these twig 'tepees' are scattered all over the property.

The western side of this slope is thickly wooded with several species, including some well-established Monterey pines (*Pinus radiata*), but the garden is wide open to the south across the valley. On this side of the roses struggle a little in the shallower soil, but none was under real stress. It was good to see a superb plant of 'Silver Moon' showing off about half a dozen flowers. This, along with three yellow Noisettes – the lovely 'Crépuscule', the delicious golden-yellow 'Maréchal Niel' and the lesser-known 'Duchesse d'Auerstädt' – grow close to the house.

I did not ask how many varieties of rose Kleine has in her garden, but there are many more than I have mentioned. I doubt if even she knows, for to her they are like the rest of the flora and fauna – to be enjoyed, not counted, dated or listed.

This garden is not open to the public, but I am sure no one would ever be turned away if they wished to see it.

LA BONNE MAISON
CHEMIN DE FONTANIERES, LYON, FRANCE

THERE CAN BE A NO MORE APPROPRIATE CITY IN THE WORLD in which to plant a rose garden. Lyon was the capital of roses during the nineteenth and early twentieth centuries, when the French – inspired first by the Empress Josephine and later by nothing more than good taste – were world leaders in the making of new roses. From France's second city came such legendary varieties as 'Souvenir de la Malmaison', 'Cécile Brünner' and 'Mme Alfred Carrière', not to mention the first-ever Hybrid Tea, 'La France', and the progenitor of all our modern brightly coloured roses, 'Soleil d'Or'. The list is endless, and they came from famous breeders with names to tingle the spines of serious lovers of old roses, such as Jean Béluze, Joseph Schwartz, Joseph Pernet-Ducher and Jean-Baptiste Guillot. No less than thirty-six breeders worked in and around Lyon during that grand period of rose history, between them introducing well over six hundred roses from about 1840 to 1924. (This information is well documented in *The Old Rose Adviser* by Brent Dickerson.)

Odile Masquelier had no idea of the important part Lyon had played in the story of the rose when she started her garden. In 1966 she and her husband Georges moved in to the house which had been Odile's family home during her early formative years and which, quite by chance, became available to them when they moved back to Lyon after their marriage. 'The fragrances here still evoke memories,' she said, 'a mixture of roses, santolina and ripening tomatoes.' A year after their return a storm washed away much of the earth. They rebuilt the garden with lots of good soil and peat, making in all six new terraces – quite an undertaking for a steeply sloping site of over one hectare.

The new layout was becoming nicely established when Odile made a visit to Lady Sarah Haddington's garden at Tyninghame, Scotland, a decade later. 'I discovered then that all I had done for ten years was wrong,' she told me as we walked together in the glorious result of her long *affaire des roses*. 'I decided to replant all my garden

The rich apricot climbing Hybrid Tea rose 'Opaline' adds colour to this part of Odile Masquelier's potager. In the background is the vigorous white rambler 'Fontanières', a seedling found at La Bonne Maison, which Odile says has the best hips of all the roses in the garden from August until February each year.

This superb unnamed velvety-red Hybrid Tea rose given to Odile Masquelier twenty-five years ago does well at La Bonne Maison. There are not many good red roses but this is one of the best.

ROSA FOETIDA

PERSIANA

ALSO KNOWN as Persian Yellow, this important shrub rose was brought to Europe from Tehran in the 1830s. The famous rose breeder Joseph Pernet-Ducher of Lyon used it along with the Hybrid Perpetual 'Antoine Ducher' to bring forth the bright orange-yellow seedling 'Soleil d'Or' (1900), the colour of which had never been seen before in a repeat-flowering rose. It then went on to become the parent to many other brightly coloured roses; some say it was also responsible for the proneness to inherit blackspot in many of today's roses.

Leaving aside its martyrdom to blackspot, *Rosa foetida persiana* makes an excellent shrub and there are few, if any, other double-flowered roses that can compete with it for unfading strength of colour. Its buds are globular and open with many petals in cupped form. They do not have the most pleasing of scents, hence its name.

As a bush it has an upright habit, with dark brownish stems, whitish young thorns and dark green leaves. Like its relatives *R. foetida* (a single bright yellow) and *R. foetida bicolor* (a single bright orange), it gives a spectacular display in late May/early June, but has little to offer after that – although this would not prevent me from planting it.

with old roses, for there I found such beautiful roses with perfumes, soft colours, agreeable habits and captivating shapes – and most of them with French names.'

Now thirty years old, this garden is a paradise all the year round. It begins in March and April with a multitude of spring flowers and builds up in a magnificent crescendo of roses in summer, which slowly gives way to the richly coloured foliage of autumn and the plenteous rose hips of winter. Added attractions are the tantalizing glimpses of the city you get from among its trees. The extra terracing allows the land to fall more gently towards a fine panorama of the city of Lyon in the east, for this garden is high up, almost suspended above the river Saône, which runs southwards in the valley below to merge three kilometres on with the more famous Rhône.

The substantial dark green door of La Bonne Maison affords no clue to the treasure behind it. Indeed, even on entering – except for 'Albertine' contented in the arms of an expansive grey-foliaged rose 'La Mortola' on the caretaker's house – you have little indication that this is anything other than the courtyard of a quality townhouse. Terracotta pots brimming with ferns are lined up on the terrace and a dozen or so tall fastigiate cypresses stand to attention along the boundary wall.

I knew there was a garden here, of course, but there had to be one, for only true gardeners would adorn the walls of their home with plants in this way. Two roses have admirably scrambled to the eaves, matching inch by inch the densely foliated exuberance of Virginia creeper, honeysuckle and wisteria. One is the early-flowering, pink climbing Hybrid Tea 'Mme Grégoire Staechelin'; the other, the very useful creamy-white climber 'City of York'. At the foot of the house, clearly loving the attention it gets as a conversation piece, is a superb bush of *Rosa primula*, its dense, aromatic, fern-like foliage wafting the fragrance of incense for yards around.

Flourishing too among all the activity on the house is one of Odile's chance finds; this one, named 'La Bonne Maison', is a lovely repeat-flowering form of 'Francis E. Lester'. Because of a climate so well disposed to germination, and such an abundance of hips, these chance seedlings occur frequently here. Odile grows them on, selecting the very best for special purposes. Another is named 'Pauline' after her daughter.

Well over six hundred different roses now flourish in this garden, but it is also full of many other interesting plants, lots of them rare and all part of the overall plan, for Odile never plants anything without thought and purpose. While roses are her first love she prefers not to be typecast as a collector. 'My only problem,' she says, 'is to find the right place for the right rose. When I like a rose I try to find the right spot for her' – a philosophy with which I most certainly concur.

Because of the terracing, of which one is mostly unaware, it is necessary to duck and weave, under arches and around trees, through little spinneys and up and down steps. The whole garden is one large, luxuriant plantation, but though sometimes the boundaries merge, there are several areas of special interest and purpose. There are open spaces, too, some of them lawns, others, albeit smaller, paved or cobbled; and, as you would expect too in France, there are plenty of strategic nooks and crannies for contemplation and the appreciation of wine and roses.

Odile has woven together some lovely combinations. Wherever there is a rose, near by is something else, perhaps a ceanothus to bring in some blue, a spring-flowering lilac, or a viburnum for winter. Perennials, too, are numerous – blue and white iris, sage and lavender, geraniums in all colours and lots and lots of peonies, which cohabit so effectively with shrub roses. Most important to this garden, though, are trees. Some are common, like apple and cherry, and host roses; others – rare and

majestic – add structure, proportion and strength. These include tall cedars and a broad catalpa, a Judas tree or two and liquidambar. One outstanding specimen is a splendiferous Japanese pagoda tree (*Sophora japonica*), almost eighty years old, its pendulous branches wide-spaced with their tips down to the ground, and with the most twisted and contorted limbs and trunk of any tree I have ever seen.

To come back to roses: whatever Odile wishes to call it, there is no escaping the fact that this is now one of the world's major collections of the genus. Everywhere in this garden they are in excellent condition and clearly enjoying life. Apart from those on the house, the first roses I met here were two spring-flowering, soft yellow species – *Rosa hugonis* and *R. × cantabrigiensis*. These grew in front of a wall on which is a sizeable plant of the simultaneously flowering *Clematis montana*. Odile loves to take roses indoors, so there is a special area planted with roses for cutting. A favourite here is a splendid bush of 'Souvenir de la Malmaison', which 'produces flowers right through into winter'. From this point arches brimming with roses extend down towards the south-eastern corner of the garden. I spotted the bright yellow and pink 'René André', the delightful lemon-white 'Madeleine Selzer', its copious dark green foliage looking particularly good, and the seldom-seen 'Primevère', an unfading yellow rambler from Barbier – a rose I really should get for my collection.

Almost all Pemberton's Hybrid Musks, essential in any garden for autumn flowers, are scattered between the shrub roses of varying sizes and colours that

*Odile Masquelier never plants anything without a purpose and this unusual combination of climber 'Alida Lovett' and giant kale (*Crambe cordifolia*) clearly works very well. 'When I like a rose I find the right spot for her,' she says.*

Pink rambler 'Mrs F.W. Flight' is one of many ramblers and scramblers in this collection of six hundred roses at Lyon. 'I don't like being typecast as a collector,' says Odile Masquelier. 'My problem is finding the right place for the right rose.' The little soft pink in the front is an unknown Noisette.

The delightful 'Opaline' is just one of the many varieties one passes when weaving through arches and walking up and down steps in this rose garden suspended above the city of Lyon. The rose on the left is 'Madeleine Selzer' (facing page).

populate the raised borders on either side of the main pathway running diagonally from the house towards the south-west. Here, too, were some species, including the rich yellow single *R. ecae* and the golden-yellow double *R. foetida persiana*.

Such is the diverse range of roses in her garden that Odile will forgive me, I know, if I indulge myself a little and concentrate more on some of the less common varieties – or at least on some that are not so often seen elsewhere, such as the lovely soft yellow Wichuraiana 'Gardenia' and the free-flowering delicate pink 'Evangeline', both merging into an informal hedge of the pink Rugosa 'Thérèse Bugnet' in a jungle-like area on the eastern boundary. Also luxuriating in this area is what Odile believes to be the true 'Princesse Marie', a lovely old soft pink rambler whose identity has been challenged in recent years – but that's another story.

Under a series of arches along a twisty narrow path one is led towards a wrought-iron gate, barely visible among unruly roses while I was there. This is the entrance to Odile's romantic *jardin secret* – totally enclosed and festooned with all types of roses, in particular, the old-fashioned-looking white hybrid Setigera, from 'Long John Silver'. I felt like an intruder, but inside little curved seats were overhung with ramblers and scramblers and enveloped by shrub roses such as the striped pink and white Bourbon 'Honorine de Brabant' and the lovely greyish-pink Gallica 'Rose du Maître d'Ecole'. Odile tells me that 'Rose de la Maître-Ecole' is the correct name: La Maître-Ecole is a district of Angers, once home to a famous school of horticulture.

NOISETTE ROSE

'DUCHESSE D'AUERSTÄDT'

T HIS ROSE is a deep golden-yellow sport of the paler 'Rêve d'Or', discovered in Lyon in 1884. They were introduced in 1888 and 1869 respectively.

Both deserve garden space anywhere in the world, but neither is really hardy enough for colder climes, coming into their own in Mediterranean areas and the southern states of the USA.

The Noisettes are among the oldest of the groups of roses with *Rosa chinensis* in their make-up, having evolved from a cross between that rose and *R. moschata*. In their ranks, in my opinion, are some of the most beautiful roses ever produced. Almost all are scented; in addition they have the ability to flower in great profusion throughout the rest of the season.

In colder areas these two varieties (along with the other yellows in their group) are best grown on sheltered warm walls. In temperate climates, they are in their element on arches, trellis and pergolas. They enjoy good fertile soils and flourish with extra loving care.

'*Cerise Bouquet' is an outstanding rose. It can be used either as a climber or as a vigorous free-standing shrub. In the garden of La Bonne Maison it thrives as both.*

Nearer to the house, next to a relatively open space of day lilies and topiary – full of bulbs in the spring, Odile said – is the part of the garden that I found the most French in style. Wide, densely clothed arches of roses surround a large classical-style birdbath on a plinth which emerges out of an encircling clump of clipped lavender. The arches sport a most interesting collection of roses, but I would like to single out two, the lovely golden-yellow Noisette 'Duchesse d'Auerstädt', discovered here at Lyon way back in 1884 by Alexandre Bernaix, and its parent 'Rêve d'Or', another locally raised rose, the creation of Claude Ducher fifteen years before.

These two roses growing together represent the reawakening of the city of Lyon to old roses – a movement attributable in large part to Odile Masquelier. She is active in forming 'Une Société des Roses Anciennes' in France and planning an International Conference on Old Roses in her city for 1999. Odile is also planting, with the blessings of the Mayor, a garden of old roses in a park to commemorate, at long last, those bygone rose-men of Lyon. Her garden is open March to September on Fridays, Saturday mornings and Mondays; otherwise by appointment.

MANNINGTON HALL
SAXTHORPE, NORFOLK, ENGLAND

ATING FROM THE WARS OF THE ROSES, MANNINGTON HALL IS a medium-sized battlemented and moated manor house constructed of a pleasing combination of knapped flint and terracotta. It stands in grand isolation amid rolling fertile farmland about seven miles from the Norfolk coast and is approached by a long tree-lined drive.

The present owners, Lord and Lady Walpole, have planted what is now recognized as one of the finest and most important collections of historic roses in the world. They have turned the former kitchen garden and orchard into a series of smaller gardens which illustrate and record, in a living museum, one thousand years of rose history. The Heritage Rose Garden is all contained within approximately one acre and surrounded and sheltered by beautiful old red brick walls. Lord Walpole's botanical background and natural aptitude for plants show clearly in the careful attention to detail and chronology. Furthermore, by leaving some of the existing fruit trees amid the various smaller gardens and some of the espaliered apple and pear trees on the lovely old walls, he has succeeded in creating the impression that the garden has been here for much longer than the fifteen years it has actually taken to achieve.

First impressions on entering the walled garden from the south-east corner belie the extent of what is to follow. On the left a deep border spanning the entire width of the garden comprises mainly species roses and near-species varieties. Although not immediately apparent, a narrower border planted in similar vein goes off to the right. Catching the eye in the north-facing border are *Rosa omeiensis pteracantha* and *R. moyesii* 'Geranium'. If you turn to the right here and into the main part of the garden, the first thing you will notice is a small Medieval Garden bounded by rose-covered wattle hurdles and designed around two seats made up of clipped grass sods. The ancient species *R. moschata* and the elderly Multiflora hybrid 'Rambling Rector' are the natural choices to cover the fences and rustic-arched entrance.

Mannington Hall is a beautifully proportioned flint and terracotta Norfolk manor house, built during the Wars of the Roses. Here Rosa wichuraiana, *a naturally procumbent species, tumbles gracefully into the moat.*

HYBRID GALLICA

'JAMES MASON'

This rose was raised by me and introduced in 1982. Clarissa, wife of the actor James Mason, wanted a red rose to be named for him and chose this one from three options. The Masons were both rose devotees and James was able to enjoy his rose in his Swiss garden for two seasons before he died.

The result of a cross between 'Scharlachglut' and 'Tuscany Superb', it combines attributes from both its parents – height and vigour from the former, texture of petals and scent from the latter, and colour from both. The two parent roses can also be seen at Mannington, 'Scharlachglut' growing up into a cherry tree in the south lawn border and 'Tuscany Superb' in the Victorian section of the Heritage Rose Garden.

'James Mason' has been described as a red version of 'Nevada', but it does not repeat, nor is it quite so tall. Apart from 'Scharlachglut', which was introduced in 1952, it is the only Gallica to be raised this century. Flowering in early July, 'James Mason' is an easy rose to grow and will tolerate even the lightest sandy soil. Although it prefers an open position such as the one it enjoys at Mannington, it will tolerate some light shade. It probably looks best in a border grown in groups of three, but it also does well in pots and will make an attractive, if informal, hedge.

Planted in small cultivated circles in the grass are specimens of ancient roses, among them Gallicas such as *R. gallica officinalis* and 'Rosa Mundi' (*R. gallica versicolor*), Damasks 'Quatre Saisons' and 'Kazanlik' and several Albas, including 'Great Maiden's Blush'. The thorny Scotch Rose (*R. pimpinellifolia*) with soft creamy-white single flowers is used here to provide interest after the others have finished flowering with its mahogany-coloured hips and rich autumn foliage. Those of us interested in rose history and the evolution of this fascinating genus could easily become embroiled in the more academic aspects of this particular part of the Mannington gardens, but during this visit we will simply enjoy its aesthetic appeal.

From the Medieval Garden you might move through the small plantation of fruit trees towards an interesting structure of trellis which is a copy of an enclosure designed by Gertrude Jekyll. On this trellis, inside and out, are ramblers and climbers that would have been used by Jekyll at the beginning of this century. Outstanding is 'Dorothy Perkins which, along with other Wichuraiana ramblers, comes into flower in mid-July. Opposite the Jekyll Garden is a fascinating re-creation of a 'Between the Wars' garden, with paved paths and a small water feature. This period produced many excellent roses and you will recognize some famous Hybrid Musks such as 'Ballerina', 'Felicia' and 'Buff Beauty', but the one that will surely catch your eye is the less well-known 'Belinda', which produces masses of deep dusky-pink flowers in large clusters from June until October.

Still going north, you will emerge from the relatively complex designs of earlier this century to a deliberately planned open space in which a number of circular rose beds have been dug into the earth. Each of these is planted with roses from different breeders of the post-war period. The contents of the beds are far more interesting than the design here – a deliberate ploy, I suspect, to typify the lack of imagination in the landscaping of the 1950s and '60s. Thank goodness for the two corner beds! Outstanding in one is the continuous-flowering German red 'Parkdirektor Riggers'; the other contains a superb example of 'Marguerite Hilling', the pink form of 'Nevada'. Each is surrounded by other modern shrub roses of distinction such as the yellow 'Graham Thomas' and creamy-lemon 'Frühlingsgold'. Dominating this area in late June/early July on the south-facing wall is a wonderful mature example of the Moschata 'La Mortola'. Its masses of pure white single flowers combine beautifully with the abundance of matt grey-green foliage and the soft red brick walls.

If you have all day to spend at Mannington, then linger a while longer in the Heritage Rose Garden. If not, there is much still to see in the extensive grounds outside these walls, so head back south along the east-facing wall, enjoying in passing the heady perfume exuding from the Mosses, Bourbons and Hybrid Perpetuals that make up the Victorian garden on your left. To your right, to add to the amalgam of fragrances, you will brush past the Sweetbriars 'Meg Merilees', red, and 'Lady Penzance', coppery-yellow, as well as dense bushes of Rugosas in the form of 'Blanc Double de Coubert', white, and the clove-scented 'Roseraie de l'Hay', purplish-red. This path takes you to a doorway in the north-east corner leading to where Lord Walpole is laying out his 'post-modernist' garden of recent rose varieties.

From here walk south past the timber-clad Information Centre to a large expanse of well-kept lawns dominated by two huge cedars, glorious in their survival of the 1986 hurricane despite the loss of a few limbs. This is a good vantage point to take in the superb proportions of the house, moat and drawbridge set against a backcloth of woodland and framed by a large expanse of sky.

There is much of interest in the gardens inside the moat, but we will return to these later. Instead, step out across the lawn towards the focal point of the south-east garden – a small classical temple which is open to the north but covered at the back with yet another 'Rambling Rector'. Your walk to this temple will take you over springy turf with, on your left, the reflections of the house in the wide waters of the moat and, on the right, large shrubberies consisting mainly of roses. Many roses of interest thrive here in the ever-moist peaty soil. I feel a particular affinity with this little corner of Mannington, for when I first met the Walpoles in the early 1980s I planted seedling roses for trial here. Three of these – 'Sadler's Wells', 'William and Mary' and 'John Grooms' – have found their way into our catalogue, but the feature I seek out most often here each year is a magnificent red hybrid Gallica, 'Scharlachglut', which has scrambled its way some twenty feet or so into the branches of a Kanzan cherry.

From this point, retrace your steps and cross the fascinating Victorian wrought-iron drawbridge leading to the gardens within the confines of the moat – pausing on the bridge itself to observe, on the east bank of the moat, a splendid, well-established, cascading white *Rosa wichuraiana* and a dense, shrubby bush of the silvery-pink Rugosa 'Fru Dagmar Hastrup', growing one on either side.

The gardens around the house are again, probably accidentally, divided up into separate 'rooms'. The first of these is a spacious lawn surrounded by deep mixed

The walled garden at Mannington is divided into several different smaller gardens, each one depicting a different period in the history of the Rose. Here an arch of 'Rambling Rector' and clumps of Rosa Mundi extend a welcome to the Medieval Garden.

45

The Medieval Garden is entirely surrounded by 'Rambling Rector'. Here the centrepiece of Rosa pimpinellifolia *is clipped and shaped as it would have been in those ancient times.*

borders which, in turn, are backed with ten-foot-high brick walls. Numerous roses grow here among a variety of shrubs and herbaceous plants; three worth special mention are 'Golden Showers', a yellow modern climber which flowers and flowers all summer, 'James Mason', a hybrid Gallica growing here since before its introduction in 1982, which produces a stunning display of crimson flowers in June each year, and an enormous white-flowered 'Kiftsgate', which is actually trespassing from the other side of the wall where its roots are growing in the courtyard at the back of the house. Natural curiosity will lead you to peep into this courtyard from under 'Kiftsgate's' branches through the ancient arched doorway, but this is a private area. Three roses which would not normally be seen in this part of the world shelter from the blasts of Norfolk winters in the courtyard: a twelve-foot-high *Rosa bracteata* with its large creamy-white flowers and masses of soft green leaves; one of the best specimens of 'Ramona' that I know of this side of the Mediterranean ('Ramona' is a deep pink form of 'Anemone Rose'), and 'Guinée', the dark red climbing Hybrid Tea from the 1930s.

From here cross the lawns past the front of the house into a formal area of beds of Hybrid Teas and Floribundas, numerous in variety and supported by pillar roses, mostly of modern continuous-flowering varieties. Thriving here is the unfading golden-yellow Floribunda 'Allgold'. I have fond memories of this rose; much of my love for roses was originally inspired by its raiser, the late Edward LeGrice, in my student days. This formal south-facing garden extending to the edge of the moat is flanked on either side by tall yew hedges and some strategically placed pieces of statuary add interest. Sharing the south wall of the house with an expansive wisteria is a fine example of the seldom-seen, rather tender *Rosa banksiae* 'Lutescens', which blooms late in May in clusters of small single yellow scented flowers and is capable of climbing to considerable heights. Its bronzy-green foliage goes particularly well with the subtle blues and greys of the flint walls. The Walpoles have extended this colour blending by the use of greyish-green foliage plants along the base of the wall, among them rosemary, rock rose (*Cistus* 'Silver Pink') and Mexican orange blossom (*Choisya ternata*).

Beyond one of the yew hedges is a small, secret, scented garden designed in the same intricate pattern as that of the moulding of the dining-room ceiling. Among numerous fragrant herbs are several highly scented roses, including 'Louise Odier', a famous Victorian Bourbon, and the more recent soft pink 'Anna Pavlova', one of the most fragrant of all the modern Hybrid Teas. To add height to this garden four Eglanterias are planted on tripods – the pink 'Amy Robsart', the crimson 'Anne of Geierstein', the rose-red 'Greenmantle' and, of course, the most fragrant of all Sweetbriars, *Rosa eglanteria* itself.

Such is the extent of the gardens here at Mannington that it would be easy to miss some of them. You can also encounter roses in the gardens of the ruined chapel and on some of the perimeter fences, not to mention the woodland walks.

The gardens are open to the public on Sunday afternoons from the beginning of April to the end of October, and on Wednesdays, Thursdays and Fridays from 1 June to the end of August. Each year, usually at the end of June, there is a weekend Festival of Roses. Parties can visit by appointment.

Mannington Hall has one of the world's major collections of roses. The Damask rose 'Quatre Saisons' is seen here in full flush. It is one of the most fragrant of roses and has been used in the production of perfume since before the Middle Ages.

MULTIFLORA ROSE

'RAMBLING RECTOR'

That 'rambling rector' crops up in almost every garden I visit is not surprising; apart from the appeal of its amusing name, it is such a good rose.

It has a wide range of uses, from covering unsightly buildings to scrambling up into trees and through hedgerows. It is quite thorny and dense in structure, so makes a good burglar deterrent when grown on walls or boundary fences.

The individual flowers consist of about ten petals and are borne in large clusters in early July. Each small bloom is white, but the pronounced boss of yellow stamens gives an overall mass effect of cream. It is sweetly fragrant and extremely healthy, as are most of the vigorous white scramblers.

Its origin is lost way back in the mists of time, but it is clearly a seedling from *Rosa multiflora*. Its alternative name of 'Shakespeare's Musk' is unlikely to have any basis in truth; as Graham Thomas pointed out, *R. arvensis* is almost certainly the 'sweet musk-roses' of *A Midsummer Night's Dream*.

At Mannington 'Rambling Rector' can be seen on the wattle fencing around the Medieval Garden, where it is pruned early each year to keep it contained. It is also planted on the north side of the temple in the South Garden where it is, once again, kept in trim, but in this case it is allowed a little more freedom to expand to its true dimensions.

36 ATLANTIC STREET
PORTLAND, MAINE, USA

AS WELL AS BEING ONE OF THE SMALLEST, THIS GARDEN IS ONE of the newest featured in this book. It is living proof that 'small is beautiful'. As for its newness, the house was built way back in 1848 and presumably there has been a garden of some sort here since then. But it is new in that its owner Suzy Verrier started planting it when she moved here only two years ago; in gardening time-scales, it thus has a mere two seasons' growth behind it. To me, it has a distinct atmosphere of maturity, partly attributable to the age of its surroundings, but not least to skilful design.

The only plants other than old irises and day lilies in the garden when Suzy came were a ten-foot American holly tree on the north-west side, an 'Alba Maxima' by the front door and a species rose which, interestingly, Suzy believes was collected from the wild by a previous owner, since it can be found growing naturally around parts of Maine; this is *Rosa virginiana*, of which there is a small hedge. Mature trees beyond the boundaries play their part – tall conifers, western red cedar (*Thuja plicata*), just outside the fence in a neighbour's garden, and a large Norwegian maple growing in the sidewalk of Atlantic Street in front of the house.

Bearing in mind that the overall size of this garden is only a hundred by fifty feet, the surrounding trees and buildings – this being a town garden – are very influential. They do not just provide that sense of time past, but their light and shade affect the atmosphere during the four seasons. Suzy has been particularly conscious of this in designing the garden, especially since up until arriving here she had a three-acre garden and owned a rose nursery. She confesses to missing the spaciousness of the previous gardens, but enjoys being liberated from the nursery – she can now 'do my own thing and grow what I like without having to pander to others' tastes'. Furthermore, in her new life as a professional garden designer and author, she is now able to lead rather than follow. Her tastes, no doubt influenced by her experience in running her nursery, are clearly quite catholic:

The beautiful single flowers of Rosa virginiana, *part of a short hedge of plants collected from the wild, hang gracefully over the fence of the porch, while* 'William Baffin' *peeps through next to the unusually designed seat.*

Landscape designer Suzy Verrier's cottage-style garden in Portland, Maine, was created recently, although the house itself was built in 1848. The rose in the foreground is 'Lilian Gibson' *with* Rosa glauca (R. rubrifolia) *behind* (facing page).

The richly coloured 'Morden Centennial' is one of the many extremely hardy roses in this garden. 'There are ample roses that tolerate the harsh climate of Maine,' says Suzy Verrier, 'so why should I grow any of the tender ones?'

'Whatever is healthy and pleases me,' she says. Her open-mindedness spills over into her choice of roses, for what I found in this garden were many varieties I had never seen before, and some I had never heard of. She is particularly fond of single roses and pink is her favourite rose colour.

The ambience of this place was in no way spoilt – it was perhaps even heightened – by the rain that fell on the day of my visit. I started my tour at the back of the house, the south-east side, on what Suzy calls her porch – a delightful raised area with a wooden floor, or deck, for sitting out on. Several roses were near by, including the *Rosa virginiana*, growing into and around the short fence which surrounds the porch. Later in the year this variety is covered in bright orange-red hips, and as winter gets nearer, its foliage changes to bright yellow and then red.

North from the porch, along the side of the house, a lawned area is surrounded on all sides by borders absolutely crammed with perennials and shorter-growing shrubs. Intermingled with them are several very interesting roses. One in particular, a recent arrival, is 'Mabelle Stearns', an American shrub rose of the 1930s, raised by Horvath. To accommodate this important rediscovery, Suzy had to dispense with some irises: 'Roses always take precedence,' she said. The hybrid Gallica 'James Mason' is beginning to elbow itself in among hollyhocks and poppies. Here, too, is 'William Baffin', a lovely deep pink, semi-double Kordesii hybrid. Until recently this rose has not been available in Europe, but it deserves to be everywhere in the world,

I think – it is so healthy. It was raised by Felicitas Svejda at the Canadian Department of Agriculture. Here also is a blush-white hybrid Rugosa I had never seen before, 'Mrs John McNabb', raised in 1941 by an American breeder called Frank Skinner, who raised several good shrub roses in his day. This rose is non-recurrent, but flowers for several weeks and, Suzy says, will eventually get to six feet. It is not surprising that Suzy Verrier grows a lot of Rugosas; in 1992 she wrote a definitive book on the subject, and she has just finished one on Gallicas.

On the east-facing wall is a climbing rose – or at least, the early stages of one – that will eventually climb up and over the top of the two-storey house if not stopped. It is the soft pink 'Dr W. Van Fleet' and it is here partly because Suzy loves it (preferring it to its more popular sport 'New Dawn') and partly because she believes that a rose does not have to flower continuously to satisfy her. Also, and perhaps more importantly, it was her first rose; she remembers it from childhood, when it also covered her house.

Another fine group of roses, of which Suzy has several here, are those raised at Iowa State University by the late Griffith Buck. Few of the very good roses he bred have ever received the credit they deserve. They are mostly very disease-resistant and very hardy, two factors which he insisted on before a rose was introduced. 'Country Dancer' is one such, a cerise-pink which becomes brighter with its second flush in the autumn. It also has lovely dark green foliage, another feature

Seen here, side by side, are roses from two continents: the semi-double 'Carefree Beauty' from Canada on the left and the fully double 'Abraham Darby' from England on the right. Roses take precedence over other genera in this garden but there are still many other interesting plants to see.

RAMBLER ROSE

THIS VIGOROUS rose is often confused with its more famous daughter, 'New Dawn', a sport of 1930 which almost immediately become one of the world's most popular roses. This acclaim is probably deserved, since 'New Dawn' has many fine attributes, not least remontancy. Its flowers are identical to those of its parent.

'Dr W. Van Fleet' is a Wichuraiana hybrid and was introduced in 1910. What it lacks by way of a long flowering season it amply makes up for in other respects. It is healthy, free from the mildew that 'New Dawn' suffers from later in the season; it has larger, slightly more shiny foliage, and is very much more vigorous.

'DR W. VAN FLEET'

It has a variety of uses, from climbing up into trees, which it does admirably, to covering up old, unsightly buildings. It is also good in the more refined roles of adorning high house walls and gracing pergolas and arches, the latter particularly effectively. Its vigour makes it more tolerant of poor soil than 'New Dawn'. Left unpruned it will grow thirty feet or more.

I know one garden where this rose has been doing stalwart service for years; it is labelled 'New Dawn', having been bought as such. 'Dr W. Van Fleet' is, in fact, the owner's favourite rose, but she confesses that had it not been wrongly labelled she would never have planted it.

of Buck's roses. On the point of hardiness, it is common practice in this part of the United States to protect roses through the worst months of winter by covering them with burlap straw, bracken or even polystyrene cones (which can be bought from garden centres especially for this purpose). Suzy never does any of this; if they are not hardy enough, she throws them out. 'There are enough roses that grow happily in this climate, so why should I grow those that need protection?' she says. A refreshing attitude. Something else I like about this plantsperson's philosophy is her willingness to have roses in the garden she does not know by name. If she likes it, she grows it – my feelings exactly.

In about the centre of Suzy's garden is a little pond, well stocked with water and bog plants and cleverly dividing the garden into two without obviously doing so. Close by is another of Buck's roses, 'Honeysweet' – a mixture of yellow and orange that coordinates well with assorted perennials of similar shades. Farther back in an adjacent border is the beautiful green-eyed, white 'Mme Hardy' and the charming pink single 'Complicata'. Also growing happily here is 'Dunwich Rose', the procumbent form of *Rosa pimpinellifolia*.

The clapboard house is painted white and the front door is dark blue, a colour enhanced by Suzy's choice of roses around it – all purplish or mauve shades such as 'Mary Queen of Scots', 'William III' and 'La Belle Sultane' (*R.* 'Violacea').

At the front of the house, a brown natural wood picket fence divides the garden from the car parking area and this is further extended at right angles to provide the boundary fence to the road. The little front gate is delightfully framed by an archway of timber, all matching that of the fence. This has all sorts of plants adorning it – honeysuckle and golden hop to name but two, plus an unknown red rose given to Suzy when she moved in. It was not in flower when I was there, but it looks suspiciously like 'Paul's Scarlet'.

Close by the fence, in what Suzy calls her 'wilderness' – among such diverse subjects as dogwoods and Jerusalem artichokes – are 'Alba Semi-plena', 'Nevada' and one of her favourites, an almost thornless rose bred from *Rosa blanda* in 1938 by a Professor Hanson of North Dakota and called 'Lilian Gibson'. It is rose-pink, fully double and very fragrant.

Alongside the brick pathway which runs from the front gate towards the front door, with a twist here and there, are borders of mixed plantings including several roses. Some of David Austin's varieties are underplanted with blueberries and strawberries, a most effective combination. In this border, too, is a foundling, a bright pink Gallica hybrid called 'William Grant' after Bill Grant of California, who rediscovered it a few years ago.

In England we would call this a 'cottage garden', and a superb example at that. It is situated in a delightful area of Portland, settled by Poles and Italians early in the last century, and where every house is a different pastel shade. It is less than a quarter of a mile from the sea.

The garden is not always open because Suzy is a working landscape designer, but she has a very relaxed view about visiting, so if she is at home it will be open.

Just one of the many unusual combinations of roses and companion plants in Suzy Verrier's newly created garden is the rose 'Country Dancer' with Allium albopilosum *(facing page).*

SPECIES ROSE

ROSA VIRGINIANA

THIS NATIVE American species, also known as *Rosa lucida*, is one of my favourites of all the wild roses. When fully open, its deep pink flowers have a lovely splash of yellow in the centres from the prominent stamens. They are faintly perfumed. For a once-flowering variety starting rather later than most, it goes on flowering for a very long time, almost to August. Following the flowers, the plant becomes covered in autumn and early winter with masses of bright orange-red hips. The foliage is a bright shiny green and without blemish or disease of any sort. In late September the leaves turn at first to a bronzy colour and later to yellow and orange before they fall.

The tallest unpruned plant of this species I have ever seen was five feet high, but most stay at about three and a half to four feet. It is dense in structure and will grow in any type of soil; in fact, it seems almost to prefer poorer, sandy ground. It has many uses; one is as a ground-coverer, for on its own roots it spreads naturally by suckering. It also makes a dense, wide-growing hedge.

There are two double forms, probably hybrids – *Rosa virginiana* 'Plena' (*R.* 'Rose d'Amour'), also known as 'St Mark's Rose', and a shorter-growing form of this variety called 'Rose d'Orsay'. A white form also exists, which I have never seen.

VILLA CETINALE
SOVICILLE, NEAR SIENA, TUSCANY, ITALY

*V*illa Cetinale is built on the site of an Etruscan settlement dating back to the eighth century BC. The present-day house goes back to the seventeenth century. Here 'Albertine' adorns one of the exterior walls of the ancient kitchen garden.

*R*amblers and scramblers share space on arches and pergolas with vines and honeysuckle in the old walled garden at Villa Cetinale. This, once the old vegetable garden, is just part of the ongoing building restoration and extensive garden reclamation being carried out by Lord Lambton and Claire Ward (facing page).

NYONE WITH EVEN THE REMOTEST SENSE OF HISTORY VISITing Cetinale is bound to get vibrations from its long and colourful past. Situated fifteen kilometres or so west of Siena, the villa stands on high ground surrounded by forests of evergreen oak (*Quercus ilex*), and is approached from the south through a valley of arable farmland. It is the home of Lord Lambton and Claire Ward, who fell for it when they first came to live in a farmhouse near by in 1972. It was then almost derelict, having been empty since 1959, but when it became available in 1978, Lord Lambton was able to buy it. Since then, revitalizing and restoring the villa, the estate and gardens has been a labour of love, a real team effort, and the place now feels wanted and lived in.

There was an Etruscan settlement on the site of the villa in the eighth century BC and much later, in the fourteenth century, the Chigi family, bankers to popes and kings, built a large farmhouse. Incredibly, this remained in their hands until Lord Lambton took over five hundred or so years later. It was remodelled in its present style in the late seventeenth century by the Roman Baroque architect Carlo Fontana, a pupil of the great Bernini. A central arch in the south facade of the villa leads to a handsome portico, or hall. It was here that we took lunch on the day of my visit, and I learned from Claire Ward something of the history of Cetinale and of her 'affair' with the garden. She also translated the Latin inscription of a seventeenth-century plaque on the wall: 'Whatever you see here, we love. If you like it, stay. If you don't like it, go away. Either is agreeable to us.' I wonder if I dare hang this translation in my office at my nursery?

The entire estate of about eighty hectares rises from the south, gently at first and then more steeply, to a high point in the north where stands the impressive fivestoreyed Romitorio, a hermitage also designed by Fontana as part of the overall grand plan. It was completed in 1713. This building, too, had become neglected and was bought by Lord Lambton in 1990, bringing it rightfully back into the estate.

BOURBON ROSE

'VARIEGATA DI BOLOGNA'

INTRODUCED IN 1909, this Italian rose is comparatively young by Bourbon standards. It is probably a sport of an old purple variety now lost to cultivation.

Its colouring is made up of pronounced stripes of purple on a creamy-white background, reminding me of the semolina with blackcurrant jam we used to have for school dinners. Each bloom is packed with petals and the flowers, when fully open, are globular in shape. They are heavily scented.

It is a shrub but can also be used as a small climber. A little temperamental, it needs plenty of good husbandry to give of its best. Its dark green leaves are not over-large, sometimes giving an overall appearance of sparsity. The main flush of flowers is fairly heavy, the later ones few and far between; even so, they are well worth while, since in autumn their colour is much more intense than in high summer.

A striking and unusual rose, worthy of a little bit of extra attention.

In the late seventeenth century Flavio, a nephew of Pope Alexander VII – who himself spent some of his youth at Cetinale – was made a cardinal. It is said he murdered a rival and was refused absolution by the Pope until, as a penance, he had daily for a month climbed on his knees the 250 steps called the Scala Santa that lead up to the Romitorio through an avenue of cypress trees.

The Romitorio was occupied until the end of the last century by an order of twelve monks. It has now been restored as an occasional retreat for family and friends. From the fifth storey there are awesomely beautiful views across Tuscany towards Siena in the east and to the south and west over the forest which stretches for seventy kilometres to the sea. I found it compelling, its refurbishment in tune with its origins.

I could go on and on about the flavour and substance of this place – describing the sixteenth-century statuary that stands around Cetinale, the fine open-air theatre now being reconstructed by Lord Lambton, the massive gate piers and their implanted larger-than-life statues that mark the original entrance. Even in a rose book, it would be criminal not to mention the Tebaide, the 'Holy Wood' which occupies twenty hectares to the north of the villa. Claire told me that the name originated from a wood near Alexandria in Egypt which was inhabited by hermit-saints. It may just have been the time of day, or perhaps my mood after visiting the hermitage, but these woods have a stillness such as I have never before experienced among trees; even the light filtering through the branches seems to have a quietness about it. The Tebaide is intersected by both footpaths and driveways, from which numerous carved, moss-clad, allegorical stone figures such as dragons, lions, tortoises and snakes peer up at you from beneath the trees. The old main road to Siena, now overgrown – and haunted, it is said – runs alongside the southern boundary of this dense, mysterious forest. There is a small crescent-shaped lake in the middle, filled with waterlilies.

The gardens at Cetinale are all around the vicinity of the house and – except for the Lemon Garden, which is Lord Lambton's province – all have been reinstated by Claire Ward. She speaks with great affection of Bruno Chompi, an aged, loyal gardener who helped her in the beginning and whose father before him had worked here, but in truth she did much of the early work herself. Nowadays, although she is still very much involved, most of the basic digging and hoeing as well as the more skilled work such as masonry is done by Fiorenzo, Fernando, Ellio and Ali. Without ever meeting these people, I could tell that a fair amount of loving care is involved in the smooth running of this estate. 'One of the joys of living here is that the people are so nice,' said Claire. The ghosts are happy too, apparently; they slam the odd door when returning by carriage from partying in Siena, but never intrude.

The structure of the gardens was in place when Claire came, but had been completely neglected. All that was here were some ancient Banksian roses, several groups of lovely, old-fashioned pink peonies and a three-hundred-year-old wisteria, which she claims is the largest in the world.

The Lemon Garden at the south of the house has been faithfully restored in nineteenth-century style, with formally arranged box topiary, citrus trees in large terracotta pots and statuary flanking a wide walk that leads from the entrance doors in the southern boundary wall right up to the villa – now the front, though Fontana designed it as the back. There is a Fattoria on one side and a Limonaia on the other. The first two roses I came upon were on the wall of the Limonaia; both, Claire said, bought unnamed from the local market. The pink I felt I should know but didn't, but the red I recognized as the beautiful highly scented climbing 'Crimson Glory'.

The old walled garden, now the Rose Garden, is approached via the north side of the Fattoria and has probably been a vegetable garden since the fourteenth century. Here I encountered the great wisteria, which could indeed be the biggest in the world; it seems to go on for ever. From the moment of entering this garden, it becomes clear that this is the domain of someone who knows and cares about plants. 'I have been gardening all my life,' said Claire. 'My father was a gardener, my mother a wonderful gardener, my aunt a gardener and when I was taken as a child to see yet another garden, I used to say to myself, "I'll never ever be a gardener, it is so boring." But then, as soon as I had a house of my own, I walked into the garden and have never been seen since.' Most of the plants came from England. 'I had an old Audi which overflowed with plants every time I came here.'

On the lines of the old layout, of two central paths criss-crossed by several others from opposite directions, Claire has developed a Rose Garden of great charm with pergolas and arches dripping heavily with such roses as 'Albéric Barbier' – white, with its lovely glossy foliage, 'Constance Spry' – pink, for its myrrh perfume, and 'Leverkusen' – yellow, for its reliability and continuity of flower. The walls that completely surround this garden are at least as old as the villa; they are tall and furnished with climbing plants of all types, including the vigorous free-flowering pink 'François Juranville', that ever-flowering, most fragrant of modern pink climbers, 'Aloha', the lovely soft yellow Noisette 'Céline Forestier' and the

A large plant of 'Constance Spry' mixed with an unknown pink climber forms part of the boundary to the orchard at Cetinale. Other roses, too, can be found in among the shrubs, fruit trees and young olives in the orchard and its surrounds. The yellow rose on the wall is 'Easlea's Golden Rambler'.

The rose 'Constance Spry' tempts one through yet another archway to discover yet more roses. As a child Claire Ward vowed never to become a gardener but the gardens here prove that the vow was not kept.

orange-lemon 'Ghislaine de Féligonde'. Here and there vines, some bearing fruit, merge beautifully with the roses.

The borders and beds are also full of roses, dozens of varieties from down the ages and in assorted sizes. 'The Fairy', bright pink, is used very effectively as an edging rose along with lavender, with the tall, lanky types such as red 'Scharlachglut' and soft pink 'Bloomfield Abundance' used in the background. Others I saw were the pink Moss rose 'Chapeau de Napoléon' (the Emperor himself is said to have come to Cetinale on one of his visits to Italy), the striped pink and purple Bourbon 'Variegata di Bologna' and the pure white 'Boule de Neige'. Modern Shrubs are here too, such as the mauvy-pink 'Lavender Lassie', yellow 'Graham Thomas' and the white Floribunda 'Iceberg'; all of these are always in flower. Without exception everything looks in good healthy condition, although the plants are seldom sprayed. The fragrance from the roses is augmented, especially in the spring, by shrubs such as viburnum, lilac, chimonanthus and osmanthus, to name just a few. In spring every bed is a mass of daffodils, tulips and lilies.

From the Rose Garden a door in the wall leads to the north side and the back of the villa. From here a wide drive flanked with tall cypress trees leads to what was the front gate at the time of Flavio. Several ancient pale yellow *Rosa banksiae lutea* thrive at intervals along a tall wall on the east side of this drive. Here Claire has also planted 'Cooper's Burmese' (*R. cooperii*) and white 'Bobbie James'.

SPECIES ROSE

'COOPER'S BURMESE'

THIS IS a hybrid of *Rosa laevigata*, the Cherokee Rose, to which it has a close resemblance. It is variously listed as *R. cooperii* and 'Cooper's Burmese'. It started life in a garden near Rangoon and was sent to the West in 1923 by one R.E. Cooper, hence its name.

It is very beautiful, with pure white flowers produced singly in June each year (earlier in warmer climates than Britain's). They have little or no scent and after the first flush, occasionally produce another flower or two. Only a few blooms set hips, which seldom ripen enough to change from green to orange in temperate regions.

As a plant it is quite vigorous and rather angular in growth. It has dark reddish-brown wood and quite vicious thorns. Its foliage is dark green and comprises three or five leaflets only. Sometimes these are variegated yellow as though infected by Mosaic virus, but this may simply be natural coloration.

I have had a plant which is only slightly protected from the north for about ten years, so it seems to be reasonably hardy where I live in Norfolk. It is, apparently, not too bothered by poor soil.

The walls of the villa itself are also adorned with climbing plants and roses, although not excessively, with the unusual combination of the yellow climbing rose 'Leverkusen' and yellow jasmine (*Jasminum nudiflorum*) taking pride of place on the north side. Also on this wall is the vigorous 'Easlea's Golden Rambler', the prolific 'François Juranville' and the even more prolific 'Seagull'.

The other walls of the villa and that of the western boundary have also been utilized effectively for plants. The modern orangey-yellow 'Alchymist', the buff-yellow Tea rose 'Gloire de Dijon', that excellent modern red climber 'Parkdirektor Riggers' and one of my favourite species, *R. laevigata*, all grow alongside pink and white jasmine and a lovely plant of Chinese gooseberry or kiwi fruit (*Actinidia chinensis*).

Both the Villa Cetinale and its gardens are very special. I was fortunate to be shown around by Claire Ward, to whom it means so much and who, with Lord Lambton, has worked so hard to bring it back to life.

Villa Cetinale is open every day in the summer.

Roses predominate in the expansive gardens at Cetinale but Claire Ward uses companion plants to great effect. Everything looks healthy and well cared for, and no chemical sprays are ever used.

HELMINGHAM HALL
NEAR IPSWICH, SUFFOLK, ENGLAND

ARGE HERDS OF RED AND FALLOW DEER GRAZE SIDE BY SIDE with rare breeds of cattle and sheep beneath ancient oaks in the 400 acres of rolling parkland which surrounds Helmingham Hall. They were grazing these pastures when they were first recorded in the mid-seventeenth century, but the history of this important Suffolk estate goes back much farther. Some of the massive oaks are estimated to be at least 900 years old. As one would expect, access can only be gained to such a substantial house by one of two drawbridges that cross the deep, wide moat which completely surrounds it. All the views of the house are pleasing, but my favourite is to see it first from the south through the perspective of the wide avenue of oaks that has stood since 1700.

The Tollemache family have owned the estate since the foundations of the Hall were first laid in 1480 and successive generations have lived here ever since, many of them keen gardeners. In fact there is evidence that gardening has been carried on here since Saxon times.

The walls of the Kitchen Garden were built in 1745 and it was here in the late 1970s that the present Lady Tollemache first started to bring her influence to bear. First she removed most of the brightly coloured roses so fashionable in the 1950s and '60s. Quite apart from having a natural inclination for the quieter colours, she had by then fallen under the spell of that 'great old man of roses', the late Humphrey Brooke, whose famous garden a few miles away at Lime Kiln, Claydon, was an inspiration to many of us in the 1970s and '80s. He loved his old-fashioned roses, and Lady Tollemache tells how she remembers him talking of them 'as though they were children'.

The walled garden, along with the extensive ornamental garden, extends to some three and a half acres and is well maintained by Head Gardener Roy Balaam, who has worked here for 38 years, since he left school. At first he worked with several

'Blush Rambler' is seen here in the foreground of the view across the walled kitchen garden towards the southern aspect of Helmingham Hall. Old roses have been growing in this part of the gardens for over a century.

The goddess Flora, seen from behind the floriferous white Damask rose 'Mme Plantier', makes an appropriate centrepiece to the formal rose garden created by Lady Tollemache at Helmingham Hall over the past twelve or so years (facing page).

CLIMBING TEA ROSE

'GLOIRE DE DIJON'

RAISED IN France by Jacotot in 1853, this lovely rose has had many imitators – none with quite its refinement and grace. It was vigorously promoted by Dean Reynolds Hole, the Founder President of what is now the Royal National Rose Society of Britain.

Some call the rose a Noisette, others a Tea; I favour the latter. It came about from the crossing of an unknown Tea rose with the beautiful Bourbon 'Souvenir de la Malmaison', from which it gets its superb fully double shape. There is seldom, if ever, a time in summer or autumn when this semi-vigorous climbing rose is without a flower. Sadly, it also inherited a profound dislike of wet weather.

The flower colour is deep straw-yellow, fading to soft primrose and becoming suffused with various shades of pink as it ages; but it is most variable, and sometimes not recognizable as the same rose from one season to the other. Its foliage is bronzy-red when young, ageing to bluish-dark-green.

As a plant it can become rather leggy, but pruning hard in its first year or two, and training its shoots horizontally, will help counteract this tendency. It prefers to be on a wall rather than on a pergola or trellis. Although it prefers sun, it will flower fairly freely on a north-facing aspect.

other gardeners, but now he manages with just two full-time men and one part-timer. When Lady Tollemache took over, the layout was cruciform in design, but it is now divided into eight segments with a wide central grass path running from east to west, flanked on either side by deep herbaceous borders. A relatively new feature running the entire length of the lateral paths is a series of tall, very sturdy metal arches making a tunnel to support sweetpeas, runner beans and ornamental gourds.

I first saw this garden in the early 1980s, when I was asked to identify some of the roses. Some of them had been growing there since before the turn of the century. Among the unrecognizable ones were several Ayrshires, subtly different to any I knew by name but not sufficiently distinctive to warrant reintroduction. (Ayrshires are hybrids of *Rosa arvensis*; they generally make ideal ground coverers and are also good for growing up into the branches of trees.) Ayrshires I knew included 'Venusta Pendula' and 'Splendens', both blush-pink, and the white 'Dundee Rambler'. All these and many others are still growing here today, trained into fan shapes on strands of wire strung between metal posts. This is a good way of taming roses which have a strong inclination to wander in all directions but the one you want.

Also trained very symmetrically on the wire supports are several plants of the hybrid China 'Gruss an Teplitz'. Like the Ayrshires, these have probably been here since they were brand-new varieties almost a hundred years ago. 'Gruss an Teplitz' is remontant with plum-coloured young foliage and dark green leaves. Its flowers, which are produced in smallish clusters, are shapely and deep crimson in colour. Graham Thomas describes its fragrance as 'spicy'. Another old favourite found here in profusion is the old purple Bourbon 'Mme Isaac Pereire', blowzy, beautiful and highly scented.

As well as the posts and wires, several supports in the form of metal and mesh arches are scattered here and there in the garden. Among the ramblers and climbers trained on them, at least two to an arch, are such old stalwarts as 'Albertine' and 'Blush Rambler', 'Alister Stella Gray' and 'Debutante'. The soft apricot-yellow 'Alister Stella Gray', a favourite of Lady Tollemache's, relishes the shelter of the walled garden. Another favourite is 'Debutante', a lovely fragrant pale pink rose which she describes as 'hanging down brilliantly'. I know exactly what she means. The delicate flowers are all perfectly spaced in their clusters, which gently tumble down among each other.

Surrounding the entire walled area to the west of the house is a second deep moat. The area inside the moat provides a corridor for wide grass paths and deep borders at the base of the walls. North of the moat a number of ancient apple trees including 'Lord Derby', 'Lane's Prince Albert' and 'Blenheim Orange' provide a partial windbreak for a number of espalier-trained pear trees on the outside walls of the garden – among them such varieties as 'Beurré Hardy', 'Doyenné du Comice' and 'Williams' Bon Chrétien'.

A most interesting collection of plants is to be found in the wide border which runs the entire length of the south-facing external wall of the Kitchen Garden. This is known as the Spring Border, for it is at its best from March through to summer and is sheltered by a belt of shrubs and trees, especially yew, which grow on the far side of the moat. In April and May this border is a riot of colour with tulips and iris particularly prominent. Spring-flowering shrubs such as ceanothus and chaenomeles also flourish on this wall, but roses are by far the most numerous. Climbing roses are placed every few yards along the walls and are mostly trained into fan

shapes on horizontal wires spaced about a foot apart; some varieties are quite rare and a delight to find. 'Captain Hayward', for example, is seldom seen these days, even in the larger collections; it is a scented Hybrid Perpetual, semi-double in form and bright reddish-pink in colour, later fading to blush-pink. It is not over-vigorous, so is ideal in a 'crowded' position such as this. Another climber here that does not grace gardens often enough these days is the thornless Boursault 'Morlettii'. This deep pink rose blooms in great profusion in June; a special feature is its young leaves, which are deep purple-red in spring.

This spot provides a most agreeable position for that most sophisticated Tea rose 'Gloire de Dijon', not just because it is sheltered and warm, but because the red bricks of the wall with their hints of blue make a perfect foil for its yellow/apricot colour. Like Teas, Noisettes enjoy a warm, sheltered aspect and this group is well represented here by several superb plants of the lovely 'Desprez à Fleurs Jaunes', whose orange-yellow colouring again looks beautiful against the old brickwork. Although sometimes temperamental, the white Bourbon 'Boule de Neige' is doing very well here, and another thriving shrub rose is the early-flowering pink hybrid Pimpinellifolia 'Stanwell Perpetual'. All the roses in this border were raised in the nineteenth century.

If the southern border is interesting to rose lovers, then the largish area between the east wall of the Kitchen Garden and the westerly aspect of the house is fascinating.

A special feature of the rose garden at Helmingham are two large beds of the Gallica Rosa Mundi. Here, the one in the foreground has reverted to its parent Rosa gallica officinalis *(the Red Rose of Lancaster), especially appropriate perhaps since* R. alba *'Maxima' (the White Rose of York) is to be seen in the background.*

This separate garden has its own character and atmosphere. It is walled on three sides and, except for a wide grass walkway which separates the two moats, only water divides it from the house to the east. Although two old mulberry trees go back much farther, the roses in this garden were planted in the mid-1960s by the present Lord Tollemache's mother. The layout consists of wide beds of roses around the inside of the three walls and a parterre of well-manicured box edging in the centre of a rectangular lawn. Everything is beautifully proportioned here, from the carefully worked out pattern of the parterre with its topiary echoing the shape of the obelisks of the main drawbridge, to the mounds of clipped yew on the banks of the moat. The beds of the parterre are filled with santolina. Somehow, too, the roses in the three perimeter beds are also in proportion. These are all Hybrid Musks and they probably represent a complete collection of these most useful shrub roses. They range from well-known varieties such as 'Penelope', 'Pax', 'Prosperity', 'Felicia' and 'Buff Beauty' planted initially, all well documented elsewhere in this book, to rarer ones introduced more recently. These include the lovely 'Danaë', a shapely deep yellow which loses nothing in fading to creamy off-white as it ages and the delightful 'Thisbe', which displays a boss of golden-coloured stamens to good effect and also fades from yellow to cream. All these borders are edged with 'Hidcote' lavender, but to me the most interesting feature is the dense carpet of London pride saxifrage which effectively provides low-maintenance ground cover all the year round. On the walls

behind the borders are several rambler roses, some of them Hybrid Musks such as 'Francis E. Lester'; these come into flower in mid-June when the shrub roses are at their peak. Outstanding is 'Gerbe Rose', a lilac-pink, glossy-leaved Wichuraiana rambler. Not quite as free-flowering in its main flush as, say, 'Albertine', it compensates with a modest succession of flowers throughout summer and autumn.

On the opposite side of the house to the Hybrid Musk garden is another formal rose garden, the newest at Helmingham, begun in 1982 by Lady Tollemache. Having fallen for old-fashioned roses in a big way by that time, she at first thought of planting a wild, informal garden here, but quickly realized that such an idea would be out of character, especially since this site is overlooked from several vantage points, including the house. Hatfield House in Hertfordshire, the seat of the Salisburys, is approximately the same age as Helmingham, so Lady Tollemache enlisted the help of her good friend Lady Salisbury in plotting and structuring its design, although she chose all the plants herself. What a successful partnership this was, for now, in maturity, the result blends perfectly and might well have been here for as long as the house – an illusion enhanced by the framework of beautifully tended dark green yew hedges, now about eight feet tall and three wide. In all this garden must consist of three-quarters of an acre. About a quarter, at the west end, comprises a knot garden of box in intricate patterns delineating the Union flag, the Tollemache fret and the initials 'T' and 'A'.

The pastel shades of the old roses predominate and fragrance is everywhere. This is a view from among the roses in the formal rose garden. The Damask rose 'Ispahan' is in the foreground.

The Knot Garden, planted by Lady Tollemache about ten years ago, is just beginning to mature. All the plants are from Tudor times or before. In the background is a splendid hedge of the ancient Rosa Mundi.

Roses take up more than half the area. Their formal beds are separated from the knot garden by two oblong borders edged with catmint and filled with closely packed plants of 'Rosa Mundi'. A large statue of the goddess Flora adds atmosphere to the Rose Garden. All the rose beds are set into lawn and each is discreetly and effectively edged with brick. They are crammed full of a wide selection of Lady Tollemache's favourite old roses, both remontant and once-flowerers. This deep Suffolk loam is good for roses. Thriving here are the Bourbons 'Souvenir de la Malmaison' and her sport 'Souvenir de St Anne's', both soft pink and highly perfumed. Likewise enjoying life to the full are the Portland Damask 'Comte de Chambord' and the striped pink-and-white Hybrid Perpetual 'Ferdinand Pichard'. Moss roses are much in evidence; worth special mention are the most heavily mossed of all, lavender-pink 'Moussu du Japon' ('Japonica') and arguably the most delicious of the many soft pinks of its tribe, 'Général Kléber'. Gallicas, of course, seem to do well whatever the conditions, and the dark purple-red 'Charles de Mills' is clearly thriving.

A problem with many of the older roses in formal situations is that they tend to become difficult to control as they get older, in good soils especially. Lady Tollemache has solved this problem by inventing her very own rose support. It consists of a stout central metal post about four feet high topped with a four-inch disc from which wires radiate at forty-five-degree angles to pegs in the ground. The long pliable shoots of the roses are arched down and fixed to the wires to form dense mound shapes. Because they retain so much more growth than is possible with pruning, they produce masses of flowers.

In the yew hedge at the east end of the Rose Garden a large 'window' is being formed to provide a vista through to the park, in the foreground of which is a huge specimen of 'Cerise Bouquet'. This modern shrub rose could not possibly fit into any of the formal settings here, but looks very much at home in its own space among weeping willows alongside the duck pond.

Helmingham is open every Sunday from April to September and I strongly advise finding the time for a visit.

HYBRID MULTIBRACTEATA

'CERISE BOUQUET'

THIS ROSE makes a strong-growing, dense, thorny shrub with a propensity for large quantities of flowers in its first flush each June. It has the pleasing habit of producing another goodly flush – although not quite in such quantity – in the autumn. It was raised by Tantau in Germany in 1958 from a cross between *Rosa bracteata* (from which it has inherited its vigour) and the Hybrid Tea 'Crimson Glory' (from which it gets its delicious cerise-crimson flower). The buds are scrolled until almost fully open, a trait which also comes from the Hybrid Tea. Although dense with petals when it is fully open the golden-yellow stamens set the flower off to perfection. A particularly attractive feature is the tidy way that the flowers in each cluster are evenly spaced. The flowers have the most lovely acidy fragrance.

This shrub can get huge if given its head. It is capable of making an effective tree climber. Another use to which it can be adapted is an informal hedge, when it will become almost impenetrable and deter the most determined of trespassers. Its leaves are small, numerous and grey-green and I have never seen this most rewarding of roses suffer from anything more onerous than an occasional attack of greenfly. At Helmingham it has been allowed to develop into a magnificent shrub outside the main garden, by the duck pond.

SONOMA MOUNTAIN ROAD
SANTA ROSA, CALIFORNIA, USA

T HIS GARDEN IS SITUATED TWENTY MILES OR SO SOUTH-EAST of Santa Rosa. The approach is through undulating wide pastures and glades of native oaks, redwoods and not-so-native eucalyptus – typical countryside in this part of California. The tall rustic gate at the entrance to the old farmstead where Michael Bates and his wife Helen have made their home emphasizes the western American ambience. Not so the garden. Over thirteen or so years Michael has defied the climate and fashioned the site in so English a way that even the temperature – in the high eighties on the day of my visit – did nothing to dispel my illusion of being in a country garden somewhere in England. Even the odd glimpse of dark green redwoods through the well-foliated perimeter, Michael remarked, could fool you into thinking you were seeing mature yew trees. Only later, espying distant mountains to the north through a gap in those redwoods, was I brought back to our true location.

It is not only skill by a professional garden designer, combined with plantsmanship, that makes this garden what it is; nor is it its Englishness. It is the result of a mixture of all three, plus – above all, I supect – devotion to an ideal. The garden is entirely Michael's creation. When they bought the property there was no garden, just the odd tree, mostly badly placed among weeds and more weeds. Michael was born in Dorset, England, and his mother encouraged him in the art and practice of gardening from an early age. He took a degree in English Literature and spent his early working life in advertising in London. He first visited northern California in 1976 and fell for it in a big way. He settled down here, combining his love of plants with his artistic flair to start a successful landscape design business.

There are many enjoyable things to write about in this garden, leaving aside the roses. Michael openly confesses that if he were to start again now he would not use so many roses. Yet what exists is very much a rose garden, for roses contribute more to the atmosphere of the place than any other single group of plants here.

*N*oisettes enjoy the agreeable climate of California. Here Michael Bates has used 'Rêve d'Or' to advantage on the arbour attached to the house, a house that he redesigned and refurbished. Alongside is the early flowering Hybrid Tea 'Mme Grégoire Staechelin'.

*C*ast-off petals on the veranda, evidence of the sheer floriferousness of 'Rêve d'Or' and 'Mme Grégoire Staechelin'.

SPECIES ROSE

ROSA PIMPINELLIFOLIA

This is the 'Pimpernell Rose' mentioned in Gerard's *Herball* of 1597. It is one of nature's most lovely single roses and has wide distribution, thriving in coastal habitats.

In its most common form it makes a dense shrub to a height of about four feet in gardens. It has its main flush in late May and will often oblige with a few intermittent flowers throughout the rest of the summer. Its sweetly scented creamy-white flowers are followed by hips which ripen to shiny black. It is very thorny (hence its earlier epithet of *spinosissima*). Its small, fern-like light green foliage were thought to resemble the herb burnet, and another nickname is Burnet Rose.

Of its other forms, the two best known are 'Dunwich Rose', which is procumbent and spreading in habit, and 'Altaica' (also known as 'Grandiflora'), taller with larger flowers. Several hybrids have been bred from this important rose and, in Victorian times, the many double forms of all shades bred in Scotland – the Scotch Roses – were popular.

Rosa pimpinellifolia makes a versatile garden plant, especially in the wilder garden. It responds well to clipping into an excellent, impenetrable hedge. Best of all, I like it as specimen shrub, allowed its own space.

Michael uses roses in many different ways – except as bedding plants. 'Why do roses tumbling out of the top of a tree do something for me which a Hybrid Tea in a rose bed doesn't?' he said. By way of confirmation, the first roses I came upon in his garden were a couple of soft buffy-yellow varieties, 'Claire Jacquier' and 'Alister Stella Gray', together cascading from a large bay tree into the tops of a dozen or so huge, purplish-blue echiums, ten or twelve feet high, a combination I had never seen before.

Using roses not only to grow up into the trees but to provide flowers high up above other plants and shrubs is part of the plan here. One shrub in this role is *Rosa glauca* (*R. rubrifolia*), eight feet high at least, its little pink flowers to be followed by hips later. 'This is not as easy-going in this part of the world as it is in England,' Michael said. Perhaps, since it grows so readily from seed, an inferior clone has somehow found its way into the system. Also playing this part well in the same vicinity, but even taller, is the lilac-pink *R. californica plena*; climbing up through its lower branches is a newly planted specimen of *Clematis texensis* 'Duchess of Albany', its purpose to provide colour when the flowering season of its host has finished. I doubt if in England this variety of clematis would ever reach the height planned for it here.

At ground level, in a mixed bed at the edge of the drive, a group of the Polyantha rose 'The Fairy' is densely packed to provide colourful ground cover without a break all through summer and into autumn. Near by is a border of predominantly light green and yellow-foliaged subjects, which Michael advocates for shady areas because they pick up the light easily. Starting to climb up into a tree from this border is the lovely soft creamy-pink and yellow Tea rose 'Souvenir de Mme Léonie Viennot', already growing and flowering well, but waiting to produce its most colourful flowers in the less intense sunshine of early autumn. Among golden-leaved feverfew which, surprisingly, I had not seen before in California, is a well-foliated bush of the pink 'Thérèse Bugnet', which seems to do well everywhere. Beneath a handsome old fig tree another Tea rose, the silvery-pink and cerise 'Mrs B.R. Cant', is performing well, like most Teas and Chinas, well suited by the climate. By the front door of the house, which is built of timber and painted greyish-white, varying sized pots are placed at random. The assortment of subjects they contain includes one or two roses, the lovely creamy-pink 'Gruss an Aachen' one of them.

Several Noisettes are among Michael's favourite roses, and examples of most of this group can be found somewhere in this garden. There is no doubt that these roses grow particularly well in California. I have already mentioned 'Claire Jacquier' and 'Alister Stella Gray' growing together up into the trees; on an arbour attached to the house are three plants of the most lovely of yellow roses, 'Rêve d'Or'. These have been in this position since the structure supporting them was built some twelve years ago, and although I missed their glorious first flush, they were still flowering and will continue to do so right through into winter. Also growing on the house is a large and expansive *Wisteria sinensis*. Again, I missed its flowering, but I can imagine the fabulous combination, a few weeks earlier, of its soft purplish-lilac flowers intermingling with those of the soft golden-yellow of 'Rêve d'Or'.

Mostly in this garden roses are used in supporting roles, but there is one place where they are major players. This is a pergola 120 feet long, twelve feet wide and nine feet tall. At least, that was its size when it started out about eight years ago; it is now much wider and taller, from the mass of roses taking advantage of the space and

support it provides. The pergola is a crucial part of the overall design and Michael has an intense love-hate relationship with it. At its peak it is glorious and produces an effect that would be impossible to achieve with anything else. At pruning time, however – which takes a full week in this garden – the temptation for Michael to dispense with its added burden is quite strong.

Along the length of this pergola is displayed the story of climbing and rambling roses. It hosts examples of Wichuraianas, Multifloras, Bourbons, climbing Teas, climbing Hybrid Teas and Sempervirens, to name but a few, but above all the Noisettes that thrive so well in this part of the world. Two worth highlighting are 'Céline Forestier', a delightful double soft yellow which is not vigorous in other gardens but is magnificent here, twelve feet high and thirty-five feet wide with copious healthy leaves; and 'Aimée Vibert', a later-flowering double white which, again, has plenty of light green foliage. Two other useful climbers dominant on the pergola are the beautiful, soft pink single 'Anemone Rose' and the lovely thornless double white *Rosa × fortuneana*, used as an understock in some parts of America. Effectively intertwined are clematis in complementary colours.

From the area immediately adjacent to the house, through an archway composed of the lovely soft pink *R. gigantea* hybrid 'Belle Portugaise' and the floriferous lilac-pink 'Blush Noisette', is an open space about thirty yards wide and roughly the same depth which has been turned into a small wildflower meadow where things natural

The richly coloured flowers of a young 'Golden Wings' planted against weather-worn rustic railings combine beautifully with the foliage and fruit of a young citrus tree, belying the 'Englishness' of this garden.

69

R. ANEMONOIDES

'ANEMONE ROSE'

Tʜɪs ɪs one of the most lovely of the single roses. It was raised in Germany by J.C. Schmidt in 1895. Its actual parentage is not known, but it is probably a cross between *Rosa laevigata* and a Tea rose. In America this rose is sometimes called 'Pink Cherokee' because it closely resembles its parent, the Cherokee Rose. It is said not to be fully hardy in less temperate climates, but I have never had problems with it, beyond a little die-back from time to time.

Its flowers, which can reach up to four inches across, are slightly scented. Their colour is a soft pink, with deeper-coloured veins; the reverse is paler, almost silvery. (There is a more deeply coloured form called 'Ramona' which, unfortunately, can revert to its parent without warning.) Its foliage is dark green, its stems reddish-coloured and very thorny. Its growth is angular. In warmer climates, where it can expand, it will grow anywhere, but it is advisable to give it the protection of a wall in Britain. Allowed its head, this rose can reach twenty feet in height and almost as wide.

It is best pruned in spring for, although it is basically a 'once-off' variety, in good summers it will continue to produce a few flowers into autumn.

grow in close embrace with lots of semi-naturalized roses. These are all on their own roots. Although in behavioural terms they are left very much to their own devices, their colour range is deliberately chosen to co-ordinate with the wild flowers and the green, unmown grass of spring. The blend of mostly deep pinks, carmines, purples and greys together with clear pure whites is achieved with Gallicas such as 'Belle de Crécy', 'Rose du Maître d'Ecole', 'Hippolyte', 'Complicata', 'Cardinal de Richelieu', 'Charles de Mills' and 'Camaïeux', Albas such as 'Mme Legras de St Germain' and Damasks such as 'Mme Hardy'. Leaving aside the wonderful effect of these colour combinations against a distant background of dark green from the redwoods, the coalescence of so many fragrances makes this area nothing less than idyllic in May each year. The scene is further enhanced in colour by blotches of deep purple-blue from *Salvia interrupta* and the soft blue of *Aster × frikartii* 'Mönch'. On the subject of wild flowers, I fell in love with the delightful little native *Clarkia amoena* growing along the roadsides here in north California.

In the garden adjacent to the Gallica meadow, Michael planted up an orchard about ten years ago with several varieties of old European apples as well as antique American varieties. Its southern boundary is fenced with very rustic split-board railing which, in turn, supports yet more roses – an aesthetic device, which keeps out deer. Here I found 'Alchymist' in its deepest orange clothes and that delightfully compatible couple, the Gallica *Rosa* 'Violacea' (also known as 'La Belle Sultane') and

'The Garland' in close embrace, respectively purple and soft pinkish-white. I found two climbing Hybrid Tea roses surprisingly in fine form (they are both temperamental with me) – the soft pink 'Ophelia' and the deep red 'Souvenir de Claudius Denoyel', each with a penetrating fragrance. Proving its worth for glossy foliage and spasmodic later flowers is the creamy-white double 'Albéric Barbier'.

Walking farther round to the east of the garden I brushed past such gems as the fully double, repeating Pimpinellifolia hybrid 'Stanwell Perpetual' and the lovely pink Damask 'Ispahan'. Here, too, but closer to the ground, is the common Scotch Rose *Rosa pimpinellifolia* (*spinosissima* as it was), which Michael remembers from his childhood, growing wild on the Dorset and Cornish coasts. On the other side of the garden Gallicas and Albas once again come into play in association with perennials and shrubs such as plume poppies (*Macleaya cordata*), catmint (*Nepeta mussinii*), yarrow (*Achillea*), rock roses (*Cistus* 'Silver Pink'), *Caryopteris* × *clandonensis* 'Heavenly Blue' and 'Worcester Gold', and *Spiraea thunbergii*.

In the midst of all the activity is a huge plant of the rose 'Bobbie James', scrambling twenty feet up into a redwood. In a year or two, when it reaches the top of this tree, it will be a spectacular sight, especially since it will be seen from the drive on the way in to this most agreeable garden – a place I felt reluctant to leave.

The gardens are open to parties only, and to others by appointment, with proceeds donated to the local chapter of the Californian Native Plant Society.

The superb and very vigorous climbing form of 'Cécile Brünner' is one of many climbing, rambling and scrambling roses to be seen in this most delightful garden, some twenty miles south-east of Santa Rosa in California.

A mixture of Noisettes 'Alister Stella Gray' and 'Claire Jacquier' cascades gracefully into a group of giant echiums, just one of many unique and fascinating plant associations arranged by English-born landscape designer Michael Bates in the gardens at Sonoma Mountain Road (facing page).

L'OUSTAOU DEI BAILEA
482 *CHEMIN DU PARADIS, BAR-SUR-LOUP,*
ALPES-MARITIMES, FRANCE

Two hundred and fifty metres up the side of a mountain in the Côte d'Azur is the home of Bruno Goris, around which he has planted a unique wilderness-style garden. Here his delightful one-time shepherd's cottage is just visible through the modern shrub rose 'La Seviliana'.

The old Hybrid Perpetual 'Souvenir du Docteur Jamain' is one of the most beautiful of its kind. Its flowers prefer to be away from the direct glare of the sun. It is just one of three hundred and fifty varieties amassed over fifteen years in this fascinating garden (facing page).

CCUSTOMED TO MY NATIVE NORFOLK, WHERE OUR HIGH-est hill gently rises to a summit of about thirty metres, I climbed higher and higher on the uneven rocky path on the mountainside above Vallée de Loup at Grasse in search of l'Oustaou dei Bailea. Getting more and more out of breath, I could not help wondering if the effort would be worthwhile. Surely no one would make a garden in such a place? Chemin du Paradis, indeed! Was this one of Vivian Russell's jokes? When I reached the top would I find only a pretty view and a shepherd's hut?

At 250 metres, almost at the top, I found both the view, truly magnificent, and the hut, a delightful little house of great character nestling into the side of the mountain and, would you believe, built for shepherds back in 1820. It is the home of Bruno Goris, who later pointed it out to me, high above on the mountainside, as we wended our way along the road below heading for Nice. It looked so tiny, and I realized then that it takes a special kind of person to plant a garden and build up such a fine collection of roses in such an improbable place.

Bruno is from Belgium, but – as he said smilingly – 'I was here before I was born.' His grandfather had found the house by chance while out walking and climbing and had bought it in 1954. As a child Bruno came to stay here on holidays rather reluctantly, for his grandfather was a strict man and Bruno had to help him tend his fruit and vegetables. Later he inherited the house and its hectare or so of terraced land from his parents, and eventually he came to live and work here as a gardener, fulfilling a burning ambition to work with plants. 'Every photograph of me from the age of four is with flowers,' he said. 'Part of my early childhood was spent in Africa, and I remember vividly the smell of arum lilies.' As he grew up his parents steered him away from gardening, believing like so many parents that it was no way for their son to earn his living. Bruno dutifully became a teacher, although gardening and flowers were always on his mind.

Somehow the purity of the beautiful single rose 'Complicata' captures the wildness of the garden at L'Oustaou dei Bailea. 'I think of a rose which I like first and then plant a bed around it,' says Bruno Goris.

The Alpes-Maritimes are seen here from among Bruno Goris's roses. In the foreground is the energetic scrambler 'Paul's Himalayan Musk', one of the best roses for climbing up into the branches of trees (facing page).

Fifteen years have now passed since he came here to live and start his garden and such is his flair and plantsmanship that he is now much sought after on the Côte d'Azur for his inimitable style of gardening. 'I am not a landscaper!' he insists. 'Here I am called a *paysagiste*, but I don't like it. I am working with plants and I try as much as possible to make my gardens natural-looking, and my clients employ me because they have seen my garden, a wild type of garden – natural, in fact.'

His garden is certainly natural and wild and beautiful – and unique. 'Once I didn't like roses because of their artificial look,' he confided. 'Then, by chance, I discovered a bush – I didn't know its name – on an old derelict house down the path. It was covered with blooms at Christmas each year, so I picked some of them and made cuttings. Despite its neglect the bush grew bigger and better each year and it dawned on me eventually that I was inadvertently pruning it, making it stronger.' He went on, 'It was the first rose I planted here and later I discovered it was called "Général Schablikine".' From this discovery roses became important to him. 'I now think of my garden with roses first and then make a bed around them,' he said reflectively.

'Général Schablikine' is a Tea rose raised and introduced by Gilbert Nabonnand in 1878. It is indeed a beautiful rose, coppery-pink and yellow. Bruno is not a rose collector, but does seek out those raised by Gilbert or Paul Nabonnand, who bred and grew roses in nearby Golfe Juan between 1870 and 1923. Teas are long-lived

TEA ROSE

'SOUVENIR DE MME LÉONIE VIENNOT'

WE SHOULD not become complacent, but in recent years it has become easier to grow Tea roses out of doors in England, especially on sheltered warm walls, for winters seem to be getting fractionally milder. Having said that, they still generally prefer sunnier, warmer climes such as the South of France and the southern US.

This variety is one of the most lovely of the climbing Teas. In parts of New Zealand it can commonly be found in older gardens, for it was a favourite there in the 1920s and '30s. Its colour is coppery-red opening to creamy-yellow, overlaid with soft hints of pink which deepen as the loosely formed flowers age. It is free-flowering, recurrent and has a lovely scent. The plant is relatively thornless, with dark green leaves. It climbs well to about fifteen feet. This is one of the few Teas that are quite good at climbing up into trees, where the weather is not too cold.

It is more at home, though, on a warm wall, where it is best left unpruned until it becomes necessary to trim it into shape. Excellent in a cold greenhouse or in a conservatory – especially in a large pot or tub, as it was most often grown in its heyday.

and enjoy this climate, and Bruno believes that many Nabonnand varieties are still to be found here somewhere. Already he has several that I had never previously heard of. Apart from the Nabonnands, Bruno has – without consciously 'collecting' them – amassed over 350 varieties of all types of roses in this incredible garden.

With mountains all around to trap the clouds, the rainfall is greater here than in the rest of the Côte d'Azur, and at this altitude the temperatures are a little lower. Together with its south-easterly aspect, even with the occasional frost and cold blow in winter, this affords a near-idyllic environment for both gardener and gardens.

The first thing Bruno did when he moved in was to plant lots of fruit trees. These are now becoming well established, performing the dual tasks of hosts to scrambling roses and bearers of fruit for Bruno to use in another of his enthusiasms, cooking.

A tour of this garden starts at the front of the house, which is hung with all sorts of exotica – abutilons, passion flowers, grape vines and roses, some scrambling high up into the branches of overhanging trees. A bright red passion flower, probably *Passiflora racemosa*, is already, only a couple of years after being planted, treble the height it is supposed to reach. Watering cans, empty flower pots awaiting use and other paraphernalia and trappings of *le jardinier* keep company with an abundance of brightly coloured *Impatiens* in the delightfully crowded area by the front door.

To the right is the potager, filled with herbs and things culinary and overhung with roses galore. Two of these were among the first roses Bruno planted when he

HYBRID MUSK

'GHISLAINE DE FÉLIGONDE'

I CAME RATHER late to this French rose: it was given to me by James Russell, late of Castle Howard Gardens, in 1975. Dating back to 1916, it is a seedling of 'Goldfinch', but – unlike its parent – is continuous-flowering; in fact it is seldom without flowers in England from early June to November.

Their colour is a little inconsistent, varying according to soil and weather. It is most usually an orangey eggy-yellow, but always fades to creamy-yellow – a change that bothers some people, but not me. I think it adds to its already considerable charm.

The flowers are about one and a half inches across, full of petals, have a slight scent and are produced in large, densely packed clusters on a tidy-growing, medium-sized plant. Its stems are almost thornless and its foliage bright green, turning orangey-brown in the autumn.

This rose can be grown either as a free-standing shrub, when it will get to six feet or more without support, or on some supporting structure; as a wall plant or pillar rose, it can grow to double that size. It is also excellent on an archway or trellis.

started the garden – 'Souvenir de Mme Léonie Viennot', a beautiful soft yellow and pink climbing Tea (1898) and 'Sénateur La Follette', a bright pink vigorous hybrid of *Rosa gigantea* growing up into the branches of a white Judas tree (*Cercis siliquastrum alba*). From his expression when telling me about this unique combination, it was obvious that their simultaneous flowering gives Bruno lots of pleasure each spring. This is a pairing that could work only in favourable climates, for although Judas trees thrive in temperate Britain, 'Sénateur la Follette' is rather tender and prefers warm, unexposed positions. This rose is distributed in the rest of the world as 'La Follette'; I have no idea why the prefix has been dropped. It was raised not far away in Cannes in 1910 by a Mr Busby, gardener to Lord Brougham, and is now very common in the South of France. Other roses sharing space with Bruno's vegetables and cascading down from the trees above are the rampant white hybrid Multiflora 'Seagull', the delicious long-flowering, soft yellow Noisette 'Céline Forestier' and the dainty but exuberant climbing form of the pink hybrid China, 'Pompon de Paris'. Closer to the ground the heady perfumes of white Rugosa 'Blanc Double de Coubert' and pink Portland 'Jacques Cartier' mingle deliciously with the subtle aromas of herbs and a profusion of ripening vegetables.

The potager is at the lower east end of two terraces but moving back past the house, a narrow pathway leads off in a westerly direction through densely packed flora with lots of roses on every side. Here I found such delights as the pink Polyantha 'The Fairy', the deeper pink 'Constance Spry' and one of Bruno's special favourites, the spritely, free-flowering white Polyantha 'Marie Parvie'. Somewhat unexpectedly, although with great pleasure, I came upon the highly scented, deep velvety-red climbing Hybrid Tea 'Ena Harkness'. This is a rose that both Bruno and I share a fondness for. Two others going strongly in the mixed company of potentillas, hebes, daisies and iris (as well as lots of spring-flowering bulbs) are the lovely purple-shaded pink, very double Tea rose 'Archiduc Joseph' and the ancient purple Gallica 'Cardinal de Richelieu'.

Ducking and weaving past tree after tree, shrub after shrub and rose after rose, we found ourselves way up above the level of the house. We could have been a thousand miles from anywhere and I felt totally in tune with nature. It is not difficult to see why mine host's 'wilderness gardens' are sought after by his clients, especially as he so obviously has the ability to mix and match colours without detriment to the natural inclinations of plants. One little glade, for example – penetrated by brushing through a thicket of *Rosa banksiae normalis* (At last I have found one! Bruno is sending me cuttings to complete my set of Banksian roses!) – is an all-the-year-round rhapsody of yellow and orange. There are mahonias in winter, golden foliage plants for both spring and autumn, hypericums in variety and potentillas, all interspersed in summer with a range of yellow and orange roses. They include the Musk climber 'Ghislaine de Féligonde', climbing Tea 'Bouquet d'Or', 'Cocktail', 'Phyllis Bide', 'Gloire de Dijon', 'Mermaid' and 'Buff Beauty'. This is quite a family gathering, for several of the roses are closely related; 'Phyllis Bide' (1923) and 'Cocktail' (1957) represent successive generations of 'Gloire de Dijon' (1853).

In a quieter mood, a little farther along this terrace, a little grassy clearing is surrounded by closely intermingled white and cream varieties, with the dark green glossy foliage of the rambler 'Albéric Barbier' providing a lovely foil for its own flowers as well as for others. Up in the grey-green foliage of the olive trees, which cohabits so effectively with the white flowers of the roses, related early-flowering

ramblers 'Rambling Rector' and 'Bobbie James' start things off in the spring. Lower down, among grey-foliaged plants such as santolina and lavender, Hybrid Perpetual 'Gloire Lyonnaise', procumbent 'Pearl Drift' and the intrepid 'Iceberg' all do stalwart service throughout summer. Later on, like the rest of the garden, this area is rich in autumn colour and the colourful fruit of roses, with an important autumn flush of flowers coming from the ancient species *R. moschata*.

I could go on and on listing the roses I enjoyed seeing and discussing with Bruno, but there were far too many to include here. One, though, cannot be missed out; new to me, it is a later-flowering hybrid of *R. banksiae* named 'Purezza', raised by Italian breeder Mansiuno. It is white, large-flowered and very vigorous – another rose that Bruno has promised to send to me to try out in England.

I do not know how many terraces make up this garden; I think it is seven. They are retained in place by dry stone walls which crumble here and there from time to time to form little extra bits of garden for Bruno to plant yet another rose, or something else he has found, adding even more variety to this glorious wilderness. I very much enjoyed the time I spent with Bruno Goris, who is assiduously doing what he likes doing most, gardening.

The garden at l'Oustaou dei Bailea is open for two weekends each year during rose season, and at other times by appointment. It is a must for anyone finding themselves in the South of France in late May and June.

One of the little glades in the wilderness of Bruno's garden is devoted entirely to yellow roses and other plants with yellow flowers, especially those with greyish foliage. Here 'Buff Beauty' cohabits happily with Jerusalem sage (Phlomis fruticosa).

BLEDLOW MANOR
BLEDLOW, BUCKINGHAMSHIRE, ENGLAND

Bledlow Manor, a seventeenth-century house situated in the Chiltern hills, has belonged to the Carrington family since 1800. Here a hint of its elegance can be seen from a large bed of the Floribunda rose 'Iceberg' and lavender.

THIS GARDEN EXTENDS TO TEN ACRES. THE PROPERTY HAS belonged to the Carrington family since 1800. When the present Lord and Lady Carrington moved in there was no garden at all and the one you see today is the creation of the landscape architect Robert Adams. Responsibility for the day-to-day gardening is in the hands of Frank Bailey, the Head Gardener, who has been here for eight years and has two gardeners working under him. Although there is no separate rose garden as such, Lady Carrington is especially keen on roses, and they feature prominently almost everywhere in the grounds.

The house was built in the seventeenth century, but its appearance is mainly early eighteenth. Built of soft bronze-pink brick, it rises to three storeys with dormer windows all round. It stands on fairly high ground at the edge of the Chilterns in the village of Bledlow, about ten miles south of Aylesbury. The chalk soil is not easy for roses, but with the loving care they receive, they are in excellent shape; they are sprayed two or three times each year with manganese to help counteract chlorosis caused by the high alkalinity.

The house is approached from the east by a sweeping metalled drive with semi-mature lime trees on the north side and the tall red-brick exterior wall of the Kitchen Garden to the south. In front of the house is a large expanse of lawn broken only by two large trees, a beech and a cedar planted by Lord Carrington in 1951. This lawn is the only substantial, uninterrupted open space in the entire grounds. Pyracanthas and honeysuckle, growing up to the eaves, clothe the walls on either side of the front door. The north-facing Kitchen Garden wall is furnished with several well-trained climbing and rambling roses. The continuous-flowering modern yellow 'Leverkusen' in particular is doing very well. Beneath the roses at the foot of the wall is a two-foot-wide border filled entirely with *Iris unguicularis* – quite a sight when in full bloom each year.

To the south of the house is what has become known as the Fishpond Garden, totally enclosed by high brick walls. Although it is of modern design, its style and proportions echo the classical lines of the house. An eight-foot-wide border running the full length of the east-facing wall is planted with a mixture of both ancient and modern shrub roses. In order to tame some of these roses and prevent them becoming untidy, and out of keeping with the ambience here, they are trained on wrought iron or wooden structures. I was particularly fascinated by one such contrivance, a low, domed cage created by bending long ash sticks into a latticework. Over this was trained the procumbent rose 'Grouse', one of the more vigorous of the modern so-called ground-coverers. It is a hybrid of *Rosa wichuraiana* and flowers profusely in mid-July. Its masses of single flowers are almost pure white; there is also a pink form named 'Partridge'. While there is clearly a need for ground-coverers in modern gardens, I cannot help feeling that the current vogue for these allegedly cost-effective landscape plants, very few of which have flowers that can be described as beautiful, is a distraction from real roses. After all, many far more lovely hybrids of *R. wichuraiana,* which make excellent ground cover and are now grown as climbers and ramblers, have been around since the turn of the century.

The Fishpond Garden is divided into two distinct areas. That farthest from the house is a sunken area with a formal pond; the part nearest the house consists of lawn with a wide shingle path in the centre, on either side of which is a short avenue of quarter-standard mop-headed *Viburnum carlesii*. These are quite a sight in the spring, and their fragrance overwhelming in the confined space. They have been here for some forty-five years but, sadly, one or two now seem to be nearing the end of their life.

To the north-east of the house a substantial walled garden doubles as an extension to the various ornamental facets of these gardens and as a source of fruit and vegetables for the kitchen. Several apple trees here are trained into mop-heads, a hark-back to Victorian times. Continuing the Victorian theme is a green-painted gazebo which stands in the centre of cruciform paths and is clothed with the yellow-and-red hybrid China climber 'Phyllis Bide' and the climbing form of the white Floribunda 'Iceberg'. On the south-facing wall of this garden are greenhouses used both for propagation and for growing out-of-season flowers for the house. On the walls, especially the warmer walls, are trained peaches and plums with, here and there, a rose. One such rose is 'Apple Blossom', an aptly named pink Victorian rambler of substance. Dominating this scene, though, are two very wide herbaceous borders containing a great diversity of subjects but, especially, large groups of peonies and delphiniums.

To the west of the walled garden is a croquet lawn, sheltered on three sides by well-clipped mature beech and yew hedges. To the east is yet another red-brick wall, on which are trained some very good specimens of climbing hydrangea, wisteria and clematis. Several roses are clearly at home in this warm spot, outstanding among them the free-flowering pink modern climber 'Bantry Bay'. All the borders surrounding the croquet lawn are planted with assorted shrubs and herbaceous plants with most species in largish groups. Colour of foliage is clearly more important than flowers, a policy which ensures interest all the year round.

Next to the croquet lawn is what has now become known as the Swimming Pool Garden. Cleverly sited adjacent to the pool is a scented garden, with all manner of fragrant flowers and herbs such as skimmia, daphne and lavender jumbled together.

MOSCHATA HYBRID

'PAUL'S HIMALAYAN MUSK'

THIS ROSE undoubtedly has *Rosa moschata* somewhere in its make-up, but it is also probable that it acquired its early-flowering ability from *R. multiflora*, its semi-evergreen nature from *R. sempervirens* and its vigour from *R. brunonii*. In other words, like its true origin, its parentage is unknown. What is certain is that it was introduced by William Paul towards the latter end of the nineteenth century.

It is a very vigorous rose, capable of attaining thirty feet or more up into the branches of trees. It turns into a dense, free-flowering plant when grown on trellises, pergolas or arches.

Its individual leaves – smallish and a greyish dark green – are produced profusely, making it a good covering rose. The shoots are usually fairly thin and pliable, with numerous hooked thorns. The plant is very hardy. The flowers, which are borne in large, densely packed clusters, are semi-double, soft lilac-pink in colour, about an inch across and made up of several slightly frilly petals. They are sweetly scented.

This variety makes a welcome change from the many other tree-climbing ramblers and scramblers that come in tones of white or creamy-white.

Landscape architect Robert Adams has been responsible for the design of most of the gardens at Bledlow Manor. Depicted here is the skilful use of 'Iceberg' roses in a supporting role to a wide variety of plants, especially purples and greys.

From here the ground rises slightly towards another beech hedge, where an assortment of small trees and shrubs has been planted randomly into grass to create a small wild garden. Again this provides a long season of activity, starting in early spring with snowdrops and daffodils naturalized in the grass. Among the taller subjects here are a fruiting mulberry and a tulip tree. Growing fifteen feet up through the branches of an elderly apple tree and now smothering it completely is a ten-year-old plant of the soft lilac-pink, floriferous rambler rose 'Paul's Himalayan Musk'.

At no time in this part of the garden is one aware of the house which stands close by. We move from one high-hedged enclosure to another, each of these variably sized separate 'rooms', so to speak, with its own particular atmosphere and character created by the selection of plants and their differing designs.

The character of the next enclosure is a contrast to the informality of the wild garden, for it is made up of a series of interlinked, straight brick-paved paths, each intersecting square or rectangular borders. Particularly interesting here from a design point of view is that within the perimeter hedges of beech and yew, which are eight feet high at least, nothing else exceeds four feet, despite the fact that a very wide variety of subjects is growing here. Once again, the differing genera are planted in large groups. As in many other parts of these gardens, emphasis is very much on texture and colour of foliage and the ultimate form and shape of the plant. Two varieties of Floribunda rose planted in largish groups here and there in this area are

the ubiquitous and reliable white 'Iceberg' and the clear yellow 'Korresia', the latter struggling slightly probably because yellow roses generally do not enjoy chalk. Positively thriving here are such evergreens as *Mahonia bealei*, *Viburnum davidii* and several different hebes.

Roses need a little extra loving care in the gardens of Bledlow Manor since its soil is so chalky. 'Iceberg', however, does not seem to mind and here is seen in its climbing form.

The next little 'room' is fascinating and unique, for standing in one corner on a large plinth is a life-size statue of St Peter overlooking a parterre-style garden of clipped box hedging twelve inches high. Each segment of this garden is filled with a different species, including lavender, iris and blue grass, and the whole is surrounded, again, by tall, well-maintained yew hedges. St Peter came here as a refugee from the House of Commons during a restoration programme carried out there in the 1970s, when Lord Carrington was Foreign Secretary.

Next door to St Peter's Garden is the Armillary Garden. This is a study in geometrics, with the armillary sphere as a centrepiece surrounded by an assortment of variably shaped clipped yew and box hedging. Here the perimeter hedges are lower to let in the sun and, once again, the house becomes visible to the south.

The Armillary Garden is the last of the separate enclosures. The gardens in the immediate vicinity of the house comprise mainly lawns, which stretch along its northern aspect towards three newly created formal lily ponds. Immediately beside the house are wide borders of shrubs and other low-growing plants divided by brick-paved paths. Roses are well represented in this section, the modern Austin rose

Adjacent to the main garden at Bledlow is a new three-acre garden commissioned by Lord Carrington to display a range of contemporary sculpture. Here the deep purple rose 'The Prince' is very effective among greens, greys, lavenders and blues.

'English Garden' having pride of place. This rose is apricot-yellow with paler edges and very full in the old-fashioned quartered style. It grows to about three feet tall and is sweetly scented. Opposite, and almost as tall as the house, is an example of a very old yew tree, which contributes a refreshingly natural informality to this area.

Farther from the house across the back drive is a relatively new garden known as Church Close, so named from its proximity to Bledlow's Norman Church of the Holy Trinity. This garden, which extends to about three and a half acres, is entirely the creation of Robert Adams and contains in its undulating levels a number of modern statues by contemporary sculptors. Apart from its entrance, which is very formal and designed around brick paths and yew hedges, the garden contains an informal arrangement of borders and beds filled with an exceptionally wide variety of small trees and shrubs.

Shrub roses are used extensively here to provide colour from early summer to autumn. The lovely semi-procumbent, early-flowering, single creamy-yellow 'Dunwich Rose' is well used at the front of one of the sloping borders, with 'Canary Bird', another early-flowering single yellow, in the background. Other taller shrub roses such as 'Nevada' and 'Cerise Bouquet' are used effectively in largish groups to break up the density of some of the clusters of evergreen shrubs. Also here is the beautiful old-fashioned double pink Alba 'Königin von Dänemark' and the more modern bright yellow 'Graham Thomas'.

Although its wide diversity of plants includes few roses, it would be quite wrong to leave unmentioned the Lyde Garden, which is just across the road from the house. It has been created from a natural dell, at the bottom of which is a series of pools fed by nine natural springs in the hillside. Two roses which can be found in this delightful setting are the early-flowering yellow shrub 'Frühlingsgold' and the purple-leaved *Rosa glauca* (*R. rubrifolia*).

The gardens are open by appointment only, and on one or two special charity days throughout the year.

No one really knows the parents of this rose, but the China rose 'Perle d'Or' must have been one of them. It was raised and introduced by the Bide Nursery of Farnham in 1923 and has been fairly widely grown ever since, for even today very few climbing roses flower continuously throughout the summer as this one does.

Too often, because of its consistent remontancy, too much is expected of it, and it is planted in a difficult position. To me this rose always does better on a wall (preferably not a north-facing one) than in open situations on trellises or arches, where it can be bothered a little by frosty winter winds. Favourably placed, it will attain a height of about

HYBRID CHINA ROSE

'PHYLLIS BIDE'

fifteen feet and spread to about eight. Its leaves, although numerous, are small and almost delicate, which can make it look rather sparse. However, any lack of substance by way of foliage is easily made up for by the sheer quantity of blooms it produces every year. Its flowers are sweetly scented, produced in small clusters and are loosely semi-double. Their colour is basically yellow, but each one is heavily flushed with a soft orange-pink which deepens with age.

At Bledlow Manor 'Phyllis Bide' grows on a gazebo, which would normally put it under stress. Here, however, it is in the walled garden, protected from the British winter.

OLD STONE HIGHWAY
SPRINGS, LONG ISLAND, NEW YORK, USA

OHABITING AGREEABLY, A LARGE, HEALTHY 'DR W. VAN FLEET' and an even larger Boston ivy adorn the east wall of this delightful timber-built house on the outskirts of Springs. 'When we planted these we were advised that both would be harmful to the house,' said joint owner Robert Jakob, 'but we believe the pleasure they will give us over the next twenty years is well worth the risk.' A stimulating philosophy, for the way the plants liven up an otherwise bare expanse of wall is magical, both when the rose is in full flush in early summer among the greenery, and later when the foliage of the creeper (*Parthenocissus tricuspidata*) is ablaze with rich autumn colours.

Growing lower down on the same wall is a very good specimen of 'New Dawn', planted to prolong the flowering season of its parent 'Dr W. Van Fleet' in this spot.

It was late morning in mid-July when I arrived at this most agreeable place. The sun was warm and the light bright on the east side of the house, where well-foliated specimens of 'Mme Alfred Carrière' are clearly thriving on either side of the door leading into the garden. I never become bored with this variety, even though it crops up everywhere I go, for from May to November it is never without at least one of its deliciously fragrant blush-white flowers. Standing beneath 'Mme Alfred', also enjoying the sun – and each bearing fruit – are two matching lemon trees in large terracotta pots. Citrus such as these have to spend the winter indoors in this region.

No other roses grow in this part of the garden, which is mainly grass, partly mown and partly left natural as a habitat for spring wild flowers. This green area, the only open space to be found anywhere in the plot, is about an eighth of an acre in size. The remaining three and a half acres consist of mixed broadleaf and coniferous woodland of varying density, much of it ancient. Other residences in the neighbourhood are well concealed and one is hardly aware of their presence. Nor is it immediately apparent that only a few hundred yards away to the east, through the woods and marshes, are Accabonac Harbour and the sea.

The first rose planted by Robert Jakob and David White sixteen years ago was Rosa gallica officinalis. *Now it is just one of several Gallicas among a variety of companion plants in this Long Island garden. In the background is 'Alba Semi-plena'.*

Shapes are as important as colour in the garden here. The rose in the foreground is 'Mme Isaac Pereire'. Rosa glauca (R. rubrifolia) *is centre right, while on the walls of the house is 'Mme Alfred Carrière' and, farther away, 'Dr W. Van Fleet'.*

ROSA MOYESII

'GERANIUM'

THE SPECIES *Rosa moyesii* is a superb shrub rose in its own right and, to some gardeners, more rewarding as a garden plant than any of its forms. It has crimson-red flowers and bright red hips. It has brought forth about a dozen hybrids. Of all its offspring, by far the most popular is 'Geranium', a selection from seedlings made at Wisley in 1938 by a man named Mulligan. It is, perhaps, not quite as vigorous as its parent, and is certainly more angular in its growth habit. Its wood is less thorny and of a lighter green colour, its foliage larger, softer and also of a lighter green. By far the biggest difference is in the colour of the flower, which is bright, flaming red.

A common feature of all the relatives of *R. moyesii* is the coronet of yellow stamens which adorns the centre of each flower. Like its parent, 'Geranium' has flagon-shaped, bright red hips, but these are slightly less whiskery and larger than those of any other of its family. In good soils 'Geranium' will reach an ultimate height of about ten feet, compared to its parent's twelve to fifteen feet. Like all its type, it tolerates poorer soils. It is probably at its best growing as a specimen shrub, but since it does quite well in shade, it can make a good woodland plant.

When artist Robert Jakob and curator David White first came here, the house needed lots of attention and the garden was non-existent, the whole plot overgrown and jungle-like with dead and fallen trees everywhere. Sixteen years on, they have not only created a substantial-sized garden but also made considerable inroads into the sensitive refurbishment of the woods and marshes leading down towards the sea. This area is the natural habitat for the sort of native flora that enjoys having its feet wet for most of the year, such as turk's-cap lilies, marsh mallows, wild iris and blueberries, and trees such as the small shrubby *Amelanchier canadensis*, known here as shadbush because its flowering coincides with the running of the shad in the local rivers.

Robert, the gardener of the team, was born in Germany and came to New York thirty years ago. He travels widely and has visited many gardens in Europe, especially in England. It was reading Vita Sackville-West that first inspired him about gardening. He loves 'the idea of a structured space in which to grow that which has nothing to do with where one is'. He also likes to experiment, finding out what will tolerate this harsh climate of hot summers and very cold winters, and how to make the best use of light and shade. His earliest recollection of growing things was as a child in wartime Germany, making ends meet as a 'reluctant helper' in his father's orchard.

As far as roses are concerned, he was first inspired to grow the older varieties from the picture of 'Fantin-Latour' on the jacket of my *Classic Roses* and by some of the captivating photographs by Trevor Griffiths in his books, *My World of Old Roses* and *A Celebration of Old Roses*. His favourite group of roses are the Albas, which he enjoys for their intrinsic beauty, as well as finding very easy to grow in this climate. Several good examples of the soft pink 'Maiden's Blush' are scattered around and there is a particularly fine plant, on its own roots, of the deeper pink 'Félicité Parmentier' growing well in semi-shade. Best of all are the sixteenth-century whites 'Alba Semiplena' and 'Alba Maxima', with very good-sized, mature shrubs of each growing in both sun and shade.

The area of the garden closest to the house, on the south side, is laid out with brick-paved paths in a cruciform pattern forming four equal-sized beds of mainly blue- and white-flowered plants with splashes of yellow, buff and deep red here and there. At the time of my visit I noted annuals such as cosmos and larkspur in full flower, and plenty of grey-foliaged plants such as *Caryopteris* × *clandonensis* and lavender, with buddlejas, cranesbill geraniums and several varieties of salvia further enlivening the blue and white theme. The buddlejas were living up to their name of butterfly bush. Yellow and buff highlights came from perennials like verbascums, several species and varieties of day lily, plume poppies (*Macleaya cordata*), champagne-coloured hollyhocks and a bushy shrub of the Hybrid Musk 'Buff Beauty'. Reds were provided by that lovely old Gallica rose 'Tuscany Superb' and beautiful old-fashioned single hollyhocks, so dark they were almost black.

Most of the other groups of roses are well represented. The Damasks, for example, are portrayed by the well-known and well-loved 'Mme Hardy' and the less well-known, but no less beautiful, 'Mme Plantier', both about four feet high. The density and shapeliness of the rose bushes here are achieved by dead-heading after flowering and light pruning before growth starts each spring. I was pleased to find a superb example of the Incense Rose, *Rosa primula*, its soft primrose-coloured flowers produced in late May and its young foliage giving off a distinct fragrance of

Rosa gallica officinalis *almost thrives on neglect. Not that it is ever neglected in this garden at Old Stone Highway where, along with other roses, it mingles easily with a host of companion plants.*

'Dr W. Van Fleet' *and* 'New Dawn' *cohabit agreeably with Boston ivy* (Parthenocissus tricuspidata) *on the east-facing wall of this house in the woods. Only a few hundred yards away to the east is the sea* (previous page).

incense all through the summer after that. This bush is pruned after flowering each spring to encourage as many new scented young shoots as possible. 'I am vague about pruning,' Robert says. What he means by this is that he does not prune for pruning's sake, but that he simply applies his experience to each individual rose bush year by year.

As well as being a conservation area for wild flowers, this whole garden has become a haven for other forms of wildlife. I have already mentioned the butterflies; the birdsong here is almost continuous. Less welcome is a small herd of roe deer, which raid the garden from time to time and have a great liking for rosebuds just before they open. I know from experience how difficult it is to become angry with these shy animals, for they are so endearingly pretty. Robert calls them 'civil', for they never eat more than they need in any one nightly raid.

On the south wall of the house are two climbers. That most beautiful of climbing Tea roses, the creamy-white 'Sombreuil', has been flowering each summer in profusion since it was planted three years ago. Planted at the same time, the lovely Noisette 'Alister Stella Gray' is growing well but quite uncharacteristically has so far failed to flower at all; its patient owners are giving it one more year to perform, otherwise it will be changed for something more floriferous. Teas and Noisettes would not normally enjoy the harsh winters of this part of the world, but this south-facing wall and the surrounding trees provide just enough protection for both.

86

Farther away from the house to the south-east, where the dappled shade of the trees softens the light, is another garden of about the same size as the south garden and crammed just as full, but this time with plants of stronger and brighter colours. Once again, roses dominate in each of the four beds, with ancient *R. gallica officinalis*, the first rose planted here twelve years ago, taking pride of place. Other Gallicas here are the striped 'Rosa Mundi' and deep purple 'Charles de Mills'.

Rising above the dense assorted ground-cover plants in the corner of one bed is an excellent specimen of the yellow 'Graham Thomas', originally a bush but now growing very vigorously and cleverly trained on to a single stem to form a standard – a tree rose, as they are called here. Another natural candidate for a bright colour scheme such as this, and doing itself credit, is the multicoloured 'Mutabilis'. Also in good shape is *R. glauca* (*R. rubrifolia*), and that richly scented, blowzy old Bourbon, 'Mme Isaac Pereire'. Again, like most roses in these gardens, their roots are shaded by dense underplantings of a wide variety of perennials and herbs.

In the shady area to the west of the house three other species, or near-species, roses are thriving: the first, arguably the brightest red of all roses, the splendid *R. moyesii* 'Geranium'; the second the white, grey-foliaged *R. soulieana* growing rampantly and beginning to establish itself in its own little corner of the garden, and the third, a shrubby plant of 'Manettii', once the understock for a named hybrid here but now quite enjoying its freedom as a rose in its own right. Although frequently listed as a species, this rose is actually a hybrid China and sometimes even classified as a Noisette. It was raised in Italy in 1835 by a man named Manetti and was popular as an understock from the 1920s right through to the 1960s. It frequently crops up in gardens such as this, probably here since the house was built in the 1950s.

Farther into the woods, beginning to climb up into a tree, is one of the nicest but one of the least often seen of the tree-climbing roses, R. gentileana (R. polyantha grandiflora). Its flowers are very large for its type, but most noticeable is its glossy foliage, again large – almost twice the size of most others of its kind.

It was very rewarding to be shown around this garden by someone who is so clearly in tune with nature. It is not open to the public, but any reader wishing to see it would, I feel sure, be made welcome.

*G*allica 'Charles de Mills' needs sun to bring out its *more subtle purple tints but in this garden it flowers freely in the dappled shade of birch trees.*

CLIMBING TEA ROSE

'SOMBREUIL'

THIS IS one of the most refined and lovely of all the Tea roses. The bush form was raised in 1850 by the French nurseryman, Robert. It is not known when the climbing form first came about; for a while it became confused with a climbing rose known as 'Colonial White', which was introduced in 1959 and bred from a cross between 'New Dawn' and 'Madame Hardy'.

The flowers are white or creamy-white, very double, quite large when fully open, and flat, being made up of a multitude of small petals. It is a deliciously fragrant rose.

Some authorities attribute Hybrid Perpetual parentage to 'Sombreuil', but clearly Tea genes figure strongly in its make-up; even so, it is one of the hardiest of its family that I know. It is almost always in flower throughout the summer, and is extremely healthy and very easy to grow. Notwithstanding its hardiness, like all of its type it still needs the comfort of a south wall in less than temperate climates before it can truly flourish.

LA LANDRIANA
TOR SAN LORENZO, ARDEA, NEAR ROME, ITALY

This study in serenity captures the essence of the gardens at La Landriana, created by the Marchesa Lavinia Taverna over the past forty years. The three hundred and fifty roses are just a small part of a wonderful collection of plants here. Accompanying the Marchesa and me on our tour of the gardens was Annalisa, the young Head Gardener, who knew most of the plants as we came to them. So too the Marchesa; for someone who knew little about gardening twenty years ago, she certainly knows her subject now.

EVELOPED BY THE MARCHESA LAVINIA TAVERNA, THIS GARden totally contradicts what she said to me when we met. 'Italians don't like gardening and don't know how to garden,' were her first words. Well, no one could be more Italian, and the Marchesa certainly knows how to garden. What she said was a generalization, of course, and might have been true a few years ago, but nowadays gardening, gardens – and roses especially – have become more and more important to her compatriots.

The ten-hectare site which is now La Landriana was a barren battlefield when the Marchesa began her garden here in 1956 – literally a battlefield, for Anzio, site of the Allied beach-head in the Second World War, is just five kilometres away. The climate is maritime Mediterranean, which means it is hard going for some species from more northerly latitudes, but opens up all sorts of possibilities for plants from regions such as Australasia and South Africa – possibilities which are exploited to the full here.

At first the Marchesa knew little about plants, her inspiration coming from memories of childhood gardens. After a while, as this one started to develop, she rather lost confidence and was advised to bring in the distinguished English garden designer Russell Page. 'You must have Russell because you are making a mess of this garden,' said a mutual friend. Page brought to the garden the rather English idea of dividing it up into lots of different 'rooms'. The Marchesa – now very much her own person – has since changed many of his plants and rearranged some of his work, but she has maintained his original basic structure. She speaks of Page with great affection: 'I learned a lot from Russell,' she said; 'I think he would approve of what I have done.'

So often large collections of plants become moribund and lacking in style; not so at La Landriana, for while its owner so evidently loves collecting, she also clearly enjoys her garden for its own sake. Hers is an original mind at work, a mind untainted by looking closely at other gardens, for she seldom travels. 'I read only books about gardens,' she said. In the mid-1980s she went through what she calls 'a crisis with my plants'. Those that were not enjoying the environment were ruthlessly weeded out and replaced with subjects more compliant.

Like most gardens, this one has evolved around a residence, in this case a tasteful, spacious, single-storey modern villa, difficult to study in detail since it is so generously draped with climbers and wall plants of all kinds and sizes. Dominant is a pergola designed by Russell Page and covering a sizeable terrace on the south side. It is swathed in a mixture of *Wisteria sinensis* and *Rosa bracteata*, both subjects extremely floriferous and effective. Other climbing plants embracing the house include *R. laevigata, R. banksiae lutea* and *R. bracteata* 'Mermaid', *Solanum jasminoides* and *S. crispum, Vitis coignetiae* and *V.* 'Brant'.

To the north-west, adjacent to the villa, is a 'garden room' full of yellow and variegated foliage plants, including trees such as *Robinia pseudoacacia* 'Frisia' and *Acer negundo* 'Elegans', shrubs including variegated forms of euonymus and hebe and a neatly kept hedge of *Lonicera nitida* 'Baggesen's Gold'. On the south-east side, accessible from the terrace, a lily pool and water fountain surrounded by several white roses sit neatly in the centre of a small enclosed garden. The roses include the semi-procumbent 'Swany' and the larger, slightly spreading 'Sally Holmes'.

Although some of the enclosures contain formal gardens, the Marchesa, surprisingly, is not especially fond of precise Italian-style gardens. Dividing hedges play a vital part in any garden such as this, and even where formality is not the rule, *Buxus sempervirens, Viburnum tinus* and *Laurus nobilis* are much in evidence, usually beautifully clipped and shaped.

The first of the formal gardens I came upon is about the size of a tennis court and now called the Orange Garden. It was actually designed by Russell Page as a rose garden, but the roses failed miserably and the Marchesa has now redesigned it with standard bitter orange trees, clipped into perfect globes like toffee-apples with, beneath them, little spherical box trees arranged in ranks. The whole effect is very precise, the geometrical evergreens emerging from ground-hugging *Solenopsis fluviatilis*, a spreading, blue-flowered Mediterranean native. Next to the Orange Garden is another enclosure in a similar style, except for a few curves; here, instead of oranges, the globular standards are fashioned from *Viburnum tinus* and the little mounds beneath from hebes.

To the north of these two gardens across a pathway edged with a mixture of different hellebores is a less formally structured area known as the Olive Garden. This is full of grey-foliaged herbs, perennials and lots of hostas, with groups of the yellow Floribunda rose 'Korresia' randomly scattered among them. In spring this enclosure is a mass of yellow tulips and daffodils. Although the roses were not doing too well, I liked the shadowy mysterious atmosphere in this garden accentuated by the overhanging branches of grey smoky-coloured olive trees and the four substantial trunks of a heavily gnarled cork oak (*Quercus suber*).

After spending some time in these gardens, the Marchesa led me through the olive trees into a very long, narrow garden consisting of paved paths broken at intervals by steps and flanked by borders of grey-foliaged and white-flowered plants of all kinds. This is known as the White Walk and is still much as Page designed it, with Hybrid Musk 'Penelope' and the semi-procumbent 'Sea Foam' flourishing among the blanket of ground cover bordering each side of the path. Inevitably,

RUGOSA HYBRID

'SARAH VAN FLEET'

WITH ONE or two exceptions, Rugosa hybrids are very, very thorny. 'Sarah Van Fleet' is perhaps the most prickly of all. As its name suggests, it was raised by Van Fleet in America in 1926. In good soil it makes a dense, upright-growing shrub to about six feet. Its foliage is lightish green and its stems greyish-brown. The younger thorns are soft yellowish-green.

The flowers of this rose are beautifully furled and pointed at first, but later open semi-double. They are silvery-pink in colour, very highly scented and produced very freely from the beginning of summer right through to winter. Unlike those of most Hybrid Rugosas, its hips are not particularly ornamental, so dead-heading is advisable and will yield many more flowers throughout the season.

This variety makes an excellent specimen shrub for a border or on its own in a lawn. Being dense and upright, it is also a good hedging rose. A white form is called 'Mary Manners'.

Gardeners who spray their roses will find this variety excellent. Those who do not, especially in poor soils, may find its proclivity to rust sadly renders it unsuitable for their site.

Hundreds of plants of 'Bonica 82' are planted along a cobblestoned rosewalk at La Landriana. This is one of the most effective and most widely grown landscape roses of all time. Here it is interplanted effectively with Pittosporum tenuifolium *'Silver Queen'.*

I suppose, in a white garden, 'Mme Alfred Carrière' is doing stalwart service as a background plant. To list all the grey and white plants along this border could become monotonous, but I was very taken by two American natives – the Californian poppy *Romneya coulterii* and a superb example of the deliciously fragrant, summer-flowering evergreen shrub *Carpenteria californica*.

Several options open up from paths leading through one or other of the tall neatly trimmed bay hedges that flank the White Garden. We chose to go east into one of the most incredible rose plantations I have ever seen, a valley of *Rosa chinensis* 'Mutabilis' in all its glory. 'I love this rose but it doesn't mix with others, so I grow it *en masse*,' said the Marchesa. Three hundred of these roses are planted in huge drifts, with mown grass walkways between. Some of the bushes are two metres high, and their soft yellow, peachy-pink, orange and crimson flowers look for all the world like thousands of butterflies nestling on millions of reddish-green leaves. They go on flowering in this part of the world right through the winter, certainly until Christmas. Grey olive trees and pencil-thin cypresses add to the effect and provide height and shape to the unique display.

North-west of Mutabilis Valley is what the Marchesa calls her 'Valley of Old Roses'. This is what I had really come to see, and I was not disappointed – a large informal area with wide grass walkways sweeping through irregular beds and borders of varying sizes and shapes, each crammed full of all sorts of older and

more recent varieties of rose. Except for the odd slender cypress reminding me where I was, this could well have been England, for the ground is covered with lavender, catmint and pinks in pastel shades, as well as by roses. In the background is a lake surrounded by moisture-loving trees and plants.

Over 350 varieties of roses can be found growing in these gardens, most of them in this delightful valley. To name them all is unnecessary, for they are planted here to form a garden, not a collection. The majority are the ancient varieties of Gallicas, Damasks, Centifolias and Albas, but interplanted between them I saw many Hybrid Musks, including a particularly fine plant of 'Prosperity' and several very good 'Cornelia'. I also spotted 'Moonlight', one of the Rev. Pemberton's first introductions way back in 1913. Other shrub roses I saw looking good were pink Portlands 'Jacques Cartier' and 'Comte de Chambord' and the very ancient fuchsia-red 'Rose de Rescht'. Austin roses are numerous but, in all honesty, none of these is really flourishing; the best here are apricot 'Abraham Darby', soft pink 'Claire Rose' and deeper pink 'Mary Rose'. I did not see any Teas; this is surprising, for they would really enjoy themselves in this soil and climate; the Chinas would, too, as evidenced by the performance of 'Mutabilis'. Several Rugosas, on the other hand, are much better than I would have expected, since these roses usually like to take a rest in winter – a luxury they certainly do not get here. The white 'Blanc Double de Coubert' and the bright pink 'Sarah Van Fleet' are particularly good. To prolong

China rose 'Mutabilis' crops up in lots of gardens but nowhere is it to be found in such quantity as at La Landriana where the Marchesa Lavinia Taverna has planted over three hundred in a large meadow to create an unique forest of them.

the flowering season *Pavonia hastata*, a plant I had never met before, is planted randomly among the roses. This interesting little southern-hemisphere shrub has masses of small pink flowers in late summer and autumn each year.

I was reluctant to leave the Rose Garden, but still had much to see and was a little pressed for time. From here I was shown the Italian Box Garden, a regular pattern of angles shaped from clipped bay and box, all underplanted with purple verbena and flanked by two rows of elegant standards of *Magnolia grandiflora*. It is impossible to do justice to this garden in so little space, so I will grudgingly hurry on past the camphor trees and a fine collection of camellias and skirt the heather garden to arrive at the Bonica Rose Walk. 'Bonica 82', to give its correct name, is a pink continuous-flowering semi-procumbent rose which is one of the best and most widely grown roses of our time. Here, hundreds are planted in line beneath olive trees and alongside a wide cobblestone pathway behind a low clipped hedge of *Pittosporum tenuifolium* 'Silver Queen'. This hedge is the only concession to formality in this area, for the rest is relative abandonment, a study in greys, with one or two specimens of *Pinus pinea* overhead. It was about here that I completely lost my bearings, but then we came to the newest part of the garden. This was once the car park but is now a wide paved walkway with borders of smoky-toned plants on each side, including euphorbia, sea holly (*Eryngium*), cotton lavender (*Santolina*).

Then there is the Blue Meadow, a large, open area of lawn edged by borders full of large drifts of blue and white subjects such as plumbago (*Ceratostigma*), agapanthus and lots of other Mediterranean plants I just did not recognize. Then there is the Lily Pool, the Australian Border, the Hydrangea Garden and so on, and so on.

On my way into the garden earlier I espied the largest *Rosa bracteata* I have ever seen. Without realizing the significance of what I said, I told the Marchesa how much I coveted the plant; thus it was that on my way out I carried a gift – a pot-grown rooted cutting of that same *R. bracteata*. I will plant it in a sheltered position in Norfolk to remind me, each time I see it, of the Marchesa Lavinia Taverna and her very special garden at La Landriana.

This garden is open every weekend from April to October.

PROCUMBENT ROSE

'Bonica 82' was raised by the famous firm of Meilland of Antibes, France. Another rose named 'Bonica', a red, raised by the same firm in 1958, now seems to be extinct in commerce.

The 'Bonica' we now have is, in my opinion, one of the most successful roses to have been raised in recent times. It came from a cross between *Rosa sempervirens* and a hybrid of *R. wichuraiana* called 'Mlle Martha Carron' which, in turn, was crossed with the modern Floribunda 'Picasso'.

Its bright pink, shapely double flowers are scented and borne freely and

'BONICA 82'

continuously on a dense, wide, spreading plant generously endowed with dark green foliage. To call it a ground-cover rose is only appropriate if the plants are grown fairly close together, but it does grow wider than it is tall.

'Bonica 82' has an extremely healthy disposition and its flowers tolerate wet weather without quibble. It will also grow well in poorer, lighter soils. It has a variety of other uses – as a bedding rose, specimen shrub and hedging plant. It also does particularly well grown as a specimen shrub in a container or else when grown as a standard or tree rose.

TYNINGHAME
EAST LOTHIAN, SCOTLAND

THE LAYOUT OF THE GARDENS AT TYNINGHAME TODAY IS, IN the main, the creation of Sarah, 12th Countess of Haddington. She obviously knew about gardens and gardening when she moved to the Haddingtons' ancestral home in 1953. Of course there had been fine gardens at the mansion for centuries; she built upon a design and layout dating back to 1829, when the last major reconstruction of both house and gardens had been effected by the Scottish architect William Burn. More recently this beautiful old house has again been re-vamped, this time in a sensitive conversion by Kit Martin (who has made a speciality of such adaptations) into a number of individually owned residences within the house and on the estate. However, the gardens have been kept more or less as they were when Sarah Haddington died. They are now controlled and cared for by a separate Garden Company consisting of the present Lord Haddington and other owners of the residences. It was three members of this Company who showed me around: Jane Clifford owns the West Wing overlooking the Parterre Garden; Daphne Merrills owns the East Wing, and Charnisay Gwyn owns the Walled Garden and Arboretum. Three dedicated lady gardeners – a daunting prospect for me at first, but it was not long before a rapport developed. My guides had been heavily involved in the garden's revitalization over the past couple of years, Jane especially. There is a lot of garden at Tyninghame and many, many roses, but three hours later, over tea, I felt I knew the garden reasonably well.

Tyninghame stands overlooking Hedderwick Bay at the mouth of the Scottish river Tyne. Facing south to the sea, it is protected from the north and east by an area of thick woodland, thus providing temperate conditions. This part of Great Britain enjoys plenty of sunshine in normal summers, but an average rainfall of only about 24 inches per annum can pose a challenge for gardeners, as can the light sandy soil.

A building of some importance has stood on this site since medieval times; the house in its present form dating from 1829 is built of soft reddish sandstone, stands

The distinctive turrets of Tyninghame are seen from the south-facing mixed border in which roses of all types, sizes and colours thrive. Here the modern climber 'Parade' has pride of place in the centre foreground.

The garden at Tyninghame today is largely the creation of the late Lady Sarah Haddington, who very much loved old roses. Seen here is the focal point of her Secret Garden, a distinctive gazebo housing the goddess Flora (facing page).

four storeys high and has imposing turrets and gables. The surrounding flat parkland is well stocked with aged trees and you approach from the west by a long, twisting drive. From this direction the house does not come into sight until you are almost upon it. When I drew up in front of its north elevation I felt, somehow, absurdly insignificant and very conscious of its noble past.

There are three main areas to the gardens immediately around the house. To the west is the Parterre Garden. Alongside this and past the front of the house is a long, wide gravel path bordered with rose beds; this area also takes in a sheltered courtyard in front of the house and extends around to the east through trellises and pergolas. The wide path actually forms the upper tier of a long, split-level terrace. This is not immediately obvious, for the whole area is well foliated, as are the walls of the house. Steps lead down from the lower terrace to a wide area of lawn edged with scattered small trees forming the boundary, but a long, deep border runs the entire length of the south-facing retaining wall of the terrace.

In Victorian times, with ample labour to hand, the emphasis would have been on colourful bedding plants. Lady Haddington by both necessity and choice introduced a less labour-intensive planting scheme. She solved the problem of the Victorian parterre garden by planting it up almost entirely with roses in just two colours — white in 'Iceberg' and yellow in 'King's Ransom' and 'Chinatown'.

I have no doubt that to begin with the roses flourished and the colour scheme worked well, but 'Iceberg' has now taken over as the dominant variety for, as so often, yellow Hybrid Teas do not enjoy growing in light, sandy soil. This does not mean that this formal area is any less attractive than it was in the beginning. A tall grey sundial, this one copied from an original at Newbattle, embellished with examples of Haddington heraldry, forms the centrepiece of this part of the garden. Standards of 'Iceberg' and pillars of yellow climbers add height to the rose beds.

The turreted west wall of the house is furnished with a variety of interesting subjects, mainly in blue and white. Effectively serving as ground cover along this

BOURBON ROSE

'ZÉPHIRINE DROUHIN'

THIS FINE rose raised in 1868 has lots to commend it besides its total freedom from thorns. Yet I cannot help wondering whether, if it had been as spiteful as, say, a Rugosa hybrid, it would have survived the intense competition for garden space from other Bourbons raised during the Victorian era. There were many, many more of these than the fifty or so that have come down to us since the last one was raised in 1919. As it is, 'Zéphirine Drouhin' is one of the most popular and willingly fulfils the many roles asked of it.

An easy rose to grow, it will tolerate a north wall but prefers a little more sun. A notable feature is the reddish tinge of the young leaves, which mature to deep green, acquiring a greyish tint as they age. In an agreeable position, with good soil, it will grow to a height of twelve feet.

The colour is probably best described as bright cerise-pink, but on some days, especially in bright evening light, the petals have a distinctive silver sheen. The sweetly perfumed semi-double flowers which open from shapely buds are produced without a break from June to December. A bloom of this rose was the only one the vicar could find in his garden to place on the font at my daughter Amanda's christening in December 1967. She subsequently used it in her wedding bouquet in November, twenty-one years later.

'Parade', one of Lady Sarah's 'acceptable' modern roses, is the rose on the gazebo. A wealth of companion plants adorn the Secret Garden at Tyninghame, almost all of them scented and none of them strident in colour or of an aggressive nature.

wall are largish clumps of *Caryopteris* × *clandonensis* 'Heavenly Blue', that most useful autumn-flowering grey-foliaged small shrub, and the hardy plumbago (*Ceratostigma willmottianum*) with its deep blue flowers. African lily (*Agapanthus*) in both blue and white is also used effectively here, as are one or two varieties of rock rose (*Cistus*) and *Senecio greyi*. Emerging from the blue and grey, close to the front door where its perfume can be fully appreciated, is a fine example of the white, continuously flowering Rugosa rose 'Blanc Double de Coubert'. Taking advantage of the benevolent climate is more blue in the form of *Ceanothus dentatus* and *C.* 'Burkwoodii'. Additional white colouring here is provided by yet more roses. One not in flower on my visit I failed to recognize, but 'Kiftsgate' was accomplishing its usual considerable climbing feats and a superb 'Mme Alfred Carrière' was effortlessly doing its duty on the turret which dominates this wall. On the south-west corner is the more modern, less vigorous climbing rose 'White Cockade', which is almost continuously in flower.

The borders on either side of the gravel path which runs west-east comprise a wide variety of roses, with the ground-covering function performed by lavender. Cleverly placed at the parterre end, to detract from the bareness of the wide path, are several bay trees growing in large tubs. Again, yellow and white feature here and there among the roses in the form of more 'Iceberg' and the well-foliated tallish yellow Floribunda rose 'Chinatown', but by far and away the predominant variety

along this walkway is the pink Hybrid Musk 'Felicia' – testimony, yet again, to its versatility and worthiness, for it shows up in almost every garden in this book.

Halfway along the front of the house, approximately one step up from the path, is the courtyard, open to the south and leading to the front door. This is a sun-trap and a natural haven for several tender plants, notable among them *Solanum jasminoides*, the delicate pale blue climber from Brazil, and the pure white *Carpenteria californica*. Tenderness, however, is not the only passport to this area, for on the walls, mixed with such diverse subjects as *Photinia* (formerly *Stranvaesia*) *davidiana* and *Garrya elliptica* can be found yet another plant of the rose 'Mme Alfred Carrière', clearly not at all out of place among such delicate neighbours.

From the courtyard, moving to the east, the shrubbery thickens. Not many roses can be found, but I did see 'Cécile Brünner' and 'Souvenir de la Malmaison' looking well and healthy and a few plants of the thornless, cerise-pink ancient climber 'Zéphirine Drouhin' tolerating, if not enjoying, the shade.

Moving now down several steps off the terrace, the long, wide, south-facing border displays a wealth of flora of all types as we move along the wide lawn towards the west. This border started life full of herbaceous plants but it has gained height and substance over the years by the addition of shrubs such as the purple smoke tree (*Cotinus coggygria* 'Foliis Purpureis'), white buddleja and hydrangeas. At equally spaced intervals, four sizeable horseshoe-shaped rustic rose arbours were erected in

Since its genesis in 1956 this garden has been the inspiration of many rose lovers and from this study it is not difficult to see why. In the centre foreground is the single pink 'Complicata'. Behind this and to the right of the picture is the soft pink 'Fantin-Latour', with 'Gipsy Boy' beneath. 'Mme Isaac Pereire' is on the left.

NOISETTE ROSE

'MME ALFRED CARRIÈRE'

DATING FROM 1879, this is not only one of the best roses from the Noisette family, but one of the most useful ever raised. While the term 'useful' describes its more prosaic virtues, it does less than justice to its many aesthetic qualities; although no such thing as a 'perfect' rose is ever likely to exist, if versatility is related to perfection, then 'Mme Alfred Carrière' is close to that ideal.

Its flowers are fully double and a little blowzy, creamy-white with a blush tint on the young buds and newly open flowers. They are produced almost perpetually throughout the summer and have the most delicious of fragrances. Its leaves are bright, light green and almost, but not quite, glossy. The young shoots are also light green. As so often with Noisettes, this rose does not have many thorns, although the few it does produce are hooked, spiteful and sharp. Except for an occasional bout of mildew in an inclement autumn, it is very healthy.

'Mme Alfred's' really big plus is her extreme tolerance, not least a willingness to do well on a north wall. She also seems quite oblivious to soil types but, in the best conditions, will reach almost twenty feet. The plant does, however, react well to pruning and can be contained to half that size if need be.

the 1950s, specifically to accommodate as many sorts of climbing and rambling roses as possible, with the emphasis on continuous- and repeat-flowering varieties. I will not list them all, but outstanding at the time of my visit were the ever-blooming 'Aloha' with its sumptuous full, deep pink and highly scented flowers, and 'Parade', an almost shocking-pink in the old-fashioned, fully double style. These are together on the same arbour with two other very good modern pinks, 'Pink Perpétue' and 'Rosy Mantle'. On another arbour farther along is the modern yellow 'Casino' together with the old Victorian yellow Tea rose 'Lady Hillingdon' and the coppery-yellow Noisette 'Alister Stella Gray'. Intermingled with all the climbing roses are carefully selected companion plants such as clematis, honeysuckle and vine.

If Lady Sarah had a favourite genus it was roses, and old-fashioned roses in particular. The formal nature of the gardens nearest the house restricted their use, so soon after moving here in the 1950s she converted an old tennis court and its surrounds to a separate rose garden. This garden is hidden from the house by trees and has now become generally known as the Secret Garden. Indeed it is, for had I not been taken there, I would not have even suspected its existence. It is quite different from the rest of the grounds, its informality exaggerated and, in a strange way, enhanced by mild neglect; not that it is uncared for, simply that in this day and age pruning, hand-weeding and dead-heading are luxuries. The original design was taken from an old eighteenth-century French gardening book. Its centrepiece is a fairly elaborate, white wooden gazebo structure, built around a grey stone statue of the goddess Flora and covered by climbing plants of all types. In particular I noticed *Clematis* 'Mrs Cholmondeley' and the climbing rose 'Parade'. This rose crops up a lot in this garden and was clearly a favourite of Sarah Haddington. The bed surrounding the gazebo is full of peonies, iris, lavender and, above all, roses of a purplish shade, including the modern shrub 'Lavender Lassie' and the heavily scented old Hybrid Perpetual 'Reine des Violettes'. On our way into the garden we had passed through a wide metal archway clothed with a fine example of the creamy-white, glossy-leaved rambler 'Albéric Barbier'. Scattered around in the other beds are such delights as the pale pink Albas 'Celestial' and 'Great Maiden's Blush', the deep pink Gallica 'Président de Sèze' and the rich purple Centifolia 'Tour de Malakoff', also known as 'Black Jack'. Suffering a little bit from neglect is an unusual tunnel made up of pleached apple trees which forms one side of the garden. Between each of the trees 'Rosa Mundi', the old pink-and-white striped Gallica, is doing well and surviving the shade. A huge, gnarled horse chestnut tree overhangs another part of this garden and I noticed – growing in the almost constant shade that this tree casts – *Rosa virginiana* with its lovely soft-silvery-pink flowers. Also here were several of the free-suckering, double white and double pink Scotch roses.

Although we came in search of roses, to leave Tyninghame without mentioning the unique espaliered apple walk just outside the southern end of the walled garden would seem criminal. It was planted about a century ago and is made up of all types of apples – from crabs to culinary varieties – and now forms a tunnel over a hundred yards long. At one end is a statue of Flora, goddess of flowers, and at the other one of Ganymede, cup-bearer to the gods.

After the demise of Lady Sarah the future of the gardens at Tyninghame was uncertain for a while, but they are now in good hands and in very good shape. Such is their appeal that I, for one, will definitely return. They are open twice a year for charity under the Scottish Gardens Scheme.

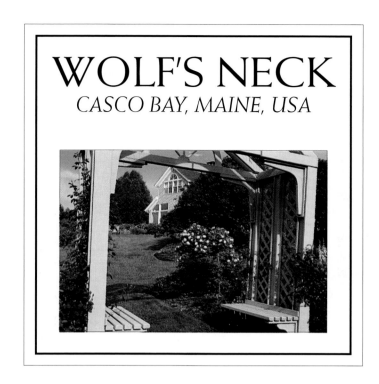

WOLF'S NECK
CASCO BAY, MAINE, USA

HIS GARDEN HAS COME ABOUT FROM THE COLLABORATION of two dedicated people – owner Carol Wishcamper and David Emery, a professional gardener. Before David arrived on the scene, Carol had found herself with an open space of about ten acres. She had absolutely no knowledge of gardening. She did, however, have the determination to find out more, and as a result has now put her own imprint on the landscape around her.

She and her husband Joe bought the property in the early 1980s. The house is built largely of timber, and parts of it date back to 1840. Some modernization had been carried out twenty years before, but further reconstruction by Joe and Carol has turned it, to all intents and purposes, into a modern building. In addition they built the extensive terracing which now forms an important part of the garden. The area at the front of the house is taken up by a raised terrace that extends around to the east side. Here stone steps lead down to expansive lawns which surround the house on all sides except the north. From this direction a long sweeping drive comes in through thick woodland.

In her desire for a garden, Carol's first move was to have the grounds shaped by a landscape architect. She also employed a specialist plantsperson with a particular leaning towards herbaceous plants and perennials. The first thing that happened when David Emery came on the scene was the dismantling of most of this work and the disposal or relocation of many of the plants. By then Carol had begun to learn more about plants and gardens and she too was feeling uncomfortable with what had been done in the garden, although she was not altogether sure why.

This is a dream site. It is situated within two hundred yards of the sea at the end of Wolf's Neck, a small peninsula which juts out into Casco Bay. The view across the Bay with its 365 islands, known as the Calendars, is superb. The maritime climate here is kind to plants, enabling the majority of them to survive most

This unusual modern structure provides seating, as well as support for two young plants of 'Dr W. Van Fleet', in the garden of Carol Wishcamper at Wolf's Neck. In the border beside is a well-balanced example of the Rugosa hybrid 'Martin Frobisher'.

HYBRID RUGOSA

'AGNES'

'AGNES' IS a Canadian rose raised from a cross between *Rosa rugosa* and *R. foetida* 'Persiana' by Dr W. Saunders at the Central Experimental Farm, Ottawa, and introduced in 1922. While its growth habit and bristliness is inherited from Rugosa, its flowers are very similar to those of 'Persiana', except that they are much less globular or cupped. Old-fashioned in style, they are delicately scented and produced in considerable quantities during its first flush in early summer and then intermittently for the duration of the season, with sometimes an extra burst in September. It is one of the few Rugosas to have yellow in its make-up.

Its foliage is distinctly rugose and very dark green, its thorns when young are greenish-yellow. Like most Rugosa hybrids it is very healthy and will grow in most soils including light sandy ones – a useful trait, for very few of the deeper yellow-coloured roses enjoy poor soil. Again, in common with most of its type, it makes a useful hedge rose.

Its Canadian origins make it tolerant of both summer heat and low winter temperatures.

winters. Whatever the season, though, this is an idyllic spot for gardening, sheltered as it is from all sides except the south – which looks straight out to sea.

Although he had had some input before then as a friend and adviser, David Emery first came actively on to the scene in 1987. Nowadays he puts in about twenty hours a week working with Carol as part of his landscaping business. He once had charge of a grand private garden in which there was a large collection of roses, which is no doubt why roses figure so prominently in this garden. Carol is now an organizational development consultant, so her personal 'hands-on' input is about ten hours per week – ten hours which are very important to her. Interestingly, she sees parallels in the garden with her work: what she finds exciting is 'having to think about, and hold in my mind at the same time, so many different elements' in order to guarantee that each garden bed has 'a "look" all through the seasons'.

The first roses I came upon on arrival were alongside the drive – two 'Dorothy Perkins' draped over a four-foot-high ranch-style fence, one on either side of the gateway leading into a sizeable paddock. Also on this fence, attractively intertwined with honeysuckle, is the myrrh-scented pink 'Constance Spry'. At the base of these roses is a most effective assortment of yellow-flowering plants such as annual marigolds, old-fashioned calendulas and coreopsis. Just inside the paddock is a bed of mixed Rugosa roses, with the lovely citrus-yellow 'Agnes' looking especially good. The paddock, which is lightly studded with assorted trees, including weeping birch, maples and willows, is full of wild flowers naturalized in the grass. By the gate are lilies; Carol is particularly fond of them, and they can be found everywhere in this garden. The house stands slightly higher than the drive, and beds which slope away from the house on the north side are filled with shade-tolerant plants, mostly with coloured foliage. One bed by the garage door is full of yellow- and silver-variegated hostas and yellow day lilies (*Hemerocallis*).

On the terrace in front of the house the skill of these two gardeners in harmonizing colours is plain to see – especially in association with the local greyish-biscuity stone of which the various levels are built. 'Spring is the best time here,' said Carol, 'with thousands of bulbs of all species and types flowering together.' Here in summer, though, my eye is taken by a group of roses on the extreme eastern edge of the terrace, used partly as ground cover and partly to achieve a shrubby definition to an otherwise herbaceous area. They are Hybrid Musks 'Belinda', rosy-red, and 'Cornelia', strawberry-pink. Also here is the modern shrub rose 'Nymphenberg', salmon-pink and, completing the group, Polyantha 'The Fairy', soft pink. All the roses are being used to their best advantage in groups of at least three.

From the eastern edge of the terrace the lawn slopes away quite sharply and a largish oval bed has been formed to conceal the extent of the slope. This holds several 'once-flowering' roses, mostly Gallicas, such as the Apothecary Rose of medieval times (*Rosa gallica officinalis*), 'Empress Josephine', 'Camaïeux' and 'Charles de Mills', the purples and magenta-pinks of these varieties charmingly combined with such shrubby plants as the blue of *Caryopteris* × *clandonensis*, the grey-foliaged, purple-spiked 'Munstead' lavender and the soft reddishy-pink clouds of *Spiraea* 'Anthony Waterer'. Deep pink heather rounds off the scheme.

Everything in this garden clearly benefits from good husbandry. One particular routine is regular mulching with composted seaweed. As well as suppressing weeds, this material is highly nutritious and especially rich in trace elements. It is also said to keep blackspot at bay.

In the middle distance between the house and the mixed woodland which forms the eastern boundary are assorted specimen ornamental flowering trees. The crab apples are especially stunning in springtime. Just in front of these, a wooden pergola or archway with seating on either side makes a focal point. This is painted the same stone-cream colour as the house. On each side of this archway are two substantial oval-shaped island beds; growing over it, one on each side, two extremely healthy-looking plants of the rambler 'Dr W. Van Fleet'. These beds are overflowing with a wide variety of interesting shorter-growing shrubs such as *Daphne cneorum*, rhododendrons and azaleas and perennials such as campanulas, phlox and salvias. Here and there among them is a rose. The deep pinkish 'William Baffin', a very popular rose in America, was looking particularly good here on the day I called.

Farther round to the north-east from this area is a well-stocked fruit and vegetable garden, the province of Joe. A novelty here is an arbour of vines concealing a kennel, the home of Mac the family dog, a German short-haired pointer. A clever facet of the landscaping throughout this garden is the subtle way the various changes in level are hidden by one feature or another – a bed, borders or perhaps a stone retaining wall. Along one such wall, which divides the vegetable garden from the main garden, several roses have been planted in a wide border to good effect, among them 'Dorothy Perkins' spilling out over the edge with 'Scabrosa' and 'Alba Semi-plena' adding height to the undulations of the mixed plantings beneath them.

A special feature of the garden at Wolf's Neck are the island beds in the lawns. Here 'Martin Frobisher' and 'Carefree Beauty' share space with foxgloves and lilies, with more roses in the background.

RAMBLER ROSE

'DOROTHY PERKINS'

THIS ROSE arose from a cross between *Rosa wichuraiana* and the old Hybrid Perpetual 'Mme Gabriel Luizet'. It was introduced by Jackson and Perkins, the famous American rose growers, in 1901. Considering how badly this old variety gets mildew towards the end of its flowering season each year, it is amazing how popular it still is. But when seen in full flush on an archway or a porch over a door, it is one of the most memorable sights in roses: the density of its small ruffled flowers is such that barely a leaf is visible. Along with most of the Wichuraiana hybrids, it also flowers later in summer than many ramblers or climbers from other families.

Its flowers are produced in huge hanging clusters that cascade downwards in swathes of bright, clear rose-pink. Its foliage is dark green, its growth is dense and pliable, enabling it to be trained in all directions. It also makes good ground cover in parts of the garden where it can be allowed to do its own thing. You can also train it as an excellent weeping standard rose.

Beautiful though she is, there are other pink ramblers that I would choose ahead of her, but this is on the strength of her proneness to mildew alone. Alternatives – not necessarily in order of preference – are 'Debutante', 'Minnehaha' and 'Ethel'.

Nearer to the house a large old apple tree hosts on its trunk the soft white-flowered grey-foliaged *R. soulieana*. Close by this tree is a shrub of *R. pimpinellifolia*. Although not in flower, looking very attractive in its summer clothes of light green fern-like foliage and green, gooseberry-like hips. Two other roses I must mention seeing are 'John Cabot', a semi-double, continuous-flowering *R. kordesii* seedling and 'Sarah Van Fleet', a lovely heavily scented pink hybrid Rugosa.

This is a delightful garden in a superb setting which has been designed and structured with skill, with the entire year in mind. Each changing season must bring with it great satisfaction to its creators. It gave me great pleasure to visit it in summer. It is not, however, open to the public.

An interesting study of the beautifully formed flowers of 'Martin Frobisher'. This rose does particularly well in the north of the United States. As you would expect from a Rugosa, it has a lovely perfume.

Adding vibrant colour to the foreground are Rosa gallica officinalis, red valerian (Centranthus ruber) and lavender. The view seen here from Carol Wishcamper's garden at Wolf's Neck is of Casco Bay (facing page).

HAMBLEDEN MANOR
HAMBLEDEN, BUCKINGHAMSHIRE, ENGLAND

HAMBLEDEN MANOR IS A HOUSE OF GREAT CHARACTER BUILT of flint and red brick in the early seventeenth century. Changes have been made to the building down the years, not least in Victorian times, but always in sympathy with its original style. It is situated where the land starts to rise out of the Thames Valley on the edge of the picturesque village of Hambleden, a compact little place with many fourteenth- and fifteenth-century buildings huddled together on either side of a twisty main street and village square. The nearest town is Henley-on-Thames and from the Manor House there is a delightful view of the beautiful old church of St Mary the Virgin.

Although standing proud, the house somehow nestles into the west-facing hillside. Behind it and rising above it, a belt of woodland provides shelter from the north and east, the mature trees adding substance to the background and accentuating the sense of the past which prevails here. Except for a large copper beech, most of the ground to the front of the house is open, being taken up with lawns and the driveway. From the front door there are superb views to the north-west, where the land rises steeply towards a long ridge of ancient woodland. During the Second World War the 3rd Viscount Hambleden felled a large section of trees on this ridge to give the village below an extra hour of sunshine in the evenings.

The Hambleden family moved to this area from Devon in the early nineteenth century and the title was bestowed posthumously on the 1st Viscount by Queen Victoria. The family have always been interested in gardening and at their last home, Greenlands, a few miles away, seventeen gardeners were employed up until the outbreak of the war. When the present Lady Hambleden moved here in the early 1950s there were five gardeners, as she puts it, 'producing bronze chrysanthemums and not much else!'

Lady Hambleden is Italian by birth and divides her time between Italy and Hambleden. She learned her gardening in Rome, but has quite consciously avoided

A glimpse of the lovely old Hambleden Manor house is seen here from the half-acre rose garden designed and laid out in 1982. It is now mature and, in June each year, is a 'happening' of soft colours and perfume not to be missed.

The highly scented Damask rose 'Leda' ('Painted Damask') is in the foreground of the view across the garden at Hambleden Manor. Here and there among the flowers is one that has reverted to 'Pink Leda', its parent; a phenomenon that occurs in this rose from time to time (facing page).

ALBA ROSE

'MAIDEN'S BLUSH'

THIS ROSE is perhaps the best known of the Alba family. It is beautifully formed, fully double, blush-pink and in the quartered style. When first introduced to England two hundred years ago – though it is actually much older – it was known as 'Cuisse de Nymphe': nymph's thigh. Without exception the Alba roses are blessed with the loveliest of perfumes, but this variety probably has the strongest scent of all. The foliage of 'Maiden's Blush' is plentiful and a leaden greyish-green in colour. It is extremely healthy, although in prolonged dry weather it can suffer a little from rust. Conversely, if prolonged wet conditions prevail at flowering time (from early June to early July), the outer petals may congeal. There are said to be two clones – 'Great Maiden's Blush' and 'Small Maiden's Blush' – with little difference between them, except that perhaps in the latter case the flowers are fractionally smaller and the growth slightly shorter; but, to be frank, I have never seen this difference and I prefer the simple name 'Maiden's Blush'.

'Maiden's Blush' was the first rose I learned to recognize; I vividly recall it growing in my grandfather's garden. It gives me pleasure that the first plants I ever grew of this variety were taken from the very bush I was so fond of all those years ago.

bringing any Italian influence to bear in this garden – except in the conservatory, which she had built with advice from Sir Martyn Beckett in the 1960s. This is not a conservatory in the accepted sense, for it has three sides without windows, the light coming in from an attractively designed, sizeable glass dome in the roof and a large window in the south wall. As with most conservatories, this one is at its best in late winter/early spring, when among abutilons a superb white jasmine, *Jasminium officinale* 'Grandiflorum', climbs right up into the dome and fills the whole room with its distinctive perfume. Outdoors Lady Hambleden's gardening skills, over the years, have been applied to redesigning the three acres so that they can be managed by just one full-time gardener.

The first rose to be found in this garden is on the north-facing wall that runs alongside the drive. Appropriately enough, this is 'Mme Alfred Carrière', for no other rose performs as well in such a difficult situation. Mentioned several times elsewhere in this book, 'Mme Alfred Carrière' is a white/blushed-pink Noisette climber. Here her companion rose is another stress-tolerant variety, the blood-red single hybrid Gallica 'Scharlachglut'. Also on this wall is the white-flowered climbing *Hydrangea petiolaris*.

On the long south-facing wall of the house, with wisteria and fremontodendron, are several roses of varying shades. Inevitably 'New Dawn' crops up, for it is invaluable in providing those last few flowers of summer each year. The sulphur-yellow 'Mermaid' seemingly enjoys this position, although you might expect to find it where it would not have to endure quite so much of the summer heat. Another rose doing stalwart service on this wall is 'Albéric Barbier', the almost thornless creamy-white hybrid Wichuraiana rambler which is also practically evergreen. A wide terrace of randomly laid flagstones, with here and there a stone removed for a variety of herbs to grow, lies between this wall and a large expanse of lawn which extends to the extreme southern edge of the garden. Both lawn and terrace are on the same level. In fact this is the only flat part of the entire gardens, being part of the area levelled at the time the building was put up. From the lawn the view extends across flat countryside towards the Thames. To avoid detracting from this important vista, the wide border of roses which forms the southern boundary is deliberately composed of less vigorous varieties, mostly in shades of yellow and white. They include the Hybrid Musk 'Buff Beauty' and the lovely soft yellow single 'Golden Wings'. Another excellent yellow shrub rose used effectively in this border is 'Lichtkönigin Lucia', a variety not seen often enough, probably because – for reasons I can never understand – it is listed by so few growers. There are two white Rugosas here too, each kept within bounds by judicious pruning. These are the double-flowered 'Blanc Double de Coubert' and the single-flowered *Rosa rugosa* 'Alba', the latter bringing to this border in the autumn the bonus of bright red globular hips. Both of these Rugosas will enhance this area in early winter with brightly coloured foliage. Another white rose which fits in well at the front of this border is the delightful little Edwardian Polyantha 'Yvonne Rabier' with its light green foliage and masses of semi-double flowers.

Cleverly hidden from view from the house and concealed from other directions by tall trees and shrubs is a swimming pool. At a much lower level than the south lawn, it is reached by steps downwards through wisteria trained on wrought-iron arches to form a tunnel. This feature was installed fairly recently and is already a delight, but will be quite magnificent in a year or two. Near the swimming pool is a bed of mixed shrub roses, including several Bourbons such as the crimson-purple 'Mme Isaac

With the tower of Hambleden's Church of St Mary the Virgin in the background, white Damask rose 'Mme Hardy' and pink Portland rose 'Jacques Cartier' are seen at the peak of their season; the latter will flower on all summer.

Pereire' and the violet-purple 'Reine des Violettes', both heavily scented. On the walls of the changing rooms are two vigorous scramblers; one I didn't recognize, but the other is the scented white *Rosa mulliganii*, so long erroneously distributed as *R. longicuspis* and frequently nowadays confused with it.

The goodly sized copper beech in the large area of lawn that forms the front garden lost one of its upper limbs in a freak storm in the summer of 1994. Surgery has been carried out to bring it back into shape, but it will take a little time before the scars are eclipsed by new growth. To help hide some of these blemishes, plants of 'Bobbie James' – a vigorous white scrambler – have been planted to grow up into and cascade down through some of the lower branches.

Running along the inside of the western boundary is a long border of mixed flowering shrubs designed to give colour and interest throughout the year. At the same time they camouflage what would otherwise be a very long, bare eight-foot-high wall. In front of the south-facing wall which forms the perimeter to the kitchen garden are two recently created rose borders. Rugosas form the bulk of the varieties in these beds, with most of the better-known sorts used: in the background the purple-red 'Roseraie de l'Hay' and the cerise single 'Scabrosa' and, in the foreground, the shorter-growing silvery-pink single 'Fru Dagmar Hastrup' and the excellent double white 'Schneezwerg'. Growing on the walls in this spot are several good climbing roses. Proving its adaptability – we encountered it earlier on a south

Damask 'Ispahan', Portland 'Rose de Rescht' and Alba 'Maiden's Blush' thrive in the beautiful tree-studded garden at Hambleden. The tall pink rambler rose on the bower is 'May Queen'.

wall – 'Scharlachglut' is once again outstanding. The centrepiece here is a tall, bower-like metal construction on which are trained several plants of the Victorian lilac-pink rambler 'May Queen'. It is pleasing to find this lesser-known rambler used in such a prominent position.

In the western corner of this part of the garden, giving form and perspective, is a large yew clipped in the form of a dome. Behind this tree, set in the wall, a door leads to the old kitchen garden. In 1982 I was asked by Lady Hambleden to design a rose garden in approximately half of this area (about half an acre). Roses today generally play supporting roles, so to be given a free hand to use them for their own sake was most gratifying. In this design I was anxious to create as much informality as possible and, at the same time, enable easy access among the roses so that pleasures experienced when they were mature would be rather more than simply visual.

I settled on the soft lines of a circular, wheel-like plan, with a round central bed as the hub and each bed thereafter separated into borders by short paths radiating outwards, with no one path opposite to another and with four large corner beds to complete the square. It is, purely and simply, a rose garden; for ease of maintenance, nothing else is used – not even bulbs in the spring or edging plants around the beds. Each year manure is lightly dug into the beds and the soil is kept free from weeds by straightforward old-fashioned hoeing. The beds are defined in cottage-garden style with flintstones set into the soil.

The whole area slopes towards the west, the rose garden being separated from the kitchen garden by a five-foot well-trimmed yew hedge. The eastern boundary is loosely defined by a shelter belt of mixed small trees and shrubs. A low brick and flint wall, on which are trained assorted rambler roses, forms the western boundary. The wide border in front is populated mostly by Nature's pure roses, with here and there a hybrid to provide a little extra colour when the once-flowering species have finished blooming in early summer. Two species flourishing in this border are the unique four-petalled white *Rosa omeiensis pteracantha* (*R. sericea pteracantha*), armed with vicious thorns, and the pink-flowered Apple Rose, *R. pomifera* (*R. villosa*). All the roses in this border are in pastel shades of pink and white.

In the main part of the rose garden some eighty varieties are growing. Care was taken in the design not to have contrasting shades growing in the same beds, but – except for the strident and garish – the whole spectrum of colour was used. For maximum effect three to five of each variety were grouped together and although consideration was given to ultimate sizes, the objective was to achieve an overall undulating effect, avoiding any semblance of uniformity.

The centre bed consists of mostly Hybrid Musks with the soft white weeping standard rose 'Félicité Perpétue' as a centrepiece. There are many examples of good reliable shrub roses in each of the beds, but two striped Bourbons – 'Commandant Beaurepaire' and 'Variegata di Bologna' – have matured into excellent plants over the past fifteen years or so, as have two shorter-growing varieties of Centifolia, respectively deep pink and pale pink, 'Spong' and 'Rose de Meaux'. Of the more recent varieties, outstanding is the pink Floribunda 'Centenaire de Lourdes', which I find combines so well with the older varieties, and the seldom-seen but equally gregarious bright pink Floribunda 'Auguste Seebauer' is also doing very well. Inevitably the pale pink Alba 'Maiden's Blush' thrives here, as it seems to do wherever I have seen it.

Lady Hambleden opens the gardens once a year at the height of the rose season for nursing charities, and it is well worth taking this chance of seeing them.

ROSA BRACTEATA HYBRID

'MERMAID' is one of the loveliest of the single roses. Its flowers are larger than those of most single varieties and are borne both solitarily and in small clusters on an almost totally evergreen plant from midsummer until the onset of the frosts of winter. Their colour is a soft sulphur-yellow which fades to creamy-white in the heat of the sun. A particularly outstanding feature of the flower is the prominent arrangement of golden-yellow to bronze stamens which remain conspicuous on the plant for some days after the petals have fallen.

'Mermaid' is a very vigorous plant and, if it likes a position, will attain a height of over twenty-five feet, with a matching width. Its foliage is glossy bright green and abundant; younger, newly produced growth is bronzy-red. A less attractive attribute is a predominance of viciously hooked thorns. While it tolerates some shade and flowers on a north wall, in more severe winters it can suffer from frost damage; however, this will seldom be terminal.

'Mermaid' came about as the result of a cross between the Macartney Rose – *Rosa bracteata* – and an unknown yellow Hybrid Tea. It was introduced by William Paul in Britain in 1918 and has been one of the most popular climbing roses for walls ever since.

'MERMAID'

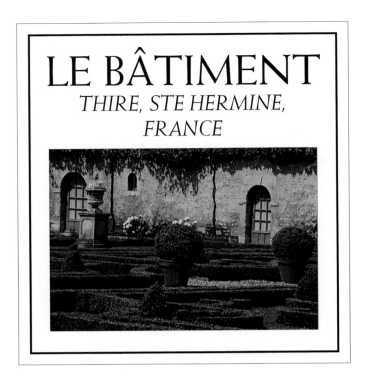

LE BÂTIMENT
THIRE, STE HERMINE, FRANCE

The parterre in the walled front garden of Le Bâtiment follows the pattern of an early seventeenth-century brick design, unearthed by Bill Christie during his restoration of this beautiful Baroque period house in the rolling farmland of the Bas-Poitou region.

HIS MOST BEGUILING GARDEN HAS BEEN COMPOSED AND arranged by musician and conductor William (Bill) Christie in the style and period of the music he loves so much, the Baroque.

The house and garden are discreetly located amid the rolling farmland of the Bas-Poitou region, thirty kilometres or so inland from the Atlantic coast, just south of Ste Hermine. Except for young trees planted by Bill on the distant horizon 'for perspective', the undulating landscape consists of cornfields and yet more cornfields.

Bill's folks had a garden in up-state New York, near Rochester, and he learned a lot about plants from them as a child. By the age of twenty he was determined, one day, to build a garden. Le Bâtiment is, therefore, the realization of an ambition.

Why this place, when there are attractive parts of France so much nearer to Paris and the Opéra? 'It is away from the tourist trail,' Bill answered, 'and there are the most beautiful clouds and skies in the world, not to mention more sunny days than the Côte d'Azur.' On the day of my visit the big sky was indeed beautiful, with hanging dark clouds to the west over the Bay of Biscay. The sun shone, too; a good day to see Bill's garden and his roses – but first his impressive house, which he bought in 1985 'on the rebound', when the purchase of another house fell through. 'This one was derelict and I bought it for a pittance. I liked it because it was late sixteenth/early seventeenth-century, with an Italianate "feel" and a lone tree inviting me to start a garden from scratch.' He bought it just in time, when its true identity as the home of a Protestant nobleman of the mid- to late 1600s was almost lost after centuries of clumsy use as a farmhouse. Now, twenty years on, it has been sensitively restored by Bill with a real feeling for its former role.

Beautifully proportioned in two storeys, its tendency to severity is considerably softened by the biscuity-coloured local sandstone walls and low-pitched terracotta-tiled roof. Early in the restoration no fewer than six Renaissance fireplaces were

uncovered along with most of the original floors. The aura of the interior, even the subdued light from the windows, brings on an acute tingle of awareness of the atmosphere that prevailed here three and a half centuries or so ago. One's imagination can have a free rein.

The sensitive appreciation of the history and origins of the building continues throughout the entire garden. Nowhere is this more so than at the front of the house where, in the early stages of restoration, to Bill's great delight, the outline of the brick surround of an early seventeenth-century parterre was unearthed. This enabled today's design of neatly trimmed box edging to follow precisely the intricacies of its true, Baroque period pattern. Bill has embellished this with several plinth-mounted urns, a central sundial and numerous terracotta pots from which sprout spherical or pyramid-shaped box trees. Other topiary adds further to the classical feel of this part of the gardens at Le Bâtiment.

The walls surrounding the Parterre Garden (except those of the house, which are, quite properly, left bare) are adorned with a wide variety of climbing plants such as *Jasminum officinale*, various clematis, *Wisteria sinensis*, honeysuckle and roses – not just climbers and ramblers, but several Gallicas which have grown very much taller than normal in this agreeable position. Among these I spotted the very ancient 'Hippolyte', a beautiful, graceful purple Gallica, and the similarly coloured 'Cardinal de Richelieu' (1840). Prominent in the corner facing south-east, and covering

The colour of the blooms of the lovely rambler 'Albertine' blends perfectly with the soft-toned, biscuity-coloured local stone of which Le Bâtiment is built. Just as perfect a blend is Albertine's young plum-coloured wood in the spring.

Cloisters run along the east side of the small white Sunken Garden at Le Bâtiment. On the south wall of the house is the blush white 'Mme Alfred Carrière'. The quarter standard rose is 'Katharina Zeimet', one of four in the concise arrangement of things in this part of the garden.

metres of wall in both directions, is 'Francis E. Lester', a delightful white/ flushed-pink rambler, its arms linked with the lovely 'Albertine'. Farther along the south-facing interior of the boundary wall is a splendid *Rosa bracteata*, which flowers in great profusion in May here and then goes on giving a smattering of flowers right through to November. I love this rose and wish I could grow it back home in Norfolk as well as it grows here.

The entire length of the western side of the Parterre Garden is taken up by a rustic timber pergola swathed with a congenial mixture of ramblers, scramblers and climbers of all sorts, but mostly roses, and with vines bearing black grapes. Among the roses on this structure I found the almost thornless, later-flowering *R. moschata* hybrid 'Aimée Vibert', white and the very prickly, early-flowering pink *R. soulieana* hybrid 'Kew Rambler', intermingling with the lovely, very fragrant pure white Musk rose 'Thalia'. Two other special features of the Parterre Garden must be mentioned before moving on: a single, tall stone pine (*Pinus pinea*), the only tree here when Bill arrived, and bright rusty-red sandstone chippings infilling the parterre, highlighting it most effectively in pleasing contrast to the dark green of the box edging.

The southern end of the rose walk is taken up by a rustic covered arbour with seating, hung with grapes, wisteria, honeysuckle and roses and discreetly lit at night by lanterns. From here a way leads through to an open area of lawn where shrub roses are scattered randomly among fastigiate conifers, medlars, quinces and the odd apple tree. Here I was pleased to find 'Comte de Chambord', a Portland invaluable for its tidy behaviour and ever-present flowers, and a couple of pink 'Complicata' – once-flowering but, in a setting such as this, very beautiful. There are several plants of the reliable shrub rose 'Nevada', likewise beautiful, but soft creamy-white. The highlight for me in this area, was a rose I had never seen or heard of before, 'Château de la Juvenie', a hybrid of *Rosa macrophylla* from André Eve's collection, producing clusters of pretty little double pink flowers with a delicious perfume.

Eastwards from this area, which is concealed from the house by a semi-mature yew hedge, one comes upon a real treat, a sunken garden. On its east side are cloisters, very cool in high summer, and on the west side a low wall supporting trellis which connects to the rose pergola. This trellis is bedecked by yet more roses, the lilac-pink 'Narrow Water' and the blush-white 'Baltimore Belle'. The Sunken Garden itself is pebbled with the same delightfully biscuity-coloured stone used everywhere in these gardens where paths are needed. This little garden is divided up into four equal-sized, square, brick-edged beds with white petunias forming the summer backcloth for classical ornaments and pot-grown topiary. Half-standards of the white Polyantha rose 'Katharina Zeimet' provide an ideal centrepiece for each of the beds. Beneath a lion-head fountain in the west wall is a raised border where several plants of 'Gruss an Aachen', that most reliable of cream Floribundas, are thriving, their colour in perfect harmony with the ancient stonework behind. Overlooking the Sunken Garden on the gable-end south wall of the house, sustaining the creamy-white theme, is a huge plant of the Noisette 'Mme Alfred Carrière'.

To the east of the Sunken Garden and cloisters, on a higher level, is a broad terrace running the entire length of the house. This is furnished with substantial pots and urns, each planted with clipped box trees, and with ten large, square ornamental wooden tubs, locally made and painted grey, each planted with a young orange or lemon tree and a group of the little pink rose 'The Fairy'. These add a pleasing extra dimension to the formality on this side of the house.

From the terrace you enjoy a wide vista of rising ground to the horizon, with ash trees and white poplars planted by Bill breaking up the view in the middle distance. Wide avenues of lime, soon to be pleached, run along either side of the expansive classical garden that makes up the entire area to the east of the house – flat, very green and some three metres lower than the terrace. Clipped yews, both fastigiate and common, are predominant in this sector, which has wide gravelled paths and a large urn centrepiece. Tiered pyramids of box occupy strategical positions along each side of the paths and four tall but as yet young stone pines occupy the centres of the grassy quads formed by the cruciform pattern of the walkways.

Farther down towards the east from this garden a wide ramp descends to an area of natural flora with a meandering stream spanned by a rustic bridge. This is where Bill has planted the spinney of ash and white poplars seen from the terrace. There is a small lake here, too – all part of the scheme to attract wide and varied wildlife. From here, looking uphill to the west, the house looks dramatic silhouetted against the azure, cloud-spun sky.

As guests arrive at the house they are welcomed by two more plants of the Noisette 'Mme Alfred Carrière' which take up the entire north wall of the house and some outbuildings. Planted on either side of the arched entrance leading through the

PORTLAND ROSE

'COMTE DE CHAMBORD'

THE PORTLAND Damasks were really the first roses to benefit from the influx of *Rosa chinensis* genes when the China roses arrived in the West in the early nineteenth century. They flower on and on all summer – what a boon those first few must have been to the gardeners of the period! 'Comte de Chambord' appeared in 1860 and, in my opinion, is second to none of its group. Its flowers are shapely at all stages of development; for those who prefer roses to be high-centred, it can compete with any Hybrid Tea for beauty of form at about the half-open stage. Later it opens farther and more to my taste – flat, full and quartered. Its colour is bright, deep pink with a sheen of soft mauve. Its fragrance is strong and heavy.

The plant grows to about three feet, is bushy and seldom without flowers. Foliage is plentiful and dark green. Like all Portlands, it makes a good bedding rose. It enjoys a little extra loving care and responds well to an annual pruning in spring. It does well under glass and is good in pots. Flowers also last fairly well when cut and used for arrangements indoors.

FLORIBUNDA ROSE

'GRUSS AN AACHEN'

THIS ROSE was raised in 1909, when it was classified as a Polypompon. It is now listed as a Floribunda and – considering its age – it is somewhat surprisingly still one of my company's best-selling varieties of the type. Perhaps not so surprising; when first raised, it was way ahead of its time. It is, in fact, not just a good bedding rose but very beautiful in its own right. I know of the extent of its popularity after its introduction, but I personally had not come across it until about 1975, when I saw a large bed of it planted at Castle Howard, Yorkshire, by James Russell.

It was bred in Germany by a man named Geduldig and may – like one of its parents, 'Frau Karl Druschki' – have suffered some rejection in England because of its German name between the two World Wars. Its renaissance occurred only when a more understanding generation of Rosarians recognized its many merits.

Bedding is its real forte, but it is also good in groups at the front of a border, for it never grows tall. I also like to see it in containers, when it outshines many a modern variety. Its colour is best described as peachy-apricot with pink flushes; in hot sunshine it fades to creamy-white. It has a superb fragrance.

Parterre Garden to the front door, these roses are six years old and already in the prime of their lives. Just to the north of the main entrance Bill has planted a small arboretum, and he has surrounded the entire garden with a tall hornbeam hedge – not so much for enclosure's sake, but psychologically 'to block out the world from the calm and quiet of my oasis'.

There is a great deal of green in this garden, and lots of shapes. Bill composes and plays his music here. The roses, he admits, are a compromise and have very little to do with the Baroque, but when the walls are hung with their flowers and the air heavy with their fragrance, it is not difficult to see why he wants them. I enjoyed this garden very much. It is open to the public by appointment only. Telephone the gardener on 51.56.89.23.

Although the garden at Le Bâtiment is still young, it is full of interest with lots of greenery and lots of shapes. Roses, although having little to do with the Baroque period, are important here for their colour and perfume. Altogether the garden is a place of seclusion and tranquillity for its owner, Bill Christie.

MILLS AVENUE
MENLO PARK, SAN MATEO, CALIFORNIA, USA

I ARRIVED AT MILLS AVENUE SOMEWHAT BEFUDDLED, JUST two hours after my long flight from London landed at San Francisco. Within five minutes I was so enthralled that I completely forgot about jet lag. The little garden measures about a hundred feet square, but there are more roses to the square inch here than in any other private garden I have seen. Besides those growing in the ground, there are many in pots and others heeled in, presumably waiting to be found a more permanent home here or elsewhere in a friend's garden. Barbara Worl is generous with her roses.

Barbara's day job is as a manager in Bells Book Store in Palo Alto, ten miles away. She also publishes books, calendars and posters on roses under the imprint of Sweetbriar Press. I first met this garden's creator during an earlier visit to California. I was taken to her garden by a mutual friend, Bill Grant, a leading American rosarian, and their conversation, and not a little banter, added considerably to the pleasure of my visit. Barbara has since visited me in England, and while I knew of her love for roses, I had forgotten just how strong it is until I saw Mills Avenue. There is a huge range of other plants, too, from native Californian wild flowers to a pink-flowered pussywillow from France. In the middle, barely visible through the foliage, is Barbara's shingle-roofed, single-storey timber house.

I suppose if you love gardening and your plot is this size, it does become full up after forty-five years, for Barbara, whose Welsh ancestors came to America at the time of William Penn, moved here in the early 1950s. In the 1930s this locality was the growing fields for the Japanese cut-flower industry, which thrived until the growers were interned at the onset of war. After the war, building began, and Barbara's house was one of the earliest to appear. In this climate the first roses come into flower in mid-February, and it is easy to get hooked.

Gradually over twenty years Barbara's rose collection and enthusiasm for plants filled this garden together with two acres of a vacant lot on the other side of town.

Roses sprout from every nook and cranny of Barbara Worl's garden at Mills Avenue, with only here and there a glimpse of the timber-built house. Here on the left of the front door is the Tea Rose 'Souvenir d'un Ami', and on the right, 'Clotilde Soupert'.

HYBRID RUGOSA

'CORYLUS'

'CORYLUS' IS a delightful rose. It was raised by Mrs Hazel le Rougetel in 1988 from a cross between *Rosa rugosa* and *R. nitida*. When grown as a specimen shrub or among herbaceous plants, it makes an attractive little low-growing shrub, but it really comes into its own when planted in groups and allowed to spread to form a dense ground cover; it is especially effective in this role since it suckers so freely when grown on its own roots. This little rose is also a first-class hedging variety.

A special characteristic is its soft, feathery, dark green foliage, which changes in autumn to rich tawny-gold and orange. At this time of the year it freely produces little orange-red globular hips, which follow on from a succession of deep silvery-pink single scented flowers. These blooms have a central boss of lovely soft yellow stamens.

'Corylus' is well bred, combining the best of both parents in a way that ensures it a good future as a trouble-free rose for all types of soils. As it becomes better known, it is bound to become more widely used, especially in the less temperate climates of the world, for it is extremely hardy.

Last spring she lost the use of this extra land, so for the past few months she has been moving most of her treasured plants back to home base, which was already well stocked anyway.

At Mills Avenue Barbara has the part-time help of Ron Debord and Janet Eldridge, of whom she speaks very highly. Ron has removed a large privet hedge from the front of the house, and replaced it with a series of raised beds over which he has built a substantial timber structure all along the front between the street and the garden, to support a range of climbers and ramblers. This splendid pergola affords complete privacy to the house from the road. By the gate is a well-grown plant of the widely grown 1930s Hybrid Musk 'Buff Beauty' and, next to it the modern lilacky-pink Austin rose 'Cymbeline'. I am pleased that, in America, David Austin's roses are most often referred to generically as 'Austin's' roses, not 'New English Roses'.

The pergola is approximately seventy feet long and consists of two top rails about three feet apart held aloft by stout uprights at about six feet apart, and it is on each of these that roses are planted, together with other plants such as clematis and honeysuckle. Having been in California for so little time I was, perhaps, slightly disappointed that my first encounter was with 'Buff Beauty', a rose I could see anywhere in England; however, the next three put things right. The first was a well-grown plant of the golden-yellow Tea 'Etoile de Lyon', the second, a lovely yellow Tea rose 'Rêve d'Or' and the third, the shapely white Noisette 'Lamarque' – all from the last century and all varieties that would not do so well for me back home. Also at home here were the delightful 'Chromatella' ('Cloth of Gold') and the free-flowering pinkish-white Hybrid Setigera 'Baltimore Belle', both bred over 150 years ago.

Also here at the front of the house are the excellent modern soft pink 'Heritage', the yellow Hybrid Musk 'Danaë', the pink Bourbon 'Blairii No 2' and the purple Hybrid Perpetual 'Reine des Violettes'. I noticed, too, a plant of *Rosa canina*. Barbara acquired it in the mid-1950s from England as the rootstock of another rose which it has long since shed. In September each year the large crop of hips it carries are superb. She treasures this rose not just for its ornamental value, but for its association with the old Sunningdale Nurseries, managed at that time by the two great plantsmen Graham Thomas and James Russell.

Less conspicuous than the pergola is another new installation in Barbara's garden at Mills Avenue – an irrigation system providing overhead spray, programmed to come on for an hour or so during the early morning and to stop in time to allow the leaves to dry before the scorching sun comes out each day in high summer. Recently – although I saw no evidence of it – they have been plagued with downy mildew, but the new system should help to keep the roses healthy. There is no better disease control than good husbandry, which includes regular watering, especially in a climate such as this. To me Barbara's roses looked in very good shape.

In the north-east corner of the garden are two trees. A deciduous oak (variety not known), Barbara explained, 'was brought to me by the birds' and now supports a modern white rambler called 'Bubble Bath', which I did not know. An acacia also came of its own volition, since it was a seedling from an older, larger tree that was blown down in a storm seventeen years ago, taking with it the rose it had supported since 1945. This rose, *Rosa brunonii*, has also regrown since then and the two continue to live happily together.

To afford maximum space for plants, a narrow path with borders on either side goes along the northern side of the house. These borders are crammed full of trees and shrubs – an eastern redbud (*Cercis canadensis*), dogwoods, maples and crab apples – as well as roses which, surprisingly, seem to flourish here despite the shade. The pink Damask 'La Ville de Bruxelles' perhaps does not flower to its full potential, but can be very rewarding if it presents just a few of its lovely flowers each year. Another doing well here, if not thriving, is the deep reddish-purple, scented Moss rose 'Capitaine John Ingram'. I cannot imagine this rose flowering so freely in such shade in England, but perhaps with the warmer, longer summers here direct sunlight is not quite so important. In this area, too, I found dahlias of all shades, delphiniums and several varieties of perennial salvia.

Round to the east of the house there is an appearance of more spaciousness – not, I hasten to say, through any lack of plants; simply that they are of a different type and generally less vigorous, at least in the middle of what is, in effect, a sort of patio. Feeling at this point that it was time to relax and enjoy the evening light, I looked for somewhere to sit, but there were no seats. Barbara explained, 'I don't want to give up the space; wherever you put a seat you can't plant something.' I should have known! Ron has in fact placed little stool-like seats here and there throughout the garden to permit an occasional rest.

Having newly arrived in California, I found the light at this time of day in this more open part of the garden quite interesting. It may have been my fancy, but it seemed, somehow, to accentuate colours – or maybe it was Barbara's skill in placing so many brightly coloured plants in this part of her garden. Flamboyance was also apparent in the roses used here. The flowers of 'Cerise Bouquet', for instance, glowed, as did the flowers of the splendid orange-yellow 'Alchymist' climbing twenty feet or more up into a 'Silver Dollar' tree, *Eucalyptus polyanthemos*, 'Alchymist's' hundreds of flowers being shared and enjoyed by at least two of Barbara's neighbours. This particular plant apparently repeats its flowers and was, even then in mid-July, on its second flush – a phenomenon which I doubt it would mimic outside California. Two roses with many years separating them were also sharing a bed, Austin's soft yellow 'English Garden' of 1986 and the first ever yellow Hybrid Tea, 'Soleil d'Or' (1900). Further enhancing this colourful area dozens, if not hundreds, of flower pots of all shapes, sizes and colours are scattered around, each one with flowers or foliage of this colour and that, not a few of them roses.

On the southern aspect of the house I found yet another change in the light, this time from the dappled shade of scattered trees, one of them a citrus. Coming from a part of the world where these are far too tender to grow out of doors, I am always fascinated when I find them in far-away gardens, especially when they are bearing fruit like the fifteen-foot Valencia orange I found here. Other exotics I discovered – at least exotics to me – were a pomegranate and a guava tree. Again, the generally pervasive air of activity was heightened by yet more flower pots. This southern side probably has the most wide-ranging assortment of different genera of this garden. The most numerous, as one might expect, are roses – far too many to enumerate – but varieties which just cannot be omitted include 'Long John Silver' raised in 1935 in America, a vigorous climber with clusters of large, fully double, fragrant white flowers; 'Souvenir d'un Ami', a lovely, soft salmon-pink Tea rose dating back to 1846; 'Marie d'Orléans', a delightful pink Tea which I had never before seen and the pretty little creamy-white Polyantha 'Clotilde Soupert'. Other roses in this part of the garden among chimonanthus, euphorbia, maples and other interesting subjects are Hazel le Rougetel's 'Corylus', a delightful *Rosa*

MODERN SHRUB ROSE

'HERITAGE'

THIS IS one of my favourite Austin roses. Introduced in 1984, it was one of the first of a new range of shrub roses now classified as 'New English Roses' – or, in America, as 'Austin's Roses'. These varieties generally have flowers in the style of the old roses but behave after the fashion of moderns, by which I mean that, unlike most shrub roses, if they are not pruned fairly hard each season they become spindly and less free-flowering. They have become extremely popular over the past decade, and seem to do especially well in temperate and warm climates.

The flowers of 'Heritage' are soft pink, deeper in the centre, with the blooms cupped until fully open, when they become attractively loosely formed. They are very fragrant and freely produced. The plant makes a useful shrub to a height of about four feet and has dark green, slightly glossy foliage.

'Heritage' is relatively disease-resistant. To keep it shrubby, as with most of the Austin roses, it is best to prune fairly hard each year. I have seen it used most effectively as a low, informal hedge; it also does well for me as a pot plant. Its colour goes particularly well with grey foliage plants and blue perennials.

*O*ne of the many superb assortments of plants arranged by rose devotee Barbara Worl in her Californian garden is, here, the Hybrid Musk 'Buff Beauty' grown comfortably alongside numerous companion plants.

*C*olours, shapes, greenery and fragrance from the ground to the tallest tree mean there is something going on every day of the year in the fascinating garden at San Mateo (facing page).

rugosa × *R. nitida* seedling with silvery-pink single flowers and rich autumn colouring, *Rosa roxburghii* 'Plena', which I coveted, since my own plant at home has died, and 'The Garland' climbing up into the trees.

I have barely touched upon the long list of Barbara's roses. Those I have mentioned will, I hope, reflect the wide-ranging tastes of this knowledgeable gardener and plantsperson *extraordinaire*. One other rose should be included, however. It is 'Barbara Worl', appropriately an unidentified, free-flowering, scented pink foundling which the Heritage Rose lovers of America have named after her. She believes it to be 'Coronet', having seen one like it labelled thus at Sangerhausen. Maybe, but since that rose, raised in 1842, is no longer in commerce, her rose should continue to be called 'Barbara Worl', for if anyone deserves a rose of her own, it is this lady.

Despite – or because of – my jet lag, my image of this garden is vivid. I remember roses and more roses, pots and yet more pots, lots of shade, lots of sun and, above all else, my first sight of a pair of humming birds, feeding on yellow abutilon. Barbara Worl's garden is not open to the public, but I am sure no reader would be turned away, especially if they were to make an appointment or arrive during sensible hours of the day.

NYMANS
HANDCROSS, WEST SUSSEX, ENGLAND

HE GREAT GARDENS AT NYMANS, OWNED BY THE NATIONAL Trust since 1954, represent all that is good in 'grand-scale', long-established English gardening. There is something to be found here in a variety of landscapes for every specialist interest, from the tiniest of alpines to the most rugged of trees.

Sitting snugly in the middle is the Rose Garden, which seems to me never to have received the attention that it deserves. Perhaps I am biased. Every so often, as one travels around visiting gardens, one comes upon a display at the peak of perfection. This happened to me on my first visit to this Rose Garden in June 1993. It was breathtakingly beautiful at that moment. A day earlier would have been too soon; an hour afterwards too late, for the early sunlight which filtered through the broken cloud to the east was exceptionally crisp and clear for England and the scent was overwhelming. As rose gardens go nowadays, this one is not large in size; just big in substance, for in what can be no more than a quarter of an acre it holds the best part of 150 varieties of old roses.

It follows a design by John Sales and Isobelle Van Groeningen devised for planting in 1987, but delayed until a year later by the intervention of the great storm of 15 October that year, which devastated not only Nymans but most of the other gardens of southern England. Now, in hindsight, it can be seen that many sites were given a new lease of life by the space and light created from the havoc – nature's way of enforcing change. There is little or no evidence today at Nymans of the trauma of the storm, and this is due in large part to the dedication of Head Gardener David Masters and his staff in working to bring forth a new order from that dreadful night of chaos.

After just seven years the new Rose Garden is fully mature, but a rose garden has been on the site since Maud Messel designed and planted one, mainly of old roses, in the early 1920s. Among the varieties planted at that time, apparently,

In the Rose Garden at Nymans there are almost one hundred and fifty varieties of old roses growing in less than a quarter of an acre. A special feature is the extra dimension achieved by tall arches and pillars. The roses seen here are 'René André'.

Bourbon 'Honorine de Brabant' is one of the most free-flowering of all the striped roses. It also has a lovely perfume. Here it thrives in the rich fertile soil of this part of West Sussex (facing page).

RAMBLER ROSE

'FRANÇOIS JURANVILLE'

THIS ROSE was raised by Barbier in France in 1906, the result of crossing *Rosa wichuraiana* with the lovely old China rose 'Mme Laurette Messimy'. These days it is sometimes confused with the well-known 'Albertine', for its colour is similar, but that is where the likeness ends; 'Albertine' is coarser, more thorny and has fewer petals. Of the two, I personally prefer 'François Juranville', for even though its flowers are made up of somewhat muddled petals, they are more refined than the admittedly beautiful 'Albertine'. They have a distinct apple fragrance. It is also a little less prone to mildew. But comparisons are odious, especially between roses, and both are ramblers I could not do without.

'François Juranville' makes a superb pillar rose and does well on arches at Nymans. On structures such as pergolas or arches, the more its pliable shoots are twisted and turned the better, for it can get quite leggy if left to its own devices. It will reach a height of twenty feet or more and will grow – if not happily – tolerably well up into the branches of small trees. It is not a particularly good rose to grow on a wall.

were many collected from the gardens of France and Italy; several were given to her by her friend, the respected rosarian of the day, Ellen Willmott. Both Maud and her husband, Lieut.-Col. Leonard Messel, were keen gardeners and, indeed, plant collectors, subscribing generously to the great plant-hunting expeditions of the day to China and the Himalayas. Leonard was the son of Ludwig Messel, who acquired Nymans in 1890 and started the great tradition of gardening associated with it.

It is not clear how much attention was paid to Maud Messel's design in the new Rose Garden, which does have a very 1920s feel about it, but even if the layout has changed she would certainly have known and loved many of the varieties now growing there. Graham Thomas, who has led the renaissance of the old garden roses since the 1950s, describes this Rose Garden as it was in 1941 as 'formal beds set in grass and interspersed with apple and mulberry trees in a pleasing cottage-garden style'. He tells of the 'special privilege' of being taken round Mrs Messel's collection and recalls 'the great beauty of "Charles de Mills" in all its glory'. Roses enjoyed then, as they do now, the rich soil here. Thomas goes on: 'It was a great experience to see them and hear all the delightful names of these rare old varieties from so knowledgeable and enthusiastic a gardener as Mrs Messel.' He was obviously much taken by the collection, and this encounter clearly inspired him in his subsequent great affair with roses. In inviting him to Nymans, Maud Messel certainly did us all a great favour.

Although the Rose Garden is the main focus for roses at Nymans, it is by no means the only place where they are to be found. When entering the gardens from the west through either of the two archways cut into the twelve-foot-tall holly hedge, we encounter 'Mme d'Arblay' growing up through the dense, dark green holly and showing itself to good effect in rose season. This is a vigorous and delightfully scented blush-white rambler, a cross between *Rosa multiflora* and *R. moschata*. Ramblers or scramblers thrive in positions like this, for they have the benefit of full protection from the north and full sun from the south in which to flower.

From these entrances a hundred-yard-long, ten-foot-wide path, flanked on either side by deep herbaceous borders, leads southwards towards two cleverly camouflaged potting sheds, both old and new, the camouflage taking the form of well-grown, dense wisteria, both white and lilac. Running the full length of this area is another tall, dense holly hedge which provides protection from the north both to the herbaceous borders and an area to the south known as the 'Top Garden'. This garden was laid down in 1910 to accommodate plants arriving from collectors working in all parts of the world. Surrounding the central grass area, the Top Garden is a fascinating range of trees and shrubs, especially a fine and diverse collection of magnolia. The two herbaceous borders have been designed to provide an interesting display throughout the year, but come into their own in late June with a real riot of colour, coinciding with the roses. In fact, along with other shrubs, several roses are to be found scattered here and there among the perennials. In particular several plants of *Rosa chinensis* 'Mutabilis' and one or two of the vigorous, early-flowering yellow Hybrid Perpetual 'Frühlingsgold' are enjoying the comfort of this sunny, warm position.

Situated roughly in the middle of the main garden, the circular Rose Garden is completely surrounded – except for entrances and exits – by a relatively young yew hedge. Its sheltered position brings it into flower early. The centrepiece is a bronze

fountain some six feet high designed by Vivien ap Rhys Pryce in the shape of an almost open single rose. A central path runs from north to south with three paths crossing it from east to west, forming a series of separate beds each holding about ten to a dozen bushes. The configuration is finished off and framed by one single bed around the circumference containing a single row of mixed shrub roses. The paths are about four feet wide and most effectively edged with plantings of geraniums 'Johnson's Blue', 'Kashmir Blue' and 'Kashmir White'. Catmint (*Nepeta mussinii*) and knotweed (*Polygonum affine* or *Persicaria affinis*) are also used to good effect as edging plants and ground cover. The simplicity of the ground plan makes viewing the roses perfectly easy and allows full appreciation of the varieties in each bed.

A pleasing feature of the central beds is that all of the various rose groups and families have been incorporated together in a grand mixture of planting. By so doing, the designers achieve maximum impact at peak rose season, from late June to early July; at the same time, when the summer-flowering non-remontants have gone over, a good continuity of flower overall is provided well into the autumn. Also cleverly done is the juxtaposition of roses of varying heights, without consideration to family or type, to achieve an undulating effect.

As well as the varieties one would expect to find in a public garden such as this – the Portlands 'Comte de Chambord' and 'Jacques Cartier', Gallicas 'Rosa Mundi' and 'Tuscany Superb', Mosses 'James Mitchell' and 'William Lobb' and

The Rose Garden is circular with criss-cross paths enabling one to walk easily among the roses. It is surrounded by trees which provide a lovely backdrop for the arches and tall pillars. Seen here in the foreground is 'Phyllis Bide' with 'Albéric Barbier' farther back.

Few rose gardens made up predominantly of old varieties are without at least one plant of Gallica 'Complicata', and Nymans is no exception. The flowering season of this rose may be fleeting but it makes up for this by the sheer number of flowers it produces when it is in bloom.

Bourbons 'Mme Isaac Pereire' and 'Honorine de Brabant' – it is refreshing to find delights such as the pink Floribunda 'Nathalie Nypels', the old yellow China, 'Perle d'Or', and the white Hybrid Musk 'Prosperity', growing happily alongside them. Even more pleasurable was to discover much rarer gems doing well here, for instance, the Tea 'Général Schablikine' – coppery-red – and the China 'Comtesse du Cayla' – orange – growing alongside such modern varieties as 'Golden Wings' and 'Fritz Nobis'. The roses in this garden are obviously cut back fairly hard each year, according to type, to keep them in shape. This is a practice I fully endorse; with timid pruning, they would soon become leggy and worn out after only a few years. This technique does not, however, benefit the old Teas, which are best pruned only sparingly, to keep them in shape.

By far and away the most important and successful element of the design in this garden is height. This is achieved by twelve arches spanning the paths and a similar number of pillars. Each arch is made of sturdy metal, eight feet wide and ten feet tall, and supports a different variety of rambler or climber; each pillar, in perfect proportion, does likewise. Mercifully, the temptation to use only continuous-flowering climbers (so often yielded to with disastrous results) on these structures was resisted. In fact some of those used do repeat; both 'Phyllis Bide' and 'New Dawn' growing on the pillars will flower on until winter, of course, and 'Mme Alfred Carrière' on two of the arches will also continue to provide her

TEA ROSE

'GÉNÉRAL SCHABLIKINE'

Tea roses do far better in warmer climates than where I garden in Britain. Until I came upon them on my travels, thriving in such diverse places as California and South Australia, I used to think of them as temperamental delicacies. Even so, I could not resist them, for among their ranks are some of the most beautiful of roses, not least 'Général Schablikine'. It was raised in 1878 by that great breeder of Tea roses, Gilbert Nabonnand, and is one of his best.

However, if any Tea will do well in Britain, this is it. It has no equal for evenness of temperament. It flowers almost continuously from June until November, grows to at least four feet in sheltered situations and has a slight but delicious perfume. It is even more worthwhile under glass. Its colour is variously described in catalogues as from coppery-orange to salmony-red; a mixture of the two is perhaps more accurate. A special feature is its delightfully muddled, almost formless shape from a scrolled, high-centred bud. Its foliage is shiny and plum-coloured when young. As well as making a good pot plant and small shrub, it is also useful on a warm wall, when it will attain a height of five feet or more.

blush-white powder-puffs throughout summer, as well as ample foliage. The rest of the structures are covered with such diverse ramblers as 'Albertine', 'Paul Transon' and 'François Juranville', all different Wichuraiana hybrids in different shades of pink, and 'Violette', 'Rose-Marie Viaud' and 'Veilchenblau', a trio of assorted bluish and lavender shades from the Multiflora range of Ramblers. Despite the fact that all these Ramblers are catalogued as 'once-flowering', there is sufficient diversity among them to give a good show until the end of July each year and some of them, especially 'Paul Transon' and 'François Juranville', will repeat with a smattering of flowers in September.

Nymans is situated near Handcross, near Haywards Heath, West Sussex and is open from 1 March to 31 October, daily except for Mondays and Tuesdays: in order to see the Rose Garden at its best, visit between mid- or late June and mid-July. People visiting for the first time are recommended to buy the delightful handbook on the gardens published by the National Trust.

This atmospheric shot shows the ancient Moss rose 'Maréchal Davoust' through the cascading clusters of flowers of the rambler 'Adélaïde d'Orléans'. Mosses seem to love the conditions at Nymans and about ten different varieties can be found enjoying life here.

BECKET'S CASTLE
CAPE ELIZABETH, MAINE, USA

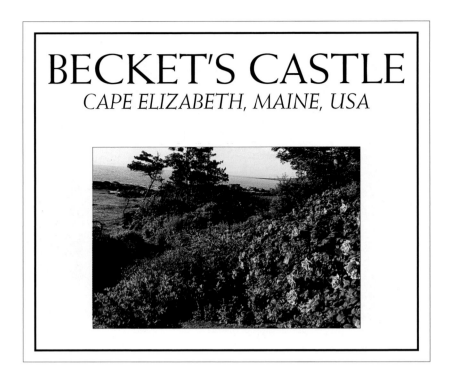

A superb example of the Rugosa rose 'Belle Poitevine' grows and flowers happily in Nancy Harvey's garden beside the sea at Cape Elizabeth, Maine. To the east there is nothing but ocean all the way to the southwestern coast of France.

Nancy Harvey believes in 'letting plants assert themselves naturally' at Becket's Castle. Seen here in the foreground is the Damask 'Celsiana', with the modern climber 'Alchymist' sitting just on the wall a little farther along (facing page).

APE ELIZABETH IS A HEADLAND JUTTING OUT INTO THE North Atlantic just south of Casco Bay. Although numerous year-round residences and summer homes are spread along the shoreline, the intrinsic wild ruggedness of this part of Maine is well preserved.

One of the first houses to be built on the cliffs was this stone building with an adjoining thirty-foot stone tower, from which, on clear days, it is possible to enjoy panoramic views of this dramatic coastline and look out over Portland Harbour. Apart from the diamond-shaped windows on the second level, it is reminiscent of a Norman church tower. Some people would call it a folly – not surprisingly, since it was built in 1874 by an English eccentric, Sylvester Becket, as his summer retreat. A lawyer, he had several other strings to his bow, including writing, ornithology, poetry, journalism, art and spiritualism. Each summer until his death in 1882 his grand parties made this the 'in' gathering place for writers, artists and the society folk of Maine. The original estate of nearly twenty acres remained intact until after the First World War, when the land was sold off piece by piece, leaving only the long, narrow strip of one and a half acres – following the line of the rocky escarpment forty feet up from the sea – on which the house stands.

The views from the house and garden are almost as dramatic as those from the tower, as indeed is the outlook from the little self-contained studio built especially for the delectation of guests such as myself. The whole site is sheltered from the west and north by rising scrubland and rocks. Although trees to the edge of the cliff afford some protection from the south, to the east there is nothing except the 3,000 miles of ocean between here and the coast of south-western France.

The secluded property is approached by a long drive, well-wooded on either side by mature trees. When its present owner, Nancy Harvey, bought the time-worn 'castle' in 1982, it was run down, and she spent the first four years renovating the house and planning the gardens. As a young girl she had often imagined living in

Blending beautifully with the stone and patchwork of lichen at Becket's Castle is Rosa glauca (R. rubrifolia). *This seat is just one of several, tempting one to sit down and enjoy both the roses and the rugged ocean views.*

a stone house by the sea in a garden of roses, so acquiring Becket's Castle was the start of a dream come true. The stark beauty of the gardenless site inspired Nancy to compose an evolving vision. 'Friends said roses wouldn't grow here,' she remembers, 'but I saw this as a challenge, and indeed it was.'

She employed an architect who had the foresight to first construct several levels of retaining walls before the garden could be built. Nancy studied art in her youth and sees her garden as a giant sculpture, its contours and shapes as important as its content, if not more so. From the start her artistic leanings influenced her every decision. Her first plantings of roses were a large group of Rugosas following the fall of the land near the entrance to the garden. 'I wanted them, from a distance, to look like they had been poured from a huge batter bowl,' she said. And they do! The varieties she chose were 'Blanc Double de Coubert' and 'Belle Poitevine'.

As the garden began to take shape, an occasional pair of helping hands became necessary; Lynn Shafer brought his own gardening expertise and creativity and encouraged Nancy to even more imaginative exploration of the capabilities of this land. Her garden is not only a sculpture; she sees the site, exposed to the ravages of the sea, as an 'experiment'. The first thing she and Lynn did together was to lay down a stone walkway from the carport to the house using rock brought up from the beach. Each side of this walkway is now crammed with a wide variety of herbaceous plants and shrubs, many ferns and foliage plants, and one or two roses. These borders, in common with all the others in this garden, are full to overflowing, with no earth showing anywhere, for Nancy likes 'letting the plants assert themselves naturally'.

A tour of this garden starts at the end of the drive which comes in from the south-west. Here cobblestones (actually ancient ballast once brought in on ships) are laid in a precise 'Catherine wheel' pattern to form a turning circle around which grow various trees including ash, willows, and elder 'for making elderberry pie'. Roses here include several plants of the species *Rosa virginiana* and its close relative, *R. carolina*, and numerous Rugosas including the single white form, *R. rugosa* 'Alba'. Honeysuckle and wild clematis scramble up into the trees and, here and there, day lilies add a splash of bright colouring to the predominance of green foliage and purplish-grey cobblestones.

MODERN SHRUB ROSE

'GRAHAM THOMAS'

THERE IS no doubt in my mind that this is the best of Austin's roses. It does everything that can be expected of a shrub rose. It is healthy; by the standards of yellow varieties of any type, it is very free-flowering – prolific in its first flush and never without a bloom all summer and well into autumn. Its clear yellow, fully double, cup-shaped flowers are well scented and all hold themselves upright on strong stems. They do not mind being cut and used in flower arrangements.

The plant is dense in growth habit and yet fairly upright, attaining a height of about four feet in most soils. It is not over-thorny. Its foliage is lightish green and freely produced. I find it everywhere I travel in the world. It does not seem to mind poorer soils and, as well as being an excellent specimen shrub, it also makes a good hedging rose. I have also seen it used effectively as a wall plant, when it will attain a height of at least eight feet. I have no hesitation in recommending it for tubs.

It has to be said, too, that there could not possibly have been a better rose to bear the name of this eminent plantsman and rosarian.

Entrance to the main garden is up two steps and through a small wooden gate in a five-foot-high stone wall. On either side of the steps are mixed plantings of roses and astilbes in all shades. Two young plants of the soft pink China rose 'Climbing Cécile Brünner' are starting to make their way up over the arch which spans the gateway. Unlike the bush form of this variety, which can be very temperamental, the climbing form will grow and grow and in a very short time, I feel sure, will look superb in this position.

Inside the gate, towards the house, is a lawned area with stepping stones leading to the door of the tower, semi-enclosed because it is open to the seaward side. At the foot of the high wall facing the sea on the west side is a border of roses, including 'Constance Spry', 'Mary Rose' and 'The Countryman', all pink, and 'Windrush', a lovely soft yellow. On the wall itself, clematis and honeysuckle intertwine with climbing roses, including the lovely pink 'Dr W. Van Fleet' and a superb climber I have never come across before, 'Viking Queen', raised at the University of Minnesota in 1963 by a man named Phillips. It has heavy clusters of deep pink, fully double flowers. It is difficult to understand why such an enchanting rose is not better known; as well as being fully remontant, it also has a delicious perfume. To descend to a lower level from this part of the garden, you follow a sloping path in the lawn, brushing past flowers and shrubs cleverly planted on either side to realize another of Nancy's predilections, encouraging the relaxed intrusion of her plants: 'I like a

The myrrh-scented 'Constance Spry' is one of the most beautiful of all roses. It can be grown as a lax shrub but here at Becket's Castle it is used most effectively in its other role as a medium vigorous climber.

There is no shortage of colour in this seaside garden. Here purple campanula and white anthemis blend into the foreground of a bank of Rugosas 'Blanc Double de Coubert' and 'Belle Portugaise'. Nancy Harvey wanted these, from a distance, to look as though they had been poured from a large batter bowl; and they do.

garden to be totally overwhelming and I enjoy brushing against things,' she says. Among plants 'brushed against' here are her 'poured' Rugosas. To the south at this point a stand of youngish trees, mostly ash and oak, creates a sort of wild secret garden – a haven for birds, judging by the birdsong, with the only other noise the ever-present sound of the sea. For here every footstep is silenced by the soft, springy pine needles laid to form the path which meanders through.

The feeling of close affinity with nature that pervades this garden is further enhanced by the wilderness on the edge of the rocky cliffs, some of it introduced but mostly nature's own, and all adding a little extra protection to the garden behind. Among shrubby plants here are old lilac, abundant sumach (*Rhus typhina*) and, as always along the coast of Maine, *Rosa virginiana*. Tucked in beneath the shrubs on the leeward side are lots of wild flowers and some colourful lupins introduced by Nancy from seed brought back from England.

Running all along the front of the house on the seaward side are two three- or four-foot-high retaining walls forming two tiers of garden. Little patchworks of greenish and gingery lichens soften the appearance of these walls and of the house. As elsewhere in the garden, seats are strategically placed along the terrace to take in the views. Growing almost to the eaves of the house is a fine shrub of *Rosa glauca* (*R. rubrifolia*), its glaucous, purplish foliage and plum-coloured hips blending superbly with the stone. Likewise harmonizing with the quietude of its surroundings is the mauve-pink shrub rose 'Lavender Lassie', one of Nancy's favourites. This is planted beside the steps, and clearly enjoys growing here.

At the northern end, where the two retaining walls peter out, a lengthy bed of mixed roses extending into the lawn is crammed full – in Nancy fashion – of roses of all types, all in pastel shades. Just a few of the many pink varieties are the floriferous Hybrid Musk 'Ballerina', the two lovely Victorian Albas 'Königin von Dänemark' and 'Celestial', 'New Dawn', and an appealing single variety I had not seen or heard of before called 'Nearlywild', raised in America in 1941. I must try to get it introduced in Britain. Also strategically placed to be 'brushed past' is the apple-scented, soft orange Sweetbriar 'Lady Penzance'.

The northern end of the garden is defined by a grey-painted trellis designed by Nancy on which are growing – a little reluctantly, it must be said – young plants of the thornless pink 'Zéphirine Drouhin' and the very thorny yellow 'Maigold'. 'Sometimes roses take time to make up their minds,' said Nancy forgivingly; as if to prove there is still hope for 'Zéphirine' and 'Maigold', close by a plant of the sometimes temperamental *Rosa × harisonii* 'Harison's Yellow' is doing very well indeed. This is the original yellow rose of Texas.

Tucked in front of the thickly wooded high ground which comprises the western boundary, and forming a mound of stronger colours between the studio and the castle, is another dense clump of many assorted roses, all intertwined with each other. Among them are 'Goldbusch', a bright golden-yellow hybrid Sweetbriar from Kordes of Germany, and 'Graham Thomas', the lovely golden-yellow rose. Mixed in here and there are blueberry bushes, which seem to go very well with roses. At the back of this little hillock, beginning to climb up into the trees, is a large plant of the white scrambler 'Kiftsgate', together with the soft pink Moschata climber 'Paul's Himalayan Musk'. At the front, several plants of the procumbent 'Raubritter', a *Rosa macrantha* hybrid, are making a wonderful display of little silvery/deep-pink cupped flowers, soon to scatter petals and exhibit yet another of Nancy's gardening choices: things 'floppy and blowing in the wind'.

This unique and enthralling garden is private and open by invitation only.

THIS IS a lovely procumbent shrub. It spreads to about six feet wide before getting to look too gaunt, and reaches to about three feet tall. It was raised in Germany by Kordes in 1936 from a cross between *R. Macrantha's* 'Daisy Hill' and a rambler rose called 'Solarium'. Few, if any, roses can rival it for sheer quantity of flowers in early summer. Each flower is globular in bud and cupped when fully open. Their colour, which is unfading, is clear, deep mid-pink with a slight silvery sheen in some lights, almost iridescent. They are also highly scented.

HYBRID MACRANTHA

'RAUBRITTER'

The shoots, which are very dense, are quite thorny and the foliage greyish dark green. The only fault is a strong tendency to mildew if not regularly sprayed.

It has several uses, but is at its best covering unsightly objects close to the ground such as manhole covers, and it will make a dense mound over old tree stumps. It also cascades down low banks and falls gracefully over low retaining walls and out of planters and tubs. It always looks good combined with purple or bluish flowers, especially those with grey foliage.

LOWER BROOK HOUSE
CLEE ST MARGARET, SHROPSHIRE, ENGLAND

WORDS LIKE DISORDER AND CHAOS WERE IN MY MIND WHEN I arrived at a substantial Georgian terrace house in a close next to historic Ludlow Castle, for I knew that the 'Shropshire Lass' I had come to visit was a specialist in wild, very English gardens and, among other widely acclaimed works, had written a book on that very subject, tantalizingly called *A Gentle Plea for Chaos*. Never having met her before (nor, I confessed somewhat sheepishly later, having read any of her books) I had no idea what I would find in the garden of the house behind the solid dark blue door in front of me. It was a little to my surprise, therefore, that what I found was quite the opposite of chaos – one of the most formal and interesting little back gardens it has ever been my pleasure to see in England. It belongs to the celebrated garden writer Mirabel Osler. Mirabel moved here six years ago when she found the wild garden at Lower Brook House, which she had created with her late husband Michael, too much to cope with alone.

'When I moved here in 1990 this was quite a nice garden,' Mirabel said, tongue-in-cheek. 'I gave it a year before touching it. There was a rose here called "Cocktail" and lots of conifers.' It now reflects her gardening skills and wide-ranging tastes as well as her deep appreciation of 'things French' gained from her extensive travels researching another book, *The Secret Gardens of France*. 'It's fun to do something more orderly than a wild garden,' she added.

The plot is only seventy feet long by thirty feet wide and within it she has planted thirty-four trees, most of them for 'taming', as the French would do. There are twelve eucalyptus to keep in order, a eucryphia, *E. cordata*, a lily-of-the-valley tree (*Clethra arborea*), a pepper tree which spends its winters indoors, a pyramid Bramley Seedling apple, and even eight limes (*Tilia cordata*) to be pleached. Shrubs, both evergreen and deciduous, are numerous, especially those that take easily to pruning and shaping, such as *Ceanothus dentatus*, *Spiraea* 'Arguta', viburnums in variety and,

*P*eonies are always good companions for old roses and here they grow together with the rambler rose 'Albertine'. Damask rose 'Celsiana' and Philadelphus 'Belle Etoile' make up the rest of this scene at the garden in the Clee hills of Shropshire.

*T*he entire garden at Lower Brook House is a riot of ramblers and climbers, all allowed, within reason, to do their own thing, which is usually to scramble into trees or on to any support available to them, man-made or otherwise (facing page).

MOSS ROSE

'CHAPEAU DE NAPOLÉON'

This is a fascinating rose, quite unique in that it is the only rose with this particular moss formation on its calyx. Its correct name is *Rosa × centifolia cristata*. It is also known as 'Crested Moss', but the name 'Chapeau de Napoléon' is now far more often applied; it originates in the resemblance of the feathery moss on the buds to the shape of a cockade.

It was introduced by Vibert of France in 1826 and is said to have been a foundling discovered growing in a crevice in a wall in Switzerland. In growth, like most of the vigorous Centifolias, this rose is somewhat sprawly, with a tendency to an open habit. Its flowers, which are produced in small clusters, are very highly scented and of a rich bright pink. They are very double and quartered when fully open, hating wet weather. The foliage is dark green and crisp to touch.

It is not bothered too much by the soil in which it finds itself planted. I have seen this rose, free-standing and lax, growing to a height of five feet. It can also be used on a wall as a short-growing climber.

of course, traditional topiary such as box and bay. There is also a trellis (in a colour matching the eucalyptus) to take such plants as clematis and honeysuckle. Amid the formality, to my delight and a little to my surprise, I found that roses had not been excluded, their summer colourfulness and fragrances very much an asset, although to remain in keeping they have to be severely disciplined from time to time with secateurs. Those I noticed were pink 'Fantin-Latour', cream 'Nevada', bright red *R. moyesii* 'Geranium' and yellow 'Frühlingsgold'. Mirabel said there were thirty-one roses there somewhere, including 'Lilac Charm', a lovely little single lilac-blue Floribunda which I remember from my youth, learning my trade – and I might say to love roses – from my mentor the late Edward LeGrice of North Walsham in Norfolk.

Peering out from a window beneath a substantial Clematis montana in a eucalyptus-coloured shed door at the bottom of the garden is a wise old barn owl – a second look reveals this to be a very clever and lifelike painting. 'It is important to incorporate humour into a garden,' says Mirabel. I agree. As in all the best French gardens, there are already places to sit and relax, but a new loggia is in the course of construction to accommodate a delightful antique bench-seat from Hungary, a recent gift from her daughters.

I very much enjoyed Mirabel's formal back garden, but it had been an unexpected diversion and I could not linger for long, especially as I had really come to see the other side of this lady's gardening skills, the glorious higgledy-piggledy style she loves best, if the truth be known. So off we went up and down the Clee Hills of Shropshire to the village of Clee St Margaret, to Lower Brook House and its unrestrained rusticity.

Once a working farm, Lower Brook House lies in a valley sloping gently upwards from either side of a delightful little stony brook which runs through the middle of the garden. It is this water feature, combined with the hills all around, that gives this garden its very own albeit somewhat capricious microclimate. The core of the farmhouse or cottage, as it has now become, probably dates back to the thirteenth century. It is full of old beams and built of randomly laid rusty brownish-blue local stone. The walls of the numerous outbuildings, like those of the cottage, have become invaluable as extensions to the garden. After Mirabel moved to Ludlow the garden became rather neglected – lacking in attention might be a better expression, for neglect of a wild garden simply means that everything, the roses especially, are free to do as they wish. Some of the more sensitive areas, of course, in particular those that took years to develop, are looking a little worse for wear. No matter; I was here specifically to enjoy the roses and in the ever-changing lifespan of a garden, this period of neglect is fleeting. In any case, Mirabel's daughter Tamsin and her family have now moved in and revitalization is already well under way.

As so often, wherever I go, there to greet me as I entered the gate on the old stone walls of what was once a cowshed was 'Mme Alfred Carrière', amicably sharing its space with a huge climbing hydrangea. Just around the corner, a dense plant of 'Leverkusen' was thrusting its way out from the wall, its dark green foliage superb with its lemon-yellow flowers. 'Thrusting' is Mirabel's term. I hadn't thought of it that way, but it succinctly describes the wayward tendencies of this rose.

Around the door and windows and going up on to the roof of the south-facing cottage is a wealth of climbers – clematis, honeysuckle, wisteria, vines and roses; name it, it's there. All this overlooks the informality of a busy and colourful herba-

ceous garden and a central pond which takes up the area in front of the front door of the cottage with the old cowshed wall and other rustic stone walls separating this enclosure from the rest of the garden. Anything that enjoys getting its feet wet is in or around the pond, including little water creatures in wide variety. Heightening the activity of what presumably was once the farmyard are pots, urns and other containers all spilling over with plants, while herbs and alpines sprout from every joint in the crazy paving. Up above – by invasion, design or both – the audacious 'Kiftsgate' is almost completely covering the mossy tiles on the old cowshed roof.

To go in any direction from the pond is to take a gentle climb upwards. From here Mirabel took me alongside the brook and introduced me to one of her favourites, *Rosa sancta* (*R.* × *richardii*). All single roses are beautiful, but despite the fact that the flowering season of this one is fleeting, and its fruit insignificant, we agreed that it is perhaps the loveliest of all: it is certainly enjoying life here. At the top of the garden, the west side, the brook runs through a little rocky ravine whose banks are densely overgrown with alder trees. From here we crossed over to the other side by way of a bridge made of planks, with rustic handrails. To board the bridge we had to brush past a huge 'Paul's Himalayan Musk' and on reaching the other side found a delightful little gazebo-like shadehouse complete with seating, its roof almost covered by that most lovely of scented white ramblers, 'Seagull'. Spilling out of the alders both above and around was yet more and more of 'Paul's Himalayan Musk'.

The velvety-red Gallica 'Tuscany Superb' happily mingles with Damask 'Mme Hardy' in the wilderness in what Mirabel Osler calls her 'chaotic garden' near Ludlow, Shropshire.

Several plants of the carefree rambler 'Seagull' enjoy an uninhibited existence in Mirabel Osler's garden. It tumbles from an alder tree over a small rustic bridge spanning the brook from which Lower Brook House gets its name (overleaf).

135

SPECIES ROSE

ROSA SANCTA

ALSO KNOWN as *Rosa × richardii*, and sometimes too as the Holy Rose, this species is very ancient, with little evidence to indicate from whence it came. It is closely related to the Damasks and could well be important in the progeny of that group. The name the 'Holy Rose' comes from the fact that it is believed to have been planted in the vicinity of Christian churches in Ethiopia (Abyssinia as it was then known) as long ago as the fourth century.

As a plant it is sprawly, almost procumbent, but dense. Its flowers are soft blush-pink to white, displaying a lovely boss of golden stamens. It has a light, sweet scent. The foliage is dark green, stems wispy and thorny. I find it a little prone to mildew, but this is not too much of a problem, since the disease usually comes on well after the flowering season is over each year.

Allowed to spread, it will achieve a width of six feet and a height of four feet. It tolerates most soils without problems. This useful and very beautiful rose should be used more extensively as a ground coverer.

As I had expected, this garden is full of trees – some, like the alders, scattered by nature's whim, others by careful human thought, enhancing the garden in specific places. Among these are whitebeams, handkerchief trees and liquidambars. Quite a few of the more ordinary trees, including a few old gnarled apples, have become hosts to scrambling roses – in this country old cider-apple trees are almost an obligatory feature of any garden once a farm. 'I wanted to see the garden from a bird's-eye view,' said Mirabel as we looked up at a tree house built high up in the branches over the brook; not exactly a house but more a platform with handrails – somewhere to sit and relax. It even has a complex pulley system to bring up the bottles of wine cooling in the water of the brook below. As well as 'Rambling Rector' and 'Paul's Himalayan Musk', many other roses enjoy the hospitality of the trees in this garden; 'Seagull', 'Wedding Day' and 'Dr W. Van Fleet' are just three.

Rugosa roses including 'Sarah Van Fleet' and 'Roseraie de l'Hay' tolerate the shade of the trees alongside the brook almost as well as several varieties of Scotch roses also growing along the banks. Taller shade-tolerant shrub roses in this area include the lilacky-pink *Rosa californica plena* and the indefatigable purple-grey-foliaged *R. glauca* (*R. rubrifolia*). The brook is an absolute delight and a major feature of the garden, essential to its wild character not only as the habitat of wide and varied flora, both natural and introduced, but as the territory of many birds, including a pair of kingfishers.

All around the house carefree roses abound, without exception varieties in keeping with the informality of the place for, even when on the walls, their growth is more or less uninhibited. None is planted in a bed, and even where they are clustered together they grow out of the grass, which is effectively suppressed by placing around each rose a mulch of damp newspaper in turn covered with lawn clippings.

A group of roses, of mostly pink shades, are growing in the lawn near to a flagstone terrace on the west side of the conservatory which juts out from the south side of the house. These include that most agreeable, highly scented, rich pink Damask rose of unknown provenance, 'Belle Amour', and two other Damasks, the very ancient lovely soft pink 'Ispahan', and the pure white green-eyed 'Mme Hardy'. Providing continuity of flower are a couple of Bourbons, the lovable pink 'Louise Odier' and that old lady, the blowzy purple-pink 'Mme Isaac Pereire'.

To the north, at the back of the cottage so to speak, is another old farm building, the granary. This is almost totally hidden by the very floriferous pink and white scrambler 'Francis E. Lester'. Near by is a huge mound composed of two single roses in full embrace, the white procumbent *R. paulii* and a similar if less thorny species, *R. macrantha*. Across the lawn, towards the back door, rustic trellis supports ramblers such as the bluish-grey 'Veilchenblau' and bright pink 'François Juranville', and the north wall of the cottage gives support to both the curvaceous creamy-white climbing Hybrid Tea 'Paul's Lemon Pillar' and that early-flowering seducer, in many shades of pink, 'Mme Gregoire Staechelin'. Also near by, not minding the northerly aspect it has to put up with one little bit, is that most unusual of Moss roses, 'Chapeau de Napoléon'.

This is the sort of garden where temptation leads one on to yet another rose spilling from a different tree, or sprawling on a bank, or adorning yet another wall or trellis. It is not open to the public, but in her inimitable way Mirabel Osler tells of its transition from farmyard and paddock to an enchanting wild garden in *A Gentle Plea for Chaos*, just republished, a recommended read.

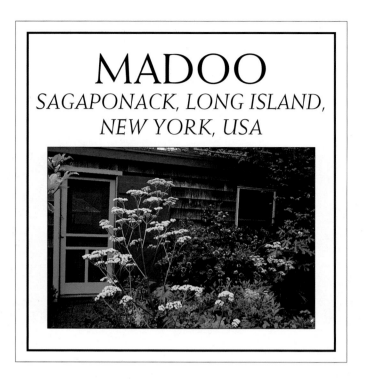

MADOO
SAGAPONACK, LONG ISLAND, NEW YORK, USA

This striking contrast of shapes and colours is one of many such 'visions' at Madoo, Bob Dash's garden on Long Island. The shrub rose on the wall is Rosa roxburghii plena.

ALL GARDENS REFLECT PERSONALITY, BUT IT IS IMPOSSIBLE TO take more than a few strides into this one without becoming aware that it is the work of a nonconformist and an artist.

I had not met Robert Dash before visiting his garden, so beyond the awareness that artists who garden are not normally inhibited by the constraints of pure plantsmanship, I had no preconceptions. Bob Dash is sceptical about the notion of artistic licence in the garden: 'I do not paint with a trowel or garden with a brush,' he says dismissively. He is obviously a knowledgeable plantsman – the garden would not work so brilliantly if he were not – but the composition of plants at Madoo and the siting of the structures that are integral to the garden relate a great deal more to artistic bent than to gardening flair.

It all started in 1967. The maturity now apparent has come about by constant subtle, and not-so-subtle, rearrangement of things since then. 'The result of an accumulation of experience,' Bob writes in his *Guide to Madoo*, 'and errors, many of them,' he adds. When he bought the site, which extends to about two acres, it had never been farmed. It was just 'turnaround' land – land where farm vehicles turned. On it stood an old 1740 barn built of shipwreck timbers, which became the core of the present substantial summer dwelling. A second timber house was built for winter use. Bob chose the site because 'The light is like Venice or Holland, and the old barn winked at me.' It was also because he could then buy land cheaply. Today this area – first settled by English people from Maidstone, Kent, in 1656 – is one of the more exclusive parts of America. The name 'Madoo' comes from old Scots and means 'my dove'.

The garden gradually evolved around the house, with no expectation in the early years of ever being grand. At first Bob used to borrow a neighbour's tractor and make patterns in the tall grass with a mower. Initially it was modelled on English lines; indeed, for a long time Bob thought of it as American flesh with English bones.

A strategically placed rose such as this 'Dortmund' adds red to one of Bob Dash's studies in yellow and green. The colour of the paintwork in the garden is often changed to suit the seasons and their flora (facing page).

138

HYBRID RUGOSA

'FRU DAGMAR HASTRUP'

THIS ROSE was raised in Denmark in 1914 and ever since has been one of the most popular varieties of the Rugosa family. In recent times its spreading nature has been especially appreciated for ground-covering purposes.

Its flowers are large, single and silvery-pink, with a large boss of creamy-yellow stamens in the centre of each. They are produced continuously throughout the summer and, as autumn comes, they share the plant with large, almost tomato-sized, crimson hips. They are delicately perfumed.

Left on its own to develop, the plant will attain a maximum height of five feet; in reaching this size it may well also spread to six feet wide. I find it best to prune it moderately to keep it to about three feet tall and wide so that it remains quite dense. Its foliage is crisply rugose, darkish green in colour, changing to bright yellow in autumn.

Besides its landscaping potential, gardeners such as myself who love single flowers will enjoy growing this rose for its own sake. Unlike some other Rugosas, it will not outgrow its welcome in smaller gardens. It is occasionally listed under the name of 'Frau Dagmar Hartopp'.

This is no longer the case. To me it is as unique as Bob Dash, with nothing else like it anywhere in the world.

Bob works as much as he can in the garden, enjoying the 'hands-on' aspects and the re-arrangement of things. Structures are often re-painted to complement or contrast with nature's changes at different times of the year. A part-time gardener helps three days a week. Bob never sprays chemicals on anything, and uses only natural fertilizer to feed his plants. I saw no pests or diseases and everything looked well nourished.

Bob's first memory of gardening goes back to childhood with visions of his mother, dressed in white and wearing white gloves, tending irises. Now ninety-five years old, she denies this.

Entry to the garden is through a wide gateway painted yellow and blue on to a gravelled reception area with a 'Dash-designed' rolling seat that looks like a wheelbarrow – but only for sitting on – in lilac and yellow; just one example of the numerous brightly coloured artefacts standing around. To walk through this garden is like walking through a large open-air gallery with lots of different rooms or spaces, each full of different shapes and forms, real or abstract, and perceived according to the depth of the visitor's comprehension or imagination, or both. This is by no means to say that this garden is lacking in botanical or horticultural interest. Quite the contrary. It has a full collection of plants, including many that are unusual. However, it is not the purpose of this book to become too engrossed in genera other than roses, tempting though it is. Bob openly admits that he prefers lilies, daisies and violets. 'Roses are too demanding,' he says, yet he cannot imagine this or any other garden without them.

The area next to the summer residence is the most densely packed with plants and, by and large, the 'rooms' here are more numerous and smaller than elsewhere, although Bob points out that some of the boundaries are more suggested than real. My most abiding memory is of the trunks – yes, trunks – of dozens of common privet (*Ligustrum ovalifolium*), which have been induced by side-shoot pruning and forced up by the shade of other trees to grow very tall, twenty feet or more, turning into ranks of lanky, smooth, greyish-white stems each about three or four inches thick. Other species of trees and shrubs not normally renowned for the ornamental value of their stems are also used to similar effect throughout the garden. In addition, as one would expect, there is no shortage of trees with natural ornamental bark of their own, such as birches, acers and planes, and also, as Bob puts it, 'the unjustly neglected *Prunus maackii*'.

Another feature fast in my memory is a group of seven or eight slender ginkgos (*Ginkgo biloba* 'Fastigiata'), standing erect above small compact globes of clipped boxwood in the grass, representing sheep grazing. Behind this scene stands an elaborate Dash-designed gazebo painted luminous mauve-magenta and encircled by eight tall slim *Juniper hibernica*. Nearer to the house is another modernistic feature, a path curving through two clipped box hedges and a frieze of busy Lizzies, the path made of perfectly round wooden discs sawn from telegraph poles and laid in white pebbles gleaned from a local beach.

Except to the west, which is fairly open, the whole garden is well enclosed with trees and hedges. It harbours within it several distinct microclimates permitting plants to thrive which one would not normally expect to find here. One such microclimate has the roses *Rosa filipes* 'Kiftsgate' and *Rosa banksiae lutea* growing in

it, both roses – especially the latter – that would not normally enjoy the climate here in winter. In another warm spot the Noisette 'Mme Alfred Carrière' thrives alongside the tender *Jasminum nudiflorum*.

One of the first roses I came upon at the start of my tour is called 'Louis Philippe' after a French barque bound for Virginia which ran aground on nearby Sagg beach in 1840. It was carrying a cargo of silk, champagne and plants, this rose among them. It is probably an old Multiflora seedling and it should remain here, for were it to go forth and multiply, so to speak, its provenance would somehow become considerably devalued.

Rugosa roses are to be found here and there in among other shrubs in this garden, but one border is devoted almost entirely to about a dozen different varieties. Most of the better-known sorts are among them, of course, but it was a great pleasure to find a plant of 'Parfum de l'Hay' doing so well. This rose can be quite difficult to grow, but at its best is one of the loveliest of its kind – fully double, deep purplish-red and highly scented. Also in this border is a fine example of the little-known pinkish-red hybrid Sweetbriar 'Magnifica', a rose worth its place in any company, but here cohabiting particularly well with the Rugosas.

There are two separate territories in this garden devoted entirely to roses. The larger is close by the Rugosa border and here a fascinating optical illusion has been employed to make it look longer than it actually is. A gradual narrowing of the centre

No chemicals or artificial fertilizers are ever used in the two acres or so that are Madoo, and in this superb study 'New Dawn' is clearly in the best of health.

*M*odern rose 'Dortmund' provides a bright splash *of colour to the greenery around the house at Madoo. Bob Dash likes lots of green shapes without too much bedeckment. 'A good garden is ruled by good geometry,' he says.*

*A*lthough Bob Dash is sceptical about the notion of *artistic licence in his garden, one does not have to be too perceptive to realize that the gardener at Madoo is an artist. The rose in the foreground here is 'Seafoam' (facing page).*

path by two feet has been effected over its length of one hundred and twenty feet. Similar gradual reductions have been made to the archways which span the path. These archways are adorned by a wide variety of ramblers such as the glossy-foliaged white 'Albéric Barbier', the deep pink single 'American Pillar' and several of the common Sweetbriar (*Rosa rubiginosa* or *R. eglanteria*).

The narrow borders that run alongside this path are planted with a mixture of shrub roses, each variety in groups. Predominant among them is 'Fru Dagmar Hastrup', the semi-procumbent, silvery-pink, hip-bearing Rugosa; these go particularly well with the reddish colouring of the bricks which make up the path and which are laid in linear fashion to add to the illusion of extra length. At the far end of the rose walk a medieval-style sod seat sits unobtrusively in the centre of a small lawn enclosed by blueberry bushes. Here I was buzzed by a mockingbird objecting noisily to my stealing its fruit.

The illusion of creating extra length by reducing the width of paths is a trick which dates back to the fifteenth century. Re-creating an even older effect (described by Xenophon from the Greece of about the fifth century BC) are four quincunx beds which occupy the open space near the rose walk. The formation of five objects, one on each corner and one in the centre, that makes up a quincunx creates a complex pattern of shadows and light; here the verticals are fastigiate yews punctuating square beds with foliage plants in an assortment of shades and shapes as ground cover.

SPECIES ROSA

BANKSIAE LUTEA

Aʟʟ ᴛʜᴇ Banksian roses will grow in the British climate but they need to be stationed in warm, sheltered positions to succeed at their best. There are four: a pair of whites, the single *Rosa banksiae* normalis and the double *R.b. alba plena*; and a pair of yellows, the single *R.b. lutescens* and the double *R.b. lutea* – this last by far and away the most popular. It first came to Europe in 1824. The little, fully double, soft lemony-yellow flowers are slightly scented and borne in large cascading clusters. They appear in colder positions in early June, but open by mid-May in warmer spots.

To all intents and purposes thornless, this rose has lovely light green foliage and its growth habit is dense. To get the best from it, prune it only sparingly by the removal of old wood – but not every year, otherwise it will never flower. The more space on a wall you can give it the better, for it will grow to twenty feet or more in most situations. It is best propagated by cuttings.

Nowhere in Britain will this rose ever reach the proportions it achieves in parts of the world with milder winters. Sometimes, too, in colder climates, it is also a little reluctant to flower as freely as it will, for example, in the Mediterranean and the southern United States.

The other rose area is in the south-eastern corner of the garden and is entirely composed of ramblers and climbers on posts and swags. The 'swags' are chains and the 'posts' rounded timber about eight feet high. It was planted up about three years ago. Among the roses adorning these structures are coppery-pinky 'Albertine', 'Sanders' White', probably the best of the white ramblers, and that most blue of all the 'blue' roses, 'Veilchenblau'. Also here is the lovely single pink native American species *Rosa setigera*, its large plentiful foliage making a most useful contribution to the site when it colours up in the autumn. Several plants of the bright red modern climber 'Cadenza' provide that important little bit of extra colour in August when the ramblers are over and done with, and most of the other climbers are taking a rest. 'Like a chocolate after a good dinner,' says the enigmatic Bob Dash. He goes on: 'The roses in this garden are an act of ingratiation to other people. Daisies are my favourite flower. I prefer green shapes without too much bedeckment. A good garden is ruled by good geometry.'

This is a most fascinating and intriguing garden. I am the richer for having seen it. It is open on Wednesday afternoons from the beginning of May until the end of September.

The Madoo Conservatory, 618 Sagg Main Street, Sagaponack NY 11962 (516 537 0802).

THE CULPEPER GARDEN
LEEDS CASTLE, NEAR MAIDSTONE, KENT, ENGLAND

Anyone wishing to learn about plant associations should study those at the Culpeper Garden here at Leeds Castle in Kent. The rose in the foreground is 'Macrantha Raubritter' and that behind the box hedge 'Alba Semi-plena'.

EEDS CASTLE IS ONE OF ENGLAND'S OLDEST, DATING FROM the reign of Henry I, son of William the Conqueror, in the early twelfth century. It is also, without any doubt, one of England's most beautiful – and romantic – buildings. Built of Kentish ragstone, which is soft orange-yellow overlaid bluish-grey, it stands on an island formed by the diverted flow of the river Len into a wide moat, the north side of which is almost a lake. In turn this is all surrounded by a large expanse of landscaped parkland.

Leeds Castle had fallen into disrepair when the last private owner, The Hon. Lady Baillie, took it over in the late 1920s, but she devoted her life to its restoration. After her death in 1974 the Leeds Castle Foundation undertook to ensure its long-term well-being, and in 1980 commissioned Russell Page to design the Culpeper Garden. This occupies a mere half-acre in the vast complex of Leeds Castle, and on the way to it you encounter a number of roses.

What few plants are growing on the island, in the grounds of the castle itself, are mostly roses. For example, a superb plant of 'Mme Caroline Testout' can be seen on the wall as you look north across the moat to the castle from the roadway between the Estate Office and the Gate Tower. Also on that warm south-facing wall, among *Magnolia grandiflora*, *M. soulangeana* and grape vines, you find a sizeable plant of the lovely white rambler 'Félicité Perpétue' and two yellows, the single-flowered climber 'Mermaid' and the early-flowering vigorous scrambling *Rosa banksiae* lutea.

To the north of the castle, overlooking the lake from the grounds, the top four feet of the retaining stone wall which rises from the moat shelter a narrow border on its south side. About fifty roses, mostly climbers and ramblers in about a dozen varieties, have obviously been growing in this bed for several years. A few are not doing as well as the others, but they still serve their purpose by providing colour in an otherwise long expanse of drab wall. The best include the vigorous yellow

climber-cum-rambler 'Easlea's Golden Rambler', the pink climber 'Cécile Brünner', the yellow rambler 'Emily Gray', the pink rambler 'Chaplin's Pink' and inevitably, I suppose, stalwarts 'Rambling Rector' and 'Mme Alfred Carrière'.

The Culpeper Garden was formerly the castle's kitchen garden and is situated on a roughly triangular piece of land which slopes to the south-west between high red-brick walls, once workers' cottages and the site of a pre-1926 lean-to greenhouse. The whole is open to the south over superb views of meadowland and a small lake known as Great Water to distant woodland.

The grounds and gardens are administered by Estate Manager and Head Gardener Maurice Bristow. The gardener in charge of the Culpeper Garden since 1987 is Chris Skinner, clearly a fine plantsman who enjoys his job. At the entrance to the garden, beneath a splendid standard variegated holly, a signboard explains that the garden is named after the Culpeper family who owned the Castle in the seventeenth century and to whom Nicholas Culpeper, the celebrated herbalist of that time, was related. Many ancient herbs are incorporated into the garden, and everything is clearly labelled, an important feature in a garden such as this.

Given half an acre of open space to work with in a setting such as this, Russell Page had wide and varied design options; he chose a cottagey style, simple in layout but complex in composition. The leaflet he wrote about the garden when he designed it in 1980 describes its transformation from a vegetable garden to 'the kind

The soft pink, sweetly scented Alba rose 'Celestial' combines with almost any non-garish colour. It also cohabits well with grey-foliaged plants.

The Culpeper Garden was designed by Russell Page in 1980. His vision was 'to enable you to walk this way and that through fields of flowers'. The rose in the background of this field of flowers is Alba 'Celestial'.

of flower garden at which the English excel. A new recruit, unpretentious to suit its modest framework, to the gardens of Kent.'

The layout is based on one main brick path across the middle of the garden running from south-east to north-west with a diamond-shaped paved centrepiece on which are placed large terracotta pots full of colourful plants. At the north-west entrance to this path is a small, brick-paved area with seats. Another central brick path makes a cross-axis to complete the cruciform. Other paths, some of them grass, dissect this at right angles and these bend and curve from all directions to connect up to the perimeter path. The result is that no two of the sixteen beds or borders are the same shape or size. Every bed is edged with carefully trimmed dwarf box, and here and there are specimens of common box expertly clipped into sizeable domes. As well as no two beds being uniform, none are in any way similar in composition; in fact, it is apparent that considerable efforts have been made to ensure as wide a variation as possible.

Russell Page went on to describe the vision of his creation: 'A simple pattern of paths has been established to enable you to walk this way and that through fields of flowers. The garden will be filled with Lilacs and Syringa and Old Fashioned roses, with Irises and Cottage Pinks, Poppies and Lupins, Lad's Love and Lavender and many other favourites old and new.' Exactly right; this is what we find, fifteen years on.

Although roses play a major part, especially during June and July, it is only their stature and shrubby nature which give them a dominant role. Except for a discreet rustic support here and there to tame an awkward variety, no structures are to be seen and the only climbers and ramblers in evidence are on the walls; one, west-facing, supports climbing 'Iceberg' intermingled with trained 'Conference' and 'Doyenné du Comice' pears; the other, south-facing, is adorned with the ever-delightful 'Mme Grégoire Staechelin', a huge plant of the climbing form of 'Cécile Brünner' and the late-flowering 'Aimée Vibert' intertwined with a splendid example of the pineapple plant, *Cytisus battandieri*.

Unlike many modern roses, old roses as landscape plants blend in well with one another, but 'a good eye' is still needed to avoid clashes when marrying them with other plants. Anyone interested in plant associations should visit this garden, for there are many examples of superb mixing and matching of colours, shapes and heights. One such combination is *Rosa glauca* (*R. rubrifolia*), 'Reine des Violettes', *Buddleja alternifolia*, *Penstemon* 'Garnet', *Berberis thunbergii* 'Atropurpurea' and *Dicentra spectabilis*. Another is 'Mme Hardy' and 'Blanc Double de Coubert' with *Pyrus salicifolia pendula*, *Lavandula* 'Munstead' and *Dicentra spectabilis alba*. If my knowledge of plants other than roses was better I could go on listing some other superb combinations – yellow-variegated plants with yellow-flowered *R. pimpinellifolia* and 'Frühlingsgold', for example, and by way of a contrast the purple Moss rose 'William Lobb' looking superb with golden elder (*Sambucus nigra* 'Aurea') and varieties of *Potentilla fruticosa*.

The roses here obviously receive a lot of loving care and they enjoy the rich deep soil so much that even the more compact growers have to be pruned fairly hard each spring. Chris Skinner explained that the Hybrid Perpetuals such as 'Reine des Violettes' and the Bourbons 'Reine Victoria' and 'Louise Odier' are pruned annually as if they were Floribundas; the once-flowering types such as the Damask 'Mme Hardy' and the Alba 'Celestial' are severely dead-headed after flowering each summer, and pruned again in February/March to keep them within bounds. Dead-heading is, of course, good rose husbandry, encouraging the once-flowering varieties to produce new growth to support next year's flowers and the remontants to make new growth for their autumn flush. Only the fruit-bearers should not be dead-headed so that they retain their autumn display – the waxy-looking mahogany-coloured hips of the already-mentioned *R. pimpinellifolia*, and the whiskery bright red flagon-shaped hips of a fine specimen of *R. moyesii* 'Geranium' that follow bright scarlet single flowers in June. Rugosas, too, are well used here; the single forms, especially, flower all summer through and bear long-lasting tomato-shaped fruit, the whole plant looking quite flamboyant in autumn and early winter with a short burst of colour before the leaves fall. One of the best is the semi-procumbent, bushy, silvery-pink 'Fru Dagmar Hastrup'.

The only modern rose I saw in this garden was the occasional 'Iceberg'. The remainder, apart from the Rugosas, are old-fashioned, divided about equally between summer-flowerers and repeaters. Were I to select just two as outstanding at the time of my visit, I would choose *R. californica plena*, eight or nine feet tall with masses of delicate, lilac-pink, semi-double flowers amid copious grey-green foliage, and a splendid, wide, bushy shrub of 'Tuscany Superb', sporting hundreds of its sumptuous red semi-double flowers with golden stamens. Who could be so greedy as to expect such a rose to flower all summer and to reject it because it does not?

SPECIES ROSE

ROSA GLAUCA

THERE ARE other roses with undistinguished flowers, but none is quite so popular as this one. This is a landscaper's rose. Used extensively as a flowering shrub, it mixes well with most other species. You can grow it as a specimen shrub, as a wall plant or to form a hedge. It is also well loved by flower arrangers.

Left to its own devices, the growth habit of *Rosa glauca*, also known as *R. rubrifolia*, is open; however, with regular pruning, it will make quite a dense shrub to about six to eight feet. The stems are plum-coloured and the foliage a glaucous grey-green. The young wood is almost, but not quite, thornless; older wood seems to develop more thorns, especially at the base.

On close inspection the small, insignificant flowers are really quite beautiful, the widely spread petals giving each one an almost star-like appearance. They are produced in clusters and have little or no scent, ending up later in the summer as drooping bunches of brownish-maroon hips.

The natural home of this species is central and south-eastern Europe. It has been a garden plant since 1830. It reproduces readily from seed and seedlings can often be found miles away, scattered by the birds.

With the possible exception of the Rugosas, of all the shrub roses Rosa glauca (R. rubrifolia) *is probably the most widely used for landscape purposes. Here at Culpeper both its flowers and foliage associate superbly with* Geranium psilostemon.

Leeds Castle is open every day of the year. The Culpeper Garden is well worth seeing at any time in spring, summer and autumn, although the roses are at their best from mid-June to mid-July. Spring is an especially good time to see the Wood Garden, when the anemones and bulbs are at their glorious best.

GALLICA ROSE

'TUSCANY SUPERB'

THE ORIGIN of this rose is not known but it was first recorded by William Paul in 1848. It is almost certainly a more refined form of 'Tuscany' itself, a very good and beautiful variety. Both are good doers in almost any type of soil but 'Superb' has more petals and is a larger flower. A special feature of both of these Gallicas is the coronet of golden stamens in the centre of the flower. Both are scented but, to me, 'Superb' slightly more so.

Gallicas generally are extremely easy going and very floriferous during their season, from late June to about mid-July in most summers. They are also tidy and reasonably compact in habit. Their foliage is dark green and plentiful; in the case of 'Tuscany', large and crinkled-looking. The stems are relatively free of thorns.

'Tuscany Superb' can be grown as an informal hedge, as a shrub, especially in groups in shrubberies, in mixed borders, as at Culpeper, or even as a pot plant in a large container. A well-grown plant of this variety in full flush is one of the pleasures of summer for me.

GIARDINO NINFA
DOGANELLA DI NINFA, LATINA, ITALY

THE GARDEN AT NINFA AS IT IS NOW HAS BEEN CREATED OVER a period of seventy-five years, but its story goes back a thousand years to when the eight-and-a-half-hectare site was a thriving little town, tiny but very wealthy. It was first settled in the eighth century, taking its name from the Roman Temple of the Nymph which once stood here but has long since gone. Ninfa quickly became strategically significant in a low-lying, swampy area, flourishing from the tolls it was able to charge travellers making their way south from Rome. These were troubled times in Europe and such was Ninfa's importance and so secure was its double row of fortified walls that in 1159 Rolando Bandinelli, newly elected pope, took refuge here from his enemies and was crowned Pope Alexander III in one of its churches.

At the peak of its affluence, this little medieval town had 160 houses, no less than seven churches and a grand town hall. Ruins of the churches still exist and the old town hall has been restored and is now a private residence. Along with parts of the old perimeter wall, the castle tower has also been faithfully rebuilt. It is this tower, from across the lake, that one first sees on approaching Ninfa from the south – a view unchanged for seven hundred years, for the tower was built in the early fourteenth century by Pietro Caetani, who started a family association with Ninfa that lasted until the line expired with the death of Lelia Caetani in 1977. The name lives on in the Roffredo Caetani Foundation now set up to adminster Ninfa and its garden.

It was late in the fourteenth century that things started to go wrong. The town became embroiled in a religious civil war and was almost destroyed. The plague followed, leaving the place totally deserted – as, incredibly, it remained until 1921, when Gelasio Caetani, a descendant of Pietro's, started a period of reclamation and restoration. After Gelasio's demise his work was continued by his successors, and so today's beautiful gardens of Ninfa have evolved. From the mid-1950s to the mid-'70s, Lelia Caetani and her English husband Hubert Howard lived here. They were

*T*he white flowers of Rosa filipes 'Kiftsgate' cascade from the top of one of the ancient walls at Ninfa, while close by is the relaxed form of rambler 'American Pillar'. The castle tower has been a landmark in this area of Latina since the fourteenth century.

*T*here is a hedge of one hundred plants of this rose Rosa roxburghii plena *at the entrance to the gardens of Ninfa.*

HYBRID MUSK ROSE

'VANITY'

THIS HYBRID MUSK is a little different from the other Pemberton Musks. It is larger in stature and much more angular in habit, making it awkward to place. It no doubt inherits this trait from its parent, 'Château de Clos-Vougeot', which also grows in an ungainly fashion.

Apart from this, 'Vanity' is still a lovely rose. Its flowers are quite large, up to three inches across, almost single in form and vibrant pink with yellow stamens – a little bright for some tastes, perhaps, when they first open up, but they quieten down to a slightly deeper shade as they age. Graham Thomas calls the fragrance sweet-pea-like.

The stems are smooth greyish-green and almost thornless. The foliage is of a similar colour but rather sparse on the plant, making it best placed as a shrub at the back of a border or on a wall, when it could well grow to a height of ten or twelve feet. Its growth habit is too ungainly for it to make an effective specimen shrub. It is, however, easy to grow and will tolerate most types of soil and, if need be, some shade.

great plant lovers and planted a wide and varied range of trees, shrubs and roses. It is largely through their influence that the gardens have become as important as they are today.

Everyone who sees the castle tower of Ninfa from across the lake on the way in and spends time exploring the ruins of the old town in its twentieth-century role as a garden cannot help but fall in love with the place. My pleasure was heightened by being shown around by Lauro Marchetti, its curator, who spent most of his childhood here and knows it intimately.

My visit got off to a good start: just inside the entrance I found a hedge of at least a hundred plants of *Rosa roxburghii* 'Plena'. This is the only hedge of this species I have ever seen, although there are doubtless others in the world, for it is so good for the purpose. From here the wall running alongside the main drive which leads down towards the castle and the old town hall is generously adorned with roses, most of them massive, having the freedom to expand at will. Some are in fact cascading down from plants growing on the other side of the wall. I recognized 'The Garland', blush-white, and 'Seagull', white; there are lots of this variety at Ninfa, as there are of the soft pink 'Dr W. Van Fleet'.

About halfway along the drive is a delightful little water feature, obviously ancient. Sparkling water emerges from a little outlet under the wall and pours down on to a rock to make a miniature waterfall which then tumbles its way into a riverlet. This babbles on beneath the road, on its way to join up with the river Ninfa, a brook which meanders its way from the lake through the garden and out across the Pontine plains to the sea. On the wall overhanging this little waterfall is an enormous plant of the lovely orange-yellow Noisette 'Desprez à Fleurs Jaunes' and, next to this beside the orangey-brown trunk of a tall stone pine (*Pinus pinea*) was the first of many huge bushes of the coppery-orange Tea rose 'Général Schablikine' that are to be found in this garden.

Water, of course, is a welcome feature in any garden and here its role has changed from a medieval necessity to an ornamental facet of the landscape. From a little pool among bamboos, in a little wooden chalice secreted near by for the purpose, Lauro gave me some Ninfa water to drink. Cool, pure and palatable it was, too. The water springs from the rocks of the escarpment to the north, on the top of which is the old Roman city of Norma. This high ground protects Ninfa from inclement weather and is the main reason for its congenial microclimate, in which almost anything flourishes in all seasons.

The restoration of the old municipal buildings, overlooked as they are by the castle tower, is an effective re-creation of part of the old medieval town. Likewise the interior of the residence I visited, the old town hall, evokes feelings of the past both in the structure of the rooms and their furnishings. Not medieval of course, but of considerable significance, is a grand piano which once belonged to the great composer Franz Liszt, godfather to the last Duke of Ninfa, Roffredo Caetani.

All around the buildings in the area of the town hall are numerous roses. Sprouting from beside one of the several buttresses on the old city wall, and scrambling ten metres up it, is an old plant of 'Seagull'. On one of the other walls are fine examples of the ever-flowering climbing form of 'Cramoisi Supérieur', a lovely blood-red China which so enjoys the more temperate climates of the world such as here, but is also tolerant of colder places like the British Isles. What is good about this particular variety is the way it seems to blend into its surroundings. Reds are not

always easy to fit into any landscape, but I have never found a discordant 'Cramoisi Supérieur' anywhere on my travels. Here at Ninfa it combines perfectly with the rusty, fawny brown stone of the old walls.

There is a particularly fine collection of trees at Ninfa, from species that you would expect to find in Italy such as the fastigiate cypress (*Chamaecyparis sempervirens*) and holm oak (*Quercus ilex*) to those that, although natural in a collection, still come as a surprise, such as *Acer griseum, Albizia julibrissin* and *Liriodendron tulipifera*. Many of the more common trees also have roses such as 'Rambling Rector', 'Paul's Himalayan Musk' and 'Kiftsgate' bustling out of their branches. The collection of flowering and ornamental shrubs is also extensive.

Botanical interest is maintained by using the whole garden in a way which makes it impossible to anticipate what is round the next corner. Sometimes what you find is the ruins of one of the old churches which, where feasible, have been put to good use supporting climbing and rambling roses. On one old wall I found at least two good plants of 'Gloire de Dijon' growing quite happily, although doing even better on a wall near by were a couple of the similarly coloured yellow Noisette 'Rêve d'Or'. On part of the ruins of what I believe is the church of St Maria Maggiore, where Pope Alexander III was crowned all those years ago, is a sizeable bush of the late-flowering *Rosa moschata*, itself very ancient, its grey foliage harmonizing perfectly with the bluish medieval stone. On the subject of grey foliage, I also found in another

Massive cascading ramblers, such as this multiflora seedling which is unique to Ninfa, are a particular feature of this garden – where ample space gives vigorous plants the freedom to expand at will.

The Ponte di Legno has been repaired only twice since it was erected across the river Ninfa in medieval times. The garden's Roman bridge, Ponte Romano, was built in the second century BC and is as sound now as it was then. The expansive rose here is 'American Pillar'.

Many vigorous rambling roses scramble among the trees and on the ruins at Ninfa; some of them, I suspect, self-sown seedlings unique to this wonderful place. I certainly couldn't name them all, this one included (facing page).

part of the garden a fine example of the highly fragrant, very vigorous *R. brunonii* 'La Mortola', which started life in the famous garden of that name on the French Riviera. Hybrid Musks, of course, are found everywhere and Ninfa is no exception. Among these are the blush-white 'Penelope' and some particularly fine bushes of the bright pink single 'Vanity'.

At intervals along its length little footbridges span the river Ninfa. Ponte Romano, a small stone humpback second-century bridge, is as sound as the day it was built; Ponte di Legno, a medieval bridge, has twice been repaired, and the relatively modern Ponte Del Macello so far has had to be renovated three times.

Of all the roses scattered throughout the gardens of Ninfa, the Chinas and Teas enjoy these idyllic conditions best of all. Already mentioned are 'Cramoisi Supérieur' and 'Général Schablikine', but there were others I recognized, some I did not and quite a few I had to look at several times before full recognition came. One such was a large bush of the China rose 'Comtesse du Cayla', a semi-double, scented, orangey-yellow growing happily by the Ponte di Legno.

Close by the gently flowing stream is a little stone temple, still as it was in medieval times. Inside are stone seats and 'The Spirit of Ninfa'. 'This is the place to come for tranquillity, to relieve stress,' said Lauro. 'If you sit in here for a while you become reinvigorated.' I am sure this is true, for the temperature was cooler, the air still and the light relaxing. However, I felt reinvigorated from the whole experience of Ninfa.

*A*rum lilies and the China rose 'Cramoisi
Supérieur' grow side by side in the ruins of one of
Ninfa's seven churches.

Ninfa is open on the first weekend of every month from April to September. I
have been able only to touch on some of its many facets. You must visit it yourself to
find out more.

CLIMBING ROSE

'CRAMOISI SUPÉRIEUR'

ALL THE good attributes of the
bush form of 'Cramoisi Supérieur'
(1835) are inherent in this rose, plus the
ability to perform considerable climbing
feats in almost any situation. It has been
around since 1885, and it surprises me
how seldom it is seen for, when found, it
is always doing an admirable job. Like
all Chinas, it prefers sunshine, so it does
better in more temperate climates. In
England it appears to be quite hardy,
but is definitely more satisfactory in
warm, sheltered positions.

Its growth habit is fairly dense, but
each shoot is thin and pliable. It has few
thorns of consequence and its leaves are
dark green and numerous. The flowers,
which are produced very freely for most
of the summer, are globular at first,
opening loosely double; they are not
large and are produced in small clusters.
Their colour is rich crimson with an
occasional white fleck in the centre
petals. They do not have much scent.

Good red climbing roses are few and
far between. If you have the right
position, this one is well worth
consideration. The bush form, too
(sometimes known as 'Agrippina'), is
most rewarding, especially in pots either
outside or under glass. It is best in good
soils.

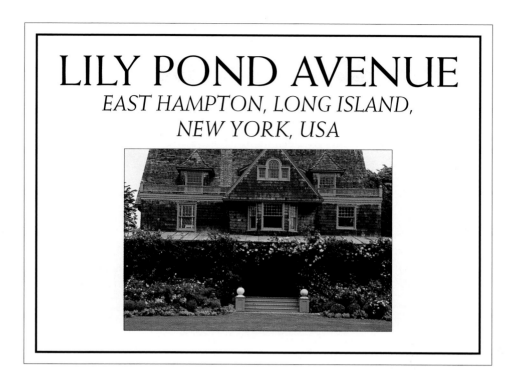

LILY POND AVENUE
EAST HAMPTON, LONG ISLAND, NEW YORK, USA

ALTHOUGH THERE ARE PARTS OF THIS GARDEN WITHOUT A rose bush, it is still difficult to walk through it in any direction without coming upon a great many of them – so many, in fact, that it soon becomes very clear that the owner, Martha Stewart, is very much a rose lover. This fact is well known in America from her writings in her books on gardening and their frequent mention in her popular monthly lifestyle magazine.

Her house is set fairly well back on the north side of exclusive Lily Pond Avenue, the 'avenue' in this case hefty plane trees (*Platanus* × *hispanica*). Most of the garden, roughly half an acre in size, is at the front of the house. It faces south and is planted up with roses which are now about six years old, in their prime and flourishing.

Entry is via a wide, biscuity-coloured gravel drive flanked on either side by narrow, well-manicured verges of lawn. This drive sweeps up towards the house around a wide roundabout full to its limit with several different kinds of ivy, effectively labour-saving but nevertheless attractively ornamental. A goodly sized *Magnolia souleangeana* stands just off-centre, adding height and structure to this area as well as colour in the spring.

About halfway along each side of the drive wrought-iron archways festooned with *Wisteria sinensis* temptingly lead through to the two separate parts of this garden. To the west is a complete rose garden and to the east a sizeable lawn encircled by rose borders. Between the verge and the rose borders a line of box clipped into small globes and underplanted with a narrow border of perennials merges into the rose beds, thus concealing the lower branches of the roses from view. Roses visible from along the sides of the drive are a mixture of old and new. Outstanding among the old are the lovely wine-coloured 'Rose de Rescht', a Portland, and the even deeper purplish-red 'Gipsy Boy', a Bourbon; among the new are the lovely soft pink 'Heritage' and the deeper pink 'Mary Rose'. Another variety looking superb in

There are a great many roses in this most attractive garden in East Hampton: several hundred in fact, in less than half an acre.

Rugosa 'Roseraie de l'Hay' enjoys the competition in the wide, mixed shrub rose border planted by Martha Stewart in the front garden of her house on Long Island. In the foreground is a lone cluster of the Floribunda rose 'Iceberg'.

Seen here through the branches of a gingko tree, 'New Dawn' performs one of the most effective of its many roles, that of covering an arch. In the background is 'Rambling Rector' (facing page).

this part of the garden is the silvery-pink Alba 'Celestial' which dates back at least to the eighteenth century. This rose, like all those in the Alba family, has lovely leaden-grey foliage.

Entering the rose garden through the left-hand archway, one is immediately taken into a rose-festooned pergola which leads through to an attractive Victorian-style wrought-iron seat at the far end. Ramblers and climbers adorning the six or so arches which form the pergola are 'New Dawn', 'Dorothy Perkins', 'Albertine', 'Rambling Rector', 'Mme Alfred Carrière' and the Moss rose 'William Lobb', not normally a climber but doing stalwart service in this role nevertheless. This area is further divided up by a pathway running north to south across the line of the pergola to form four roughly equal-sized beds of shrub roses, at least twenty-five or thirty in each. In mixing the roses no consideration is given to type or family, only to height and colour compatibility – a policy I applaud in a garden such as this, where visual effect is more important than academic considerations. As a result Hybrid Musks such as the lovely bright reddish-pink 'Belinda' and the apricot-yellow 'Buff Beauty' are merged delightfully with the old bright pink Bourbon 'Louise Odier' and the purple-red of the clove-scented Rugosa 'Roseraie de l'Hay'.

Once upon a time, before becoming a rose garden, this north-westerly corner was, no doubt, an orchard. Ancient pear trees and apple trees are scattered here and there, adding both lofty informality and a sense of maturity to the scene. Growing healthily

HYBRID PERPETUAL

'FERDINAND PICHARD'

THROUGHOUT THE history of the rose, striped varieties have always been much celebrated. The *Rosa gallica officinalis* sport 'Rosa Mundi', which dates back at least to medieval times, is perhaps the most famous and best loved. The majority of striped roses came about as sports; 'Ferdinand Pichard' has so overshadowed its parent that no one remembers what it was. It was introduced in 1921 and is the youngest of the remontant bicoloured roses.

The colour of the flowers is variable, from quiet pink heavily striped and spotted with bright crimson to deeper pink splashed magenta-purple. It is sweetly scented. The foliage is dark green and perhaps a little coarse; the plant is bushy and will grow to about four feet. In good soil it always has a tremendous first flush and then is seldom without flowers until the autumn when, again, in good seasons it has another burst of blooms – these late ones much deeper in colour. I have seen it used quite successfully as a hedge. Like all Hybrid Perpetuals, it responds well to hard pruning.

beneath one of the pear trees is what is clearly one of Martha's favourite roses, judging by its frequent appearances here – 'Sally Holmes', that most congenial of modern shrubs, with large, ever-present trusses of soft blush-white flowers.

When you cross over to the other side of the garden by way of the other wisteria-embellished archway, the lawn's spaciousness is striking after the 'busyness' of the rose garden. It is not that roses themselves are scarce; quite the contrary, for the entire circumference of the beautifully tended lawn is even more closely packed with them, in some places as many as five or six deep. Again modern shrubs are mixed in with genuine heritage varieties. Several of the moderns are Austin's, including some of his more brightly coloured ones such as peachy-orange 'Perdita', with its highly fragrant, quartered-style flowers, and apricot-and-cream 'Abraham Darby'. Most of these reproduction-style roses can get quite leggy as they get older; they are obviously pruned quite hard in this garden each year to keep them bushy. Other modern roses here are the Hybrid Rugosa 'Thérèse Bugnet', a double, deep pink, very healthy rose, and 'Martin Frobisher', with light green feathery foliage and semi-double soft pink flowers. Both are very hardy and seem to do well in this part of the world.

By far and away, though, the old varieties predominate in this collection. Albas like the fifteenth-century 'Maiden's Blush' and the 1826 'Königin von Dänemark' comfortably mingle with the purple-crimson Bourbon 'Mme Isaac Pereire' (1886), the ancient deep purple Gallica 'Charles de Mills' and the striped pink and white Hybrid Perpetual 'Ferdinand Pichard' (1921) – all adding more fragrances to the heady air of this garden in June each year.

Facing the house on the opposite side of the lawn is a rose arbour with seats painted in attractive greyish-blue, the same colour as the woodwork on the house. By midday this structure is shaded, partly by the tall privet boundary hedge behind it but mostly by the tall plane trees forming the avenue in Lily Pond road.

Over on the extreme eastern side of the house is a long narrow stretch of garden which runs all the way along the boundary. This is divided from the rest of the garden by a well-maintained *Viburnum tinus* hedge. There is not a rose to be found in this area, just trees and evergreen shrubs and perennials selected mostly for their coloured foliage. One is *Berberis thunbergii atropurpurea*, used as a background for a charming little stone statue, fitting in well here but looking even better when seen, as a focal point, from the distant archway of wisteria along the drive. Resplendent against the dark green of the privet at the shady north end of this enclosure is a superb bright clear blue Hortensia hydrangea.

Flanked by yet more roses, a creamy-pink brick pathway runs all along the front of the house, midway along which three steps lead up to a wide, covered veranda or portico. Its roof is supported by six eight-foot-high brick piers. Among the ramblers and climbers adorning these piers are the pure white 'Rambling Rector', bright pinks 'Zéphirine Drouhin' and 'Constance Spry' and, next to the steps, strategically placed to waft their perfume to those who brush past, two plants of the Sweetbriar, *Rosa rubiginosa*. The portico returns at a right angle along the west side of the house and here the piers support such delectable roses as that universal favourite 'Mme Alfred Carrière' and the purple Moss rose 'William Lobb'. Also along this side of the house in a border filled with bush roses I was pleased to find 'Perle d'Or', the beautiful little golden-yellow China rose, and delighted by the unexpected discovery of the seldom-seen single Hybrid Tea rose 'Dainty Bess'.

Trellising festooned with ramblers and scramblers extends from the house across to the western boundary; this serves to give privacy to the swimming pool, which takes up most of the north end of the garden. In front of this is a narrow border of assorted roses from all ages such as the Hybrid Musk 'Lavender Lassie' and the ever-blooming pink Modern Climber 'Bantry Bay' and that most lovely of the Bourbons, the silvery-pink 'Mme Pierre Oger'.

I believe there are almost eight hundred roses packed into this garden; I have only briefly touched on the wide range of varieties and types. They are well cared for and in excellent condition. The garden is private and not open to the public.

A wonderful plant of the Hybrid Musk 'Belinda' flanked by others of her family group: 'Felicia', soft pink, and 'Prosperity', white. These three roses continue flowering throughout the summer in this garden of mainly classic roses.

HYBRID TEA

'DAINTY BESS'

SUCH IS the influence of fashion that it is difficult to imagine a new single-flowered Hybrid Tea being introduced today. More's the pity, for those that were raised in the first half of this century are some of the most beautiful of their kind. Fortunately, a few are still available. I generally avoid putting roses into league tables, but I do rate 'Dainty Bess', introduced in 1925, as one of the loveliest. Its flowers, produced in clusters, are soft pink with deeper reverses and in the centre of each is a large boss of golden-brown stamens; the final touch to this simple charm is the ragged edge to each of the silky petals. The flowers are also scented.

As a plant this variety is bushy and yet upright in growth. Like all Hybrid Teas it prefers good soil, but it is seldom without flower in any situation. It does very well in pots and is also good under glass. There is a climbing form which I have yet to see.

Two other good single Hybrid Teas worth growing are 'Ellen Willmott' (1936), soft creamy-pink, and 'Mrs Oakley Fisher' (1921), a rich golden-yellow.

WRETHAM LODGE
NEAR THETFORD, NORFOLK, ENGLAND

AST WRETHAM IS A SMALL VILLAGE JUST ON THE EDGE OF Breckland, a large flat area of heath and woodland straddling the Norfolk/Suffolk borders and renowned for its dryland flora and fauna. Much of Breckland belongs to the Forestry Commission, but large tracts are owned by the Ministry of Defence and, until recently, were used for military manoeuvres; in fact the grounds at Wretham Lodge were commandeered for use as a hospital during the Second World War and there is still an army camp close by today. When Anne Hoellering, the present owner, moved here with her husband twenty-five years ago she had to remove several concrete runways and massive hut foundations before embarking on the creation of her now extensive gardens. Soldiers are not generally well known for their respect for property and landscape in times of war or peace, but Anne believes that the local CO must have been sensitive to the beauty of the house and the wonderful trees around it. Apart from this period of unwelcome intrusion by the Forces, its air of pastoral tranquillity has remained almost unchanged since the house was built as a rectory in 1810.

Although the house is surrounded by trees, it is not overwhelmed by them, standing as it does at the highest part of the grounds. It is substantial and, even for a rectory of that era, large. It is built almost entirely of blue-grey flint in the delightful proportions of houses of all sizes of this period of Georgian architecture. The entire eleven and a half acres are surrounded by well-maintained walls. An area of about one acre forms a sheltered walled garden in the north-eastern corner of the grounds; until its renovation, this had been allowed to fall into neglect and was virtually a jungle of massive weeds. This garden, now restored, once again fulfils its original purpose and provides the house with much of its culinary needs, although today it doubles as a rose garden. The walls here are quite beautiful and although I have lived with flint for much of my life, never before have I seen so many variable tints of colour in its make-up. Anne Hoellering explained that one wall has been entirely

The pleasing proportions of Wretham Lodge, built of Norfolk flint, are seen amid old-fashioned roses which now share space with vegetables and fruit trees in the walled garden. The red is 'Tuscany Superb' and the taller striped pink 'Honorine de Brabant'. In the centre of the picture is the rare Gallica 'Orpheline de Juillet'.

The sheltered walled garden at Wretham Lodge, entered by way of this stunning blue door, has been restored by the present owner, Anne Hoellering, and now supplies the house with herbs as well as roses, such as the 'Stanwell Perpetual' in the foreground (facing page).

Although roses play the major role in Anne Hoellering's garden at Wretham Lodge, they are just a part of a wide and varied cast. Here 'Adam Messerich' and 'Duc de Fitzjames' harmonize with a range of herbaceous plants.

rebuilt by one of the few remaining specialist flint-wall craftsmen of the area who, before he retired, taught one of her gardeners some of the skills of the trade so as to continue with the maintenance of the extensive walling. When this wall was rebuilt in 1976 the system of paths in the garden was also laid down.

Although roses are by far the predominant genus in these gardens, they form just a small part of a wide and varied cast and are, most certainly, not there for their own sake. I have already mentioned the trees and will return to these for a moment; there are two huge copper beeches, one very large specimen close to the house on the south side with its lower boughs bending right to the ground, forming a natural domed shadowhouse for seclusion and relief from the dry heat of Breckland in high summer, and another standing alone in the open on the north side, which is even bigger. To the east of the house is a straight, upright lime, which must be the tallest of its type I have ever seen. All these trees are at least as old as the house, perhaps older; in addition, well over two hundred younger trees planted by Anne are now thriving here and, in spring, a number of different hawthorns are a delight both to see and to smell.

To the west of the house a large, roughly crescent-shaped bed has been formed in the grass. This is filled with a wide variety of geraniums and monardas to form an illusion of a self-sown wilderness of wild flowers. One or two *Rosa glauca* (*R. rubrifolia*) and a few low-growing shrubs add further interest, the whole coming into its own in high summer. This bed blends well with the rustic hedge of wild plum

behind it, the base of which is liberally frilled with cow parsley – altogether a charming vista for guests relaxing on the terrace after dinner on warm summer evenings. To call it a terrace is perhaps too pretentious, for it is really a seating area among hard-wearing herbaceous plants and carpeted by wild strawberry plants. The hedge itself has never yielded fruit and probably developed naturally from suckers of understocks of named varieties of plums which have since disappeared.

Several years ago, unannounced, a rose appeared in this hedge and was brought to my nursery by Anne for trial. I have had it growing in the nursery gardens ever since under the name 'The Wretham Rose'. It is an unfading deep rosy-pink, bordering on crimson, very full, cupped and flat when fully open, similar in form to 'Baronne Prévost'. It has a spicy fragrance. It flowers profusely in late June and July and is very healthy. The original plant, now intertwined through the plum trees, must be ten feet tall and several cuttings have been rooted to grow elsewhere in the grounds. This orphan probably emerged as a seedling from a seed deposited there by birds. It is difficult to classify but, being fairly thorny, must be closely related to the Centifolias. It has not done as well for me as it has here at Wretham, and seeing it this year has convinced me that it should be given a name by Anne and made available to the world at large.

To the south of the house is an old six-foot-high red-brick wall which, apparently, once supported an array of discordant outbuildings. In order to hide the unsightly

The temperature in the walled garden at Wretham Lodge is usually a degree or two higher than the rest of the gardens there; thus China rose 'Mutabilis' thrives and enjoys life beneath the south wall. Alongside is Philadelphus *'Belle Etoile'.*

163

CHINA ROSE

'MUTABILIS'

NOTHING MUCH is known about this unusual rose. It is probably an old Chinese garden variety dating back far beyond its first appearance in Europe around 1894. The Victorians also knew it as 'Tipo Ideale'. Sometimes it is referred to as a true species, but its behaviour is far too inconsistent for this to be the case.

One could be forgiven for not immediately recognizing it as a rose. The plant is dense and twiggy, with plum-red shoots and glossy dark green leaves. Its height and girth varies from three up to ten feet or more, making it useful as both a border and a wall plant. Its flower colouring is also variable, starting off usually as honey-coloured and changing with maturity to rose-pink, plum-red and orange-red. The blooms are papery in texture, loosely formed and single, with a pronounced boss of stamens. A flower head can be made up of flowers of all these colours at once, which makes this variety useful where bright colouring is needed.

Like most of the China roses, its hardiness is suspect and therefore, in the colder zones, it will need protection from the worst of winter chills. Usually, though, even if it is cut down by frost, it will recover quickly to give a good display by midsummer. It is a must for Mediterranean gardens.

bricks left by the demolition of the old outhouses, it has been almost completely covered by a range of climbing plants, several of them evergreen. It is some thirty yards long and nowadays affords shelter from the north to an irregularly shaped border of mixed plantings. The highlight to me is several clumps of the Damask Moss rose 'Alfred de Dalmas' (also sometimes called 'Mousseline'). The term 'clump' is most appropriate in this instance, since the roses are growing on their own roots and constantly multiplying themselves. It is noticeable that quite a number of the roses in the light loamy soil of this garden now grow on their own roots, succeeding in doing so by virtue of the deep planting of budded plants. Also growing in this border and, in this case, providing substantial additional camouflage for the wall, is the seldom-seen 'Nyveldt's White', a single white Rugosa. Here, too, is the lovely soft pink Portland rose 'Jacques Cartier'.

A little farther on is an informal area consisting of trees, shrubs and conifers. Some of these have been allowed to grow naturally and others were planted deliberately to conceal evidence of the old army buildings. With its large collection of hellebores, this is a particularly good area in winter and early spring – not that the rest of the garden is dull at that time of year, for everywhere you can find aconites, snowdrops, crocuses, daffodils and species tulips, both naturalized in the grass and planted in many of the numerous borders. Dominant amid the informality in this part is another substantial lime tree, this one with its trunk completely hidden by a dense thicket of young suckering shoots at its base, a haven for varied wildlife. One or two wild plants of *Rosa canina* have also been allowed to form themselves into dense, untamed shrubs. Colour enhancement here is provided through summer into autumn with species tulips, fritillaries, perennial honesty (*Lunaria rediviva*), erythroniums, species peonies, foxgloves, martagon lilies and colchicums. Shrubby lilacs are also found here in abundance.

From here the garden takes on a more cultivated and formal look as we pass through an enclosure which eventually leads to the walled garden. On the one side are several plants of *Rosa woodsii fendleri* and, on the other, a well-used, lean-to greenhouse designed by Anne, with a large fig tree taking up the whole of the wall area. *R. w. fendleri* is a first-class lilac-pink species which grows into a dense yet graceful shrub and produces a good crop of large red hips in the autumn. Here, as elsewhere, it makes an excellent hedge. Farther along the wall on which the greenhouse stands (actually the exterior of the walled garden) are some espalier-trained pear trees. In a narrow border at their feet grow dense clumps of *Fritillaria meleagris*, and a vast planting of *Tulip bakeri* 'Lilac Wonder' comes into flower at the same time as the pears. The end of this enclosure is taken up by an outhouse, not the most inspiring of buildings, but useful as a store shed and effectively supporting four very well-trained climbing and rambler roses. On the west side is an outstanding white rambler which my nursery has been guilty for a number of years of listing erroneously as 'White Flight', and which is clearly a sport from 'Mrs F.W. Flight'. It appears that when first introduced by Hilliers of Winchester in the 1950s it was named 'Astra Desmond', and it has been distributed since under both names. On the front and south side an excellent example of the climbing Hybrid Tea 'Mme Grégoire Staechelin' reaches to the eaves. This rose is also known as 'Spanish Beauty' and is one of the first to come into flower each summer. Its large, blowzy flowers are made up of several shades of pink and, if not dead-headed, the urn-shaped hips provide interest throughout the winter. Two other climbing roses

admirably enhance this building, the reliable and easy-to-grow Noisette 'Mme Alfred Carrière', which crops up in almost every garden, and a rose I have never before seen called 'Mrs Honey Dyson'. It is exquisite in both blossom and behaviour. Its flowers are creamy-white and fragrant, loosely cupped in form and produced in drooping clusters. I intend to see much more of it in the future.

Hybrid Musk 'Thisbe' looks good against the flint that is everywhere at Wretham Lodge. This is just one of a fine collection of roses built up by Anne Hoellering over the twenty or so years that she has been gardening here.

You enter the walled garden through a discreetly positioned blue door on the east side. Inside time again seems to have stood still, for the ambience remains historical, even with its new layout. Originally, perhaps, several lean-to greenhouses would have been in place, but now the walls are clad with thick and sinewy vines planted when the garden was restored, the spaces in between being filled with climbing roses. Constructed at the same time, at the opposite corners, are two attractive, open-fronted summerhouse-type buildings of brick and flint, used for storing tools and the occasional sit down.

It was quite cold on the day of my visit but the temperature was several degrees warmer inside this garden and roses clearly relish both the congenial atmosphere here and the attention they receive from Anne and her two skilled gardeners. Quite a large collection of different varieties has been built up over the years, selected for enjoyment rather than as part of any botanical or historical plan. It would be boring now simply to list and describe them all, but many cannot escape attention. Outstanding on the walls is the orange-yellow climber 'Alister Stella Gray', which

MOSS ROSE

'ALFRED DE DALMAS'

THIS LOVELY little rose – also known as 'Mousseline' – was raised in France in 1855 and is one of the most useful of the Moss roses. If it were not a Moss it would be placed among the Portland Damasks. It is short in growth and bushy and even if left unpruned (which would be a mistake) will never attain a height of more than three feet. With annual pruning each spring and regular dead-heading each summer, it remains more consistently at two feet.

Its foliage is light green and soft to touch when young. Both the young shoots and the calyces are well covered with light green moss, sometimes with a slight purple or pinkish tinge. The flowers are almost fully double and richly fragrant, their colour soft pink to blush; when fully open the prominent yellow stamens serve to give the blooms a creamy look *en masse*. They are produced at first in June in great profusion and then regularly, although in lesser quantities, through to the first frosts of winter.

Like most of the shorter-growing old roses, this adapts easily to being grown in a container, but its most effective role is as a bedding rose. When grown on its own roots it rapidly reproduces itself by suckering, so it can also be massed in semi-ground-covering schemes.

Anne has fallen in love with over the years because 'it has such nice manners'. Also there is a sizeable plant of the soft pink 'Dr W. Van Fleet', the flowers of which are indistinguishable from those of the ever-flowering 'New Dawn' which it spawned, but which, unlike its offspring, blooms just once each year. Examples of 'The Wretham Rose', which so clearly enjoys the conditions here, are dotted about the borders and on the walls. As always, 'Rambling Rector' is doing stalwart service, as is the less often seen 'Easlea's Golden Rambler', healthy, vigorous and fragrant.

Beneath each wall are wide borders in which are planted many shrub roses. In the warmest of these borders, that beneath the south wall, is a superb specimen of 'Mutabilis' which, although to be found in many other gardens, is seldom as good as here. In this border too are the lesser known, deep pink, shrubby 'Adam Messerich' and the soft pink, fully double, richly fragrant 'Gros Choux d'Hollande'. The vigorous striped pink 'Honorine de Brabant' is also very much in evidence, and the strikingly beautiful deep purple-magenta Moss rose 'William Lobb' (Old Velvet Moss) enjoys the support of the wall.

Some of the more 'awkward' of the old roses have been trained on supports in a fairly unique fashion. Two tall bamboo canes are pushed vertically into the ground with half a dozen or so other canes wired on to them horizontally at roughly six-inch intervals to form a sort of ladder to a height of about five feet. Other roses are trained on wigwams, again formed by canes. Interesting in the overall layout is that groups of roses have been planted randomly among plots of vegetables, with each group consisting of a grand mixture of types and varieties. Gallicas predominate, though, such as the deep purple 'Cardinal de Richelieu' and the striped pink and white 'Camaieux'. Both of these, but especially the latter, have become established on their own roots and are now in a constant state of rejuvenation. Doing likewise is the rich greyish-purple Gallica 'Belle de Crécy'. A plant of the old vigorous Gallica 'Gloire de France' is allowed each year to grow long shoots which, at pruning time, are bent to the ground and pegged down, giving the plant a dome-like shape and encouraging many more flowers as a result. But the pick of the Gallicas in this garden has to be the double, crimson-purple 'Orpheline de Juillet', seldom seen but – in the words of Anne Hoellering – 'deserving of much more attention everywhere'.

This garden is full of interest and variety. There can be little doubt that the twenty-five hours or so a week that Anne and her helpers and friends spend dead-heading during peak rose season each summer contribute greatly to the wellbeing of the roses; but apart from this, everything else is in good heart and clearly enjoys growing here. In assessing her abilities as a gardener Anne is very modest, saying, 'I simply dive in like a mole following my nose and letting it happen', and acknowledging the help she gets. All the same, assistance needs good directing, and Anne's instinctive approach really has worked. There has to be much more to this labour of love than simply 'letting it happen'.

The gardens at Wretham Lodge are open four times a year, once in April, twice in May and once in rose season for the National Gardens Scheme, the Church Fund and the Red Cross. Wretham Lodge Garden is to be found in *The Good Gardens Guide*, marked with a star.

Gallica 'Charles de Mills' in the foreground and 'Alba Semi-plena', 'Reine des Violettes' and 'Mme Hardy' share a spot at Wretham Lodge with verbascums and dracocephalums (facing page).

VALLERANELLO
CASTEL DI LEVA,
NEAR ROME, LAZIO, ITALY

Roses burst from every part of the one and a half hectares that make up the rose garden of Valleranello, near Rome. This wonderful rambler, supported by a Judas tree (Cercis siliquastrum)*, is one of Maresa Del Bufalo's own raising, a seedling from 'Robin Hood' and named after her husband Luciano Del Bufalo.*

IT WAS EVENING WHEN I VISITED VALLERANELLO, WITH ONLY an hour or so of daylight left. It was raining a little too, but mild, so I was determined not to allow a few drops of Roman rain to spoil my enjoyment of the roses.

The garden is situated at Castel di Leva, about eight kilometres south of Rome in low-lying, open Lazio countryside. It extends to about one and a half hectares and contains an important collection of well over a thousand varieties of rose. 'I was first inspired to grow roses when I saw the huge collection of famous Italian Rosarian Dr Fineschi,' landscape architect Maresa Del Bufalo told me as she showed me her creation, the results of twenty-two years' work.

As we talked it soon became clear that this lady really loves roses, enjoys growing them and knows a great deal about them. She speaks reasonably good English but my Italian is nil, so Elena Pizzi, herself a lover of roses, who had kindly brought me here, acted as interpreter when, occasionally, language difficulties got in the way.

Although Maresa started her rose collection in 1973, she came to live here and started the garden when she married the architect and builder of the house, Luciano Del Bufalo, in 1956. Maresa showed me pictures of the house just after they moved in. It stood in a totally barren expanse of land without a blade of grass or a tree in sight. What has been achieved in only forty years is incredible, but then Maresa is a landscape architect in a family of architects, after all.

The property is approached by a long drive with wide, tree-scattered lawns on either side. The trees become more numerous as you approach the house, cleverly concealing it from full view – not that it can be seen easily from close range, as its walls are densely furnished with climbing and rambling plants of all types, especially roses. There is no formality, I was to discover, but, as expected in an Italian garden, no shortage of ornaments either; in fact, at the entrance to the garden two ancient marble columns, now a little the worse for wear, stand majestically erect as they did

a couple of thousand years ago in another place, when they formed part of a grand colonnade or supported a Roman portico.

A cascading cluster of the lovely 'Paul's Himalayan Musk' is captured among the branches of a Melia azedarach *at Valleranello. There are many such unusual associations of roses and trees and shrubs in this garden.*

As we walked Maresa told me that this was her real garden, the garden where she is free from the constraints of her profession of designing formal gardens for such clients as the City of Rome. 'Roses as plants are so individual that it is impossible to contain them in a line,' she said. 'In Italian-style gardens, if the line is more important than the plant, then roses cannot be used.' She went on: 'In my work when I use roses, I put them into beds and borders, but not in my garden – here they grow free.' As I soon discovered, for everywhere here roses more or less do their own thing.

In the time available it was impossible to explore every little nook and cranny, coppice or spinney, so with occasional diversions, we followed the wide grassed walkway which weaves its way through the garden from north-east to south-west.

Maresa has help from a gardener for only one day a week, so she attends to her roses herself all the year round, including week after week of pruning in winter. She believes that a garden, as well as being a labour of love, should be a place of enjoyment and somewhere to relax with her family, and soon we came upon a sizeable gazebo furnished with a suite of comfortable cane chairs and tables.

This gazebo is an attractive structure, hexagonal in shape and built of criss-cross trellising, open on two sides. Its covered roof is awash with a huge plant of the climbing China rose 'Cécile Brünner' in the peak of health with luxuriant foliage and

*A*ll the China roses, including 'Mutabilis', enjoy the climate around Rome. The whole garden at Valleranello is irrigated so that the roses, without exception, are in excellent condition.

copious flowers. Other hybrids of *Rosa chinensis* are planted in little groups around this area. I noticed the lovely soft yellow 'Perle d'Or' and the more vigorous replica of 'Cécile Brünner', 'Bloomfield Abundance', both looking in excellent shape, as was 'Mutabilis', which so loves the climate around Rome. Scrambling up into a sizeable tree near by I spotted the effervescent climbing form of 'Cramoisi Supérieur', which Maresa told me she had brought here as a cutting from the garden at Ninfa (see page 149). Also flowering away to its heart's content was a bush of 'Général Schablikine'; this, too, came from that same garden. Maresa knows Ninfa intimately, of course, and has recently published, in collaboration with friends Rita Biuso and Alberto Galli, a beautiful book on the garden there. Planted close by the gazebo I also saw one or two older varieties of Hybrid Tea. I was especially thrilled to find the bright crimson 'Soraya', which I remember from my youth. Near by a large group of several different varieties of Rugosa creates a haven for birds; they love to feast on the huge crop of succulent hips these thorny shrubs yield.

Each of the garden groups of old roses has been allocated its own space by Maresa. This is useful to anyone who is not familiar with the structure of the genus, for the different habits of each family are then more easily recognized. As if to make this point, on opposite sides of the walkway are two quite different groups, on the one side the ancient once-flowering Gallicas, with *Rosa gallica officinalis* and its historic sport, the striped 'Rosa Mundi', much in evidence and, on the other, the ever-flowering Hybrid Musks, including the semi-double bright pink 'Belinda' and a special favourite of Maresa's, the floriferous, scarlet 'Robin Hood'.

I remarked on how well all the roses looked. 'The whole garden is irrigated, and in high summer the irrigation is turned on at least every other day,' Maresa said. No wonder the ramblers and climbers all scramble so energetically high up into the trees, and the shrub roses grow with such exuberance. She also explained that every three weeks, starting in May, the whole garden is sprayed with fungicide and insecticide to keep at bay any dreaded blackspot, rust and aphids.

Sadly, I will probably never see this garden at its peak because it is at its best during the last ten days of May, dates which will always clash with Chelsea Flower

---

THIS ROSE was introduced from China in 1917. It is valuable as a garden plant, since it comes into flower a week or so later than many of the other tree-climbers. It is very vigorous, attaining a height of thirty feet or more without any difficulty.

The foliage is fine-textured, darkish green and glossy, but such is its speed of growth that its leaves are sometimes fairly wide-spaced. It blooms profusely on wood produced in the previous season, which makes it slow to begin flowering; however, once it does start, its large corymbs make for a spectacular display.

SPECIES ROSE

ROSA MULLIGANII

The individual flowers are about one inch across. Creamy-yellow in bud, they open to pure white, with a lovely boss of yellow stamens setting them off beautifully. They have a distinct perfume of bananas. Later they turn into small, orangey-red hips, themselves quite a sight up in the branches of a tall tree in autumn and early winter.

For some time, until the mid-1980s, this rose was distributed as *Rosa longicuspis*, so anyone who bought it under that name should re-name it *R. mulliganii*. The true *R. longicuspis* has much larger leaves and is similar to *R. gentileana* (1907).

Show; but, such is the abundance of roses that I can imagine its magnificence – especially the scramblers pouring out of every other tree, some six or more metres high. Among the many harmonious combinations, one example is the climbing form of 'Souvenir de la Malmaison', cascading from a *Prunus cerasifera* 'Nigra', the pastel pink flowers of the rose superb among the plum-coloured leaves of the tree; another has the bright pink blooms of 'Blush Rambler' drooping out of the purple foliage of *Malus × purpurea*. Less tall but just as effective is the golden-yellow climbing Tea rose 'Lady Hillingdon' contrasting with the bronzy-red foliage of a little copper beech tree.

As we neared the western edge of the garden, we found a large assembly of Bourbons, invaluable for autumn flowers – 'Variegata di Bologna', striped red and pink, and 'Louise Odier', bright pink – in fine shape among lots and lots of others of their kind. Next to these was a sizeable collection of Centifolias. '*Bellissimo*!' Maresa exclaimed. 'There's the star of the garden,' she said, pointing to a most prolific shrub of 'Fantin-Latour' in their midst. 'Who can resist this most beautiful rose?' None of us can; it is in every garden in this book. As we hurried on, for by now it was twilight, I saw a huge dense clump of assorted *Rosa pimpinellifolia* hybrids including the Burnets 'Double White' and 'Double Pink', 'Mary Queen of Scots' and 'Single Cherry', invaluable in any garden for their early-flowering virtues, autumn foliage and mahogany and black hips in winter.

Throughout this garden there is no shortage of species. I found a fine example of *Rosa roxburghii plena* full of flowers, and huge plants of both the lateish-flowering pink single *R. virginiana* and the early-flowering, mauvy-pink *R. californica*, as well as a large shrub of *R. hibernica*, repeating a few of its bright shell-pink flowers.

In the far western corner of the garden, making use of the tall wire fence surrounding a tennis court, is an interesting congregation of ramblers and climbers, especially yellows and whites. 'The Garland' and 'Desprez à Fleurs Jaunes' were outstanding as well as the lovable white 'Félicité Perpétue'. Close by here, doing a magnificent job covering a water-tower three metres high is a huge plant of the pink, myrrh-scented 'Ayrshire Splendens'. Next door, on an old tree and smothering it completely, is an inspired combination of the creamy-white flowered evergreen honeysuckle *Lonicera japonica* 'Halliana' and the soft apricot and milky-white flowered 'Wedding Day'.

Farther along the drive we came to *Rosa mulliganii* performing one of the biggest feats of tree-climbing by a rose I have ever seen. I neglected to note the name of the over-burdened tree, but Elena Pizzi remarked how, in the fading light, the pair together looked like a giant mushroom. On our way back towards the house were yet more tree and rose liaisons – *Prunus sargentii* and the pink Bourbon 'Blairi No 2', and *Acer saccharinum* with the pink free-flowering Wichuraiana hybrid 'François Juranville' were just two of them.

Chance hybridization has brought forth many a fine rose, and up to about the middle of the last century, this was the most common means by which new varieties came into the world. Maresa has such a rose which she treasures. She has named it for her husband Luciano. A seedling from 'Robin Hood', it is bright pink in colour and very vigorous. In only a few years it is completely covering a small tree. I have asked her to send me a cutting for trial.

Any serious student of 'The Rose' should see this garden. It is a fine collection. It is open during rose season, by appointment only.

CLIMBING TEA

'LADY HILLINGDON'

THE CLIMBING form of 'Lady Hillingdon' came along in 1917 and soon outshone its parent, the bush form (itself very popular), which had been raised in England in 1910. Its popularity was well deserved, for there were few yellow roses to compete with it for continuity of flowering at that time – a fact which holds true to this day.

Its flowers are rich yellow in colour, almost unfading, and are beautifully shaped in classical high-centred form, with a delicious, slightly fruity fragrance.

A special feature of this variety is its stems and thorns, which are a deep plum colour. Its foliage is dark green and heavily veined with purple.

The plant is hardier than many Teas and even in my garden in Norfolk, where we have quite cold winters, it grows to twenty feet on more sheltered walls. In less harsh climates it will perform well if grown up into trees, over arches and on trellis. The bush form, too, is a useful garden plant and is especially good grown in pots in a conservatory or greenhouse.

Both climbing and bush forms do not seem to mind being planted in poorer soils but, like most roses, flourish in heavy clay.

BROUGHTON CASTLE
BANBURY, OXFORDSHIRE, ENGLAND

 LIVER CROMWELL'S SUPPORTERS SECRETLY PLOTTED against King Charles I in 'a room that hath no ears' at Broughton Castle in the 1630s, and one William Fiennes, an ancestor of the present Lord Saye and Sele, whose family has owned the Castle since the early fourteenth century, actively and openly supported the Parliamentarians, raising his own regiment to fight in the Battle of Edgehill in 1642. This area, however, was staunchly Royalist and, for a while, Broughton was occupied by the Cavaliers. After the Restoration of the monarchy, the family was pardoned and William again took an active role in affairs of state.

Earlier, during the latter part of the sixteenth century, William's grandfather and father (both named Richard), had, between them, reconstructed Broughton in the grand Tudor style that you see today, considerably enlarging a manor house built by Sir John de Broughton in the early fourteenth century. Other alterations to this important building were carried out in the mid-1800s. More recently, with aid from the Historic Buildings Council and English Heritage, considerable refurbishments have been effected, first in the 1950s and again in the 1980s.

Although called a castle, this beautiful building would be more accurately described as a battlemented manor house. It is moated and built from an attractive mellow biscuity-coloured local stone. A very special feature of the place is a fifteenth-century gatehouse, which sits securely over the main drive on the inside of the moat. Just outside the moat alongside the main drive is the delightful fourteenth-century parish church of St Mary.

The interior of Broughton is a history lesson in itself, with every room furnished in one or other of the styles of its long and chequered life. Lots of important works of art and many genuine artifacts from the past are on display, from cannon balls used by the Royalists to capture the castle to a Cromwell-style greatcoat hanging in the Great Hall. There is much high-quality oak panelling throughout and some

The grey-foliaged cotton lavender (Santolina) flanks the archway leading into the walled Ladies' Garden at Broughton Castle. Four fleurs-de-lis of box edging form a parterre in this part of the garden in which are planted roses 'Gruss an Aachen' and 'Heritage'.

Roses thrive here in the deep rich loam of Oxfordshire, where Lord and Lady Saye and Sele grow them among a wide variety of companion plants. Here the Sempervirens rambler 'Félicité Perpétue' festoons an archway on the east wall (facing page).

The modern shrub rose 'Magenta' blends beautifully with lychnis and salvia in the Ladies' Garden at Broughton, a part of the garden where quiet colours and gentle perfume are the rule, in the choice of both roses and other subjects.

exceptionally fine ceilings: that in the Great Hall dates back to the 1760s and one much older and even more impressive in the Great Parlour is dated 1599.

The house is not without its royal connections. There is a King's Room in which both James I and Edward VII stayed, and a Queen's Room, where James's wife, Anne of Denmark, slept.

Broughton is situated a few miles south-west of Banbury amid the rolling countryside of the northern edge of the Cotswolds. The Castle is surrounded by a wide, deep moat in oak-studded parkland. The building and gardens extend to about three acres. The entire enclosure at the front is lawn, divided only by a wide gravel drive. Except for climbing and rambler roses on the east-facing wall which runs along the west side of the grounds, and a large wisteria on the south wall of the old stables facing the Castle, there are no plants at all in this part of the gardens; nor are there any on the house. An admirable constraint, this permits full frontal appreciation of the lines and proportions of an impressive building.

Although missing out on the sun from late afternoon onwards, the roses on the east-facing wall are in excellent shape. Here is 'The Garland', a soft pinkish-white free-flowering scrambler and 'Elegance', a seldom-seen shapely soft yellow with good dark green foliage. The Sempervirens hybrid 'Félicité Perpétue' is also here, as is the lovely yellow Noisette 'Alister Stella Gray', which in a position such as this flowers freely for most of the summer.

I was fortunate to have Chris Hopkins, the young Head Gardener, to show me around. Both Lord and Lady Saye and Sele are keen gardeners and Chris clearly enjoys working here. From the front of the house he led me through a door in the wall to the west borders; these are wide and run the entire length of the walls on that side of the Castle. Protected as they are from the north and east and with the full benefit of the sun from mid-morning onwards, the huge range of plants in these borders really thrives. One border is the special province of Lord Saye and Sele, where he allows himself to indulge in the use of bright colours – brighter than is possible anywhere else in the gardens at Broughton. Yellow, in particular, is reflected in the predominance of hypericums and potentillas and his choice of roses, among which are the Hybrid Musk shrub 'Buff Beauty' and, on the wall behind, the thorny but excellent early-flowering modern climber 'Maigold'. Other shrub roses in this border in glorious full flush for me were the lovely sulphur-yellow, free-flowering, almost single 'Golden Wings' and one of its offspring, the excellent fragrant ever-flowering 'Windrush', a semi-double soft yellow rose which fits comfortably into any colour scheme. This attribute also applies to the white Hybrid Rugosa 'Schneezwerg', which Lord Saye and Sele has used effectively in this border; although relatively unobtrusive during summer, its crop of bright red hips are really brilliant in autumn and early winter.

Quieter colours are the rule in the rest of the west borders, where the range of different subjects is huge and no square inch of soil is visible anywhere. Roses always enjoy westerly aspects and on the wall behind one of the borders are several plants of 'Albertine', all intertwined with clematis and wisteria. I also noticed that loveliest of climbing red roses, 'Ena Harkness'. Who cares about her proverbial weak neck when she has such a wonderful fragrance? I was pleased, too, to find among all the exuberance of these borders 'Purity', a semi-double, pure white climber that usually brings forth a few flowers each autumn, after its prolific first flush. With such a wealth of activity around them, several shrub roses, mostly of various shades of pink, are positively flourishing – among them the lovely single pink Gallica 'Complicata' and another variety which usually gives a smattering of flowers in late summer, the semi-double pink 'Marguerite Hilling'. Another pleasing find was the excellent Modern Shrub 'Fritz Nobis', which to my mind should always be forgiven for having no more than one floriferous display of two-toned pink flowers each summer. *Rosa glauca* (*R. rubrifolia*), with its greyish-purple foliage, and 'Cornelia', the continuous-flowering pink Hybrid Musk, both occupy their space with vitality. Adding weight to the foreground are several plants of the shortest-growing and yet most free-flowering of the fruit-bearing hybrid Rugosas, 'Fru Dagmar Hastrup'.

A large shrub of 'Fantin-Latour', that most lovely of old Centifolia roses, takes pride of place at the south end of a long box hedge which runs between the west borders and the moat, breaking up the otherwise wide expanse of lush green lawn. Here and there this little feature is interrupted by a taller plant, one such being the soft pink 'Paul's Himalayan Musk' growing unsupported, its long branches cleverly intertwined at pruning time each year to form a shrub. Also in this vicinity, completely smothering an old apple tree, is the white 'Bobbie James' in all its glory.

Around the corner from here, facing south, is another border of roughly the same width. The roses find this hot aspect a little difficult; even so, the indomitable 'Albertine' is thriving, as are the vigorous large-flowered 'Easlea's Golden Rambler' and the less-vigorous, smaller-flowered yellow rambler 'Goldfinch'.

CLIMBING ROSE

'ENA HARKNESS'

THIS ROSE has its critics, mainly because of its rather weak neck. This fault is difficult to live with in a bush rose – especially nowadays, when there are some good modern reds with strong stems – but I would never let it put me off the climbing form. I still consider that the performance of this rose when in full flush is a difficult act to follow.

The bush form was raised in 1951 by an amateur rose breeder, Albert Norman, and the climbing sport came along three years later. Its rich velvety-red, fragrant flowers are shapely, high-centred and quite large even for a Hybrid Tea. They are produced very freely in clusters. Another advantage 'Ena Harkness' has over many other red climbing Hybrid Teas is an ability to produce a second flush of flowers.

As a plant it is vigorous, with plentiful dark green leaves. Its stems are very thorny, making an almost 'burglar-proof' barrier when grown on a wall, but it also does quite well on a trellis or arch.

HYBRID MUSK

'PROSPERITY'

Throughout this book I continually expound the many virtues of the Hybrid Musks. There is no doubt that as a group, along with the Rugosas, they are the most versatile of all. Although most of them were introduced over seventy years ago, few modern shrub roses can outshine them today.

It is difficult to put the Hybrid Musks into any order of preference, but 'Prosperity' would most certainly be in my top three or four. It was raised by Pemberton – who else? – in 1919. It is scented and fully double, with a touch of soft lemon colour visible in the centre of the fully open blush-white flowers. The blooms are borne in large clusters on strong, almost thornless branches. There are only a few days each summer when this rose is not in flower. Its foliage is dark green and, in common with the other Hybrid Musks, very healthy.

As a free-standing shrub it will easily attain a height of five feet, but it is probably best treated as a tall Floribunda and kept to about four feet by regular pruning. It also makes a good hedge and is quite long-lasting as a cut flower.

Once upon a time entry to the Castle was from the south-east, and good use is now made of the old medieval entrance arch which still stands here. Festooning its west side are jasmine, clematis and *Euonymus fortunei* 'Silver Queen'; on its east are two climbing roses, the lemon-milky-white 'Wedding Day' and the soft yellow 'Leverkusen'.

From this archway, which is at right angles to the south border, another bed, this one east-facing, runs towards the Castle. Its backing wall hosts a variety of climbing roses, of which I will mention just two: the oddly named, highly scented pink Bourbon 'Blairi No 2', once-flowering but irresistible; and the more modern 'Parade', an excellent rose – scented, fully double and deep pink. Also in this border are several good shrub roses. From these I single out the white Hybrid Musk 'Prosperity' as being outstanding at the time of my visit.

In the lawn of the eastern garden several yews are clipped into large 'pouffe' shapes to add a nice touch to an otherwise bare lawn. I saw displayed in the house an old sepia photograph of the East Garden taken in 1900, when it was a complexity of parterres and arches of roses. In those days, too, the south facade of the castle was awash with what looks like ivy, or perhaps Virginia creeper. Another old picture on display, taken from the roof at roughly the same time, shows a very complex, over-the-top Victorian garden on the west lawn – in the days of plentiful gardeners, of course.

From the east lawn a little door leads into the Ladies' Garden. This is completely enclosed by high walls on three sides and the Castle to the north. A veritable sun-trap, as witnessed by such plants as *Cytisus battandieri* and *Rosa banksiae lutea* thriving to their hearts' content alongside such ramblers as the prolific pink 'François Juranville' and the creamy-white, larger-flowered, glossy-foliaged 'Albéric Barbier'.

All around the edge of this most delightful part of the Broughton gardens are borders composed of a wide range of shrubs, perennials, herbs and roses. While somewhere among them there is every colour imaginable, nowhere did I see any abrasive combinations.

Between the Castle and the parterre is a narrow border of the pink Hybrid Musk 'Felicia', always useful for such purposes. The parterre consists of four fleurs-de-lis radiating around a circular central bed from which rises an attractive dish-shaped urn. In the centre of each fleur-de-lis is a mop-head standard pink may tree and beneath these, filling each parterre, Austin's pink 'Heritage' and 'Gruss an Aachen', peach-pink and cream, both looking superb.

I visited Broughton in September, so missed the roses at their best, but I can picture it in high summer, and assure you that this garden, and indeed the Castle, is very well worth a visit.

The garden is open from April to October.

The Ladies' Garden is a sun trap. Here Polyantha 'The Fairy' excels itself as a large shrub in the foreground and the white 'Félicité Perpétue' enjoys its position on the ancient stone wall.

A border of that lovely Hybrid Musk 'Felicia' is seen here behind the massed planting of pinks and the modern rose 'Magenta' at Broughton Castle. Although this grand Tudor building is known as a castle it is actually a beautiful battlemented manor house built of local Cotswold stone (facing page).

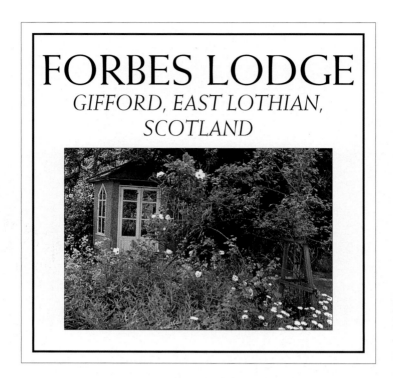

FORBES LODGE
GIFFORD, EAST LOTHIAN, SCOTLAND

Around the summer house at Forbes Lodge, Rosa multibracteata *hybrid 'Cerise Bouquet' and* R. rugosa *'Alba' are allowed to grow freely. In front, among other herbaceous subjects, is the useful, long-flowering if slightly tender osteospermum.*

I RECALL WITH GREAT PLEASURE THE SUNNY MORNING SPENT in the company of Lady Maryoth Hay in the gardens of Forbes Lodge. Although this was our first meeting and my visit was at short notice, the common ground of roses soon allowed us to relax and enjoy together a tour of her beautiful gardens.

It was September, too late for many of the roses still to be in flower, but it was not difficult to imagine the scene in July, when they would be at their peak. In any case, roses were still blooming among a wide mixture of other plants which were already beginning to take on their mantle of autumn colour.

Lady Maryoth purchased the property in 1970. It stands on the outskirts of the village of Gifford in East Lothian, and was part of the Tester Estates. Built in 1765 for one of her ancestors, from sandstone from a local quarry, the house sits roughly in the middle of a fairly long, narrow garden extending almost to five acres. The ground slopes to the east with unspoilt, ancient woodlands forming the south-eastern boundary. The cultivated ornamental gardens occupy about two acres. Flowing through the trees and cleverly incorporated into the garden is the shallow, rock-strewn burn of Gifford Water.

Only after passing beneath trees that overhang the entrance to the gardens does the house become fully visible. Just inside the gates the sweeping drive divides to lead to the front and to the rear of the house respectively. As so often in Scotland, the house faces east and, being sheltered on either side, the split-level front garden provides the ideal enclosure for a very wide range of plants. A large part of the top tier is taken up by a turning area and lawns. It is bounded to the north by an attractive old stone wall and bordered on both sides with shrubberies. The overall landscape gives an impression of informality achieved by irregularly formed, densely packed beds and borders with, here and there, unpretentious statuary. You enter the lower garden by descending approximately ten steep steps placed roughly in the centre of

Lady Maryoth Hay has clothed Forbes Lodge with a variety of climbing plants, roses among them. Here the modern climber 'Pink Perpétué' and the climbing form of 'Cécile Brünner' share space with hops (Humulus lupulus). *Beneath them, among catmint* (Nepeta mussinii), *is Hybrid Musk 'Felicia' (facing page).*

White flowering plants of any kind always work well with old roses. Here white delphiniums share a space at Forbes Lodge with rambler rose 'François Juranville'. Colour co-ordination is a special feature of the garden here.

an abrupt bank. Planted on either side of the steps and extending into the peripheral borders are numerous roses, among them several Portlands still flowering and proving their worth as relatively easy-going, unobtrusive, autumn-flowering shrub roses – especially 'Jacques Cartier', with its flat, full-petalled, soft pink, scented flowers and healthy foliage. Several plants of 'Fantin-Latour' are mingled together to form a tangled mass which in high summer would be a glorious mound of fragrant and delicate soft pink. On the other side of the lawn, still on the upper tier, the upright-growing, very thorny Rugosa hybrid 'F.J. Grootendorst', with clusters of brick-red, fimbriated, perfumed flowers and light green foliage, is giving good value at this time of the year.

In the lower section of this garden, without being too 'fussy', Lady Maryoth has colour-coordinated the borders, although this was not so immediately obvious in autumn. Some of the very interesting plant associations would be worth exploring if our quest was not concentrating on roses, which are much in evidence everywhere in these two acres. Outstanding in this area are the aptly named 'Cerise Bouquet', a very vigorous hybrid of *Rosa multibracteata*, the lovely Rugosa hybrid 'Blanc Double de Coubert' and the seemingly ever-blooming Hybrid Musks 'Moonlight' and 'Buff Beauty', creamy-white and buff-yellow respectively.

Underneath the wall at the extreme southern end of the garden are some very good specimens of *Rosa glauca* (*R. rubrifolia*), its masses of hips just turning to the distinctive mahogany-red which goes so well with its soft grey-blue foliage and dense purple stems. Another rose I spotted on that wall was the bluish-purple Multiflora hybrid 'Veilchenblau', not then in flower, but an ideal choice of bedfellow for *R. glauca*.

Roses do not feature in the delightful woodland garden which straddles the rippling waters of the burn. I made a mental note to try to return in the spring, for such a garden would really come into its own at that time of the year, and crossing the bridge to explore the inviting wetland woods would also be worthwhile then. The predominant tree species in this low-lying woodland is alder (*Alnus glutinosa*). Apparently charcoal derived from these trees was used as an ingredient for gunpowder in the Napoleonic Wars.

Continuing upwards in a westerly direction through the gardens behind the house, the path leads through an assortment of ornamental trees and shrubs where, among flowering cherries and crab apples, I noticed a nice example of *Exochorda × macrantha* and, in an open space where it has been allowed to develop its naturally tidy form, a lovely example of the Judas tree (*Cercis siliquastrum*). Not far away and supported by – or supporting – an old collapsed apple tree is a fairly expansive plant of a pale pink, single, fragrant rose brought back from China by Sir George Taylor, a former Director of Kew Gardens; this is at least twelve feet high. Much taller and climbing into an old holly tree is the white, single-flowered *Rosa filipes* 'Kiftsgate', its ever-healthy leaves beginning to change from bright green to russet-red and its trusses of orange berries looking good among the dark green holly leaves.

Farther up on the south side of this part of the garden, again among other shrubs, are several very colourful shrubby roses, some, such as *R. moyesii* 'Geranium', bearing a good crop of fruit. 'Geranium' is the brightest of the hybrids of *R. moyesii*. Its single, waxy, bright red flowers are produced abundantly in June, but its main claim to garden space is through its large, whiskery, flagon-shaped orange-red hips.

As you make your way up this part of the garden, it becomes clear that Lady Maryoth's intention when laying it out over the past twenty-five years was to contrive in each section a 'peep' to encourage you to venture on to the next. For example, a tantalizing glimpse through white *Spiraea* 'Arguta' leads on to more rose discoveries, notably 'Dortmund', a rose not seen often enough, especially in this type of informal, more natural garden. Almost single when fully open, it flowers more or less less continuously from early summer until the frosts of autumn, and then its sizeable hips still continue to provide interest into the early winter months.

Once you reach the top end of the garden and turn around to go back down towards the house, the scene changes. It is now more open and, at the same time, more formal – the formality emphasized by a clipped yew hedge dividing a cut-flower and vegetable plot from a rose walk. This walk is made up of shrub and pillar roses, ramblers and climbers, several of which were still in flower in September. Its rich yellow colour accentuated by the dark green background of yew, the excellent modern shrub rose 'Graham Thomas' was looking good. 'New Dawn' also flourishes here, as do two other good, orange-toned remontant modern climbers, 'Compassion' and 'Schoolgirl'. The climbing form of 'Mrs Sam McGredy', an older orange dating back to the 1920s, was not in flower, but I easily recognized its distinctive coppery-red foliage and stems and large, hooked thorns. (I remember these from scratches collected as an apprentice in the 1950s, when this rose was at its most popular.) In the 'cutting' garden – formerly the kitchen garden – alongside dahlias,

MODERN CLIMBER

'ALCHYMIST'

WORKING IN Germany during the 1940s and '50s, Wilhelm Kordes produced some marvellous shrubs and climbing roses. Because of man's persistent assumption that 'something new is something better', many have since disappeared from all but the most specialist rose catalogues. Even the 1956 introduction 'Alchymist', with its popular colouring and strong scent, is available from only a few growers. When fully open, the flowers are fully double in the old-fashioned style. Their colour varies according to weather or soil (and, I sometimes think, whim); from time to time, there can be both soft creamy-yellow and rich orange-buff flowers on the plant at the same time.

In the garden 'Alchymist' can be either a vigorous tall shrub or a medium-sized climber. It is not remontant, but flowers freely in early summer for a period of about three weeks. Its growth is sturdy and almost unyielding, so it has to be pruned into place rather than bent. It is very thorny, with plentiful bronze-green foliage to help compensate for the lack of flowers later in the summer. It will attain a height of about twelve feet. In very hot, dry seasons or on sunny, south-facing walls it is a martyr to blackspot. It fares well on a north wall, provided it is not too shady.

CHINA ROSE

'CÉCILE BRÜNNER'

'Cécile Brünner' is one of the loveliest little roses ever raised. Although sometimes temperamental, it has been a favourite of gardeners and non-gardeners alike since it first came on the scene in 1881. (Non-gardeners appreciate it as a buttonhole rose.) In America it is delightfully known as the Sweetheart Rose. Originally named 'Mlle Cécile Brünner', it has also, over the years, been called 'Mignon' and 'Maltese Rose'. It came about as the result of a cross between a Polyantha rose (Victorian Polypompon) and the Tea rose 'Mme de Tartas'.

Almost thornless, it grows into a compact, dense plant, usually to a height of no more than two feet, although in good heavy soils I have seen it up to almost three feet. Its foliage, which is a little sparse, is semi-glossy and darkish-green. Its delicate, beautifully scrolled little flowers, like miniature Hybrid Tea shapes, are fully double and produced in clusters throughout the summer. It is quite at home when grown under glass. 'Soft pink' is the best colour description I can come up with, but its subtle hues and reflections portray a far more lovely colouring than that. There is also a white form, equally charming.

The climbing form, introduced in 1904, is vigorous to a fault and best used as a scrambler.

chrysanthemums and so on were serried ranks of relatively modern Hybrid Teas and Floribundas. I saw several of interest, but felt I should not trespass too far into what is obviously the domain of Mr Bissett, Lady Maryoth's long-time gardener.

The rose walk finishes with a rustic arch bearing a well-foliated specimen of that stalwart Noisette, 'Mme Alfred Carrière', still exhibiting a few of its creamy-white, lightly blushed-pink, scented blooms. At this point the path takes you south, back towards the main drive, but just before you reach the house, a wrought-iron gate invites entry to a 'secret' garden. Constructed on the site of an old roadway that used to lead to the coachhouse on the old estate, this garden is totally enclosed and mixed beds of herbaceous plants, shrubs and roses border three sides, with the house itself completing the rectangle. Among the roses enjoying what must be a very pleasant microclimate are one of the most beautiful Bourbons ever raised, the soft pink, scented 'Souvenir de la Malmaison', the delightful little white Polypompon from the Victorian era, 'White Pet', and from the same period the lovely little soft pink China rose 'Cécile Brünner', a favourite for buttonholes at that time. More recent roses include 'Marguerite Hilling', the pink form of 'Nevada', and the floriferous pale pink Hybrid Musk 'Ballerina'.

As one would expect, each aspect of the house has its fair share of climbing roses among a wide diversity of other climbers such as clematis and jasmine. Not all were in flower, of course, during my visit, but there was a specimen of the modern climber

'Pink Perpétue' intermingling with hops (*Humulus lupulus*). To the right of the front door the climbing form of 'Cécile Brünner' was doing very well above a mass of purple geranium and so, too, was the Hybrid Musk 'Felicia', with its silver-pink to salmon flowers. Earlier in the summer the blowzy old cabbage-shaped satin-pink climbing Hybrid Tea 'Mme Caroline Testout' would be well worth seeing. Quite different, and even earlier perhaps, 'Alchymist' would give much pleasure wafting its perfume for yards around from variable soft orange to yellow flowers.

It might seem from what I have written that the only plants populating this garden are roses, trees and shrubs, a misrepresentation brought about partly by my autumn visit and partly by a hangover from what I sometimes think of as my misspent youth – when I very early on concentrated my learning on hardwood subjects. Autumn crocus particularly caught my eye in September, but from snowdrop time onwards, this garden always has something in flower.

Lady Maryoth Hay's gardens at Forbes Lodge are open two days a year for charity under Scotland's Gardens Scheme.

Quite apart from being a lovely shrub rose in its own right, 'Felicia' is an outstanding performer with the ability to bloom continuously throughout the summer, especially if deadheaded after each flush of flowers.

This interesting study in contrasting shapes highlights the sword-like leaves of New Zealand flax (Phormium) and the mass of flowers of an unnamed rose from the Himalayas. The rose was given to Lady Maryoth by Sir George Taylor, one-time director of Kew Gardens (facing page).

28 FAUBOURG D'ORLÉANS
PITHIVIERS, LOIRET, FRANCE

The delicate soft pink clusters of 'Belvedere' tumble gracefully from one of André Eve's rustic trellises in his beautiful rose garden. Just one of hundreds of old roses to be found there, this variety is also listed as 'Princesse Marie' and 'Ethel', just one of the many conundrums in the world of roses.

The rare Rosa gallica *'Splendens' here shows off the richness of its golden stamens. Gallicas abound in André Eve's garden, not surprisingly, since he is the founder of a nursery specializing in old roses.*

THE APPROACH DID NOTHING TO SET THE SCENE FOR THE sumptuous feast of roses I was about to enjoy. Secret gardens abound the world over and there are at least three others in this book. They, though, are tucked away within other gardens. This one is a garden in itself. Hidden behind a substantial early 1900s terrace house in an ordinary street in a little town about seventy kilometres south of Paris, the garden is not so much a secret – it is well known to rose lovers – as *secretive*, since you are not aware of its presence until you are actually standing in it, among the roses. You find it, by invitation of its owner André Eve, through a substantial front door, a long passage, a sitting room and a back door. When the roses are in flower in June and July, it becomes a mecca for five thousand or so rose lovers each year.

André Eve is a famous French rosarian and nurseryman. Although I found the lengthy street with relative ease, no one had told me that Number 28 was just a door in a wall, so I drove on seeking a nursery. Had Jérôme Paris, André Eve's partner, not been waiting outside for my arrival, I might never have found this garden and so missed a unique experience, a half-acre eruption of the genus *Rosa*. Later, during lunch, such a lunch as only the French can do, Jérôme and his wife Marie told me much about André's total dedication to roses. André himself had appointments to keep, with roses, down in the south.

André's first memories of gardening are of weeding his father's vegetable garden under duress as a thirteen-year-old. Instead of turning him away from the land, this experience led him to plant up his own personal flower garden. After military service, he worked as a landscape gardener in Paris, learning about flowers and plants while tending many small gardens in the city.

By chance in 1960 he met Monsieur Robichon, a rose nurseryman of Pithiviers, and became so fascinated by the process of breeding and growing roses that he came to work for him. When that business came up for sale, André bought it and started on his own. At first he grew and sold only modern varieties. Soon he realized that no one in France was offering the old roses, despite the fact that so many had been bred in this country, and – having by then fallen under their spell – he started to specialize. Today, from a nursery just outside the town, his firm sells over 50,000 plants each year from a choice of 550 sorts, and plans are afoot to expand even more.

As a specialist in old roses myself, I was curious to hear André's views on why the mid-twentieth-century renaissance of old roses in the rest of the world had bypassed France until only recently. 'We are not a nation of gardeners as you are in England,' he said, 'and not many small nurseries here grow roses, so the larger ones control the market and they, until now, have publicized only modern types, tending in the process to depreciate the older ones.' André Eve and his company have set about redressing the balance and now publish a most comprehensive and informative catalogue, mailing roses to an increasingly sophisticated clientele all over France.

His garden in Faubourg d'Orléans, where he and his charming wife first started their business in 1980, is an absolute must for any gardener who is even remotely interested in roses. Not only is it packed full of old varieties, but it also has lots of 'new' roses on trial, including many seedlings from his own hybridizing programme, which has absorbed him over the past few years. 'I am constantly seeking remontant roses in the old style,' he said.

The language difficulties between us faded when we talked of roses, for we had their nomenclature and the recognition of varieties in common and, even more, a mutual understanding of the pride and satisfaction gained from working together with Mother Nature to create new roses. I fell for one of his creations and, with his permission, will introduce it into Britain soon. As its name 'Red Perfume' suggests, it is a deliciously fragrant, deep velvety-red climbing rose bred from 'Souvenir de Claudius Denoyel'. I believe this rose has a big future: not only is it remontant, but it seems completely free of disease, judging by its healthy foliage and the knowledge that no chemicals are ever used in this garden. I also brought back to England with me a few more of André's roses for trial.

Around the garden to a height of about two metres is a wall built of local greyish-buff sandstone. Not that this is easily seen, being swathed on all sides with climbers and ramblers as well as many vigorous shrub roses. Inevitably 'New Dawn' is much in evidence, but as I expected, Teas and Noisettes are everywhere in this French garden, many of them described in detail elsewhere in these pages. Two, though, must be mentioned here since they are so quintessentially French, the lovely 'Gloire de Dijon', perfumed buffy-yellow with hints of pink, and the less double but equally beautiful, similarly coloured 'Souvenir de Mme Léonie Viennot'. I am told on good authority, incidentally, that 'Gloire de Dijon' is found more often in the rest of the world than in Dijon itself.

Numerous trees, both deciduous and evergreen, add strength and substance to the garden's essentially simple design, and play host to various vigorous scramblers. One of these, 'Bobbie James', shows off its richly golden-anthered white flowers and glossy green foliage to effect as it drapes itself all over the flowering cherry *Prunus* 'Kanzan', and climbing 'Cécile Brünner', of which André is particularly fond, adorns a substantial group of silver birches.

Growing roses up into the branches of trees has become quite fashionable over recent years, so partnerships such as these are by no means unique; one combination that I have never seen anywhere else is a six-metre albizia supporting a substantial

SPECIES ROSE

ROSA MOSCHATA

MYSTERY SURROUNDS the origin of many of our roses, no more so than in the case of *Rosa moschata* – its place of birth being variously ascribed to North Africa, Spain and Western Asia. It is said to have first come to England in the reign of Elizabeth I, but this, too, is uncertain. Not only are its origins puzzling, but until Graham Thomas discovered a plant growing at Myddleton House, Enfield, Essex, in 1963, its true identity had also been something of a conundrum. It had been confused, from time to time, with several other species, but most of all with *R. brunonii*.

As a garden plant, *R. moschata* is very useful. It will attain a height of twelve to fifteen feet in good soils. Its foliage is soft to touch, greenish-grey in colour and profuse, on almost thornless, upright-growing stems. It is probably at its best when grown on a warm wall rather than on a trellis or archway, for there has to be some doubt about its hardiness in colder climates. Its flowers, which are fragrant, single and almost pure white, have creamy-yellow stamens and are produced on large, well-spaced, branching heads from August onwards. Over the centuries it has played a significant part in the parentage of several roses, most importantly, perhaps, the whole group of Noisettes.

The masses of white-centred deep-pink flowers of the little-seen rambler 'Maria Lisa' are always a joy to behold when discovered. Here at 28 Faubourg d'Orléans they make a striking display in front of an old garden shed, itself covered in rambler 'Albéric Barbier'.

plant of 'Albertine'. Albizias are not hardy in Britain and I was surprised to find one looking so happy not far south of Paris, but this is a sheltered garden and clearly has its own microclimate. There is no shortage of seats in this garden, or tables for that matter – tables on which to set glasses transiently filled with good French wine.

So far I have mentioned only climbers and ramblers; indeed, it is tempting to write on and on about them, but this would do this garden an injustice for whenever there is a space, it is filled with a shrub or species rose.

I was impressed by the health and vigour of the roses in André's garden and struck by the superb shape of one plant of *Rosa roxburghii* 'Plena' – achieved, I suspect, by regular pruning each year. Three other species are also conspicuously well grown: the dense and thorny *R. omeiensis pteracantha*, some two and a half metres high, the seldom-seen Swamp Rose, *R. palustris*, with its healthy dark green foliage, and a fine plant of *R. carolina* doing extremely well in the dense shade of a group of silver birches. Of all the roses in this garden, an excellent specimen of the almost evergreen hybrid of *R. multibracteata*, 'Cerise Bouquet', stands out for me. Here its head is allowed, as it should be, to grow into a wide, dense shrub.

Although very British in origin, Hybrid Musks are universal. André has planted a wide selection of them here – 'Felicia' and 'Buff Beauty' inevitably, and a couple of less common ones in 'Nur Mahal', a semi-double red that ought to be more popular, and the soft pinkish-white 'Kathleen', which was a pleasure to find.

Highlighting André's wide-ranging taste are two fairly modern roses from the North American continent, the glowing pink 'Prairie Dawn' from Canada and 'Golden Wings', a continuous-flowering shrub rose from the United States, a very hardy hybrid of *R. pimpinellifolia*. Several shrubs other than roses also grow happily in André's garden, as do perennials, but these come into their own later when the roses have quietened down from their frenzy in high summer.

I have discussed only remontants so far, but the many summer-only roses include many of the old French Damasks, Gallicas and Centifolias – for example, the white 'Mme Hardy' rubbing shoulders with the beautiful deep purple 'Charles de Mills', the sumptuous bright pink 'Chapeau de Napoléon' cohabiting easily with the much simpler, very lovely bright pink single 'Complicata' and, making up the threesome, a lovely specimen of the very ancient Apothecary Rose (*R. gallica officinalis*). Another ancient rose thriving here is the autumn-flowering species *R. moschata*. I was not surprised to find this progenitor of many roses, including all the Noisettes, in the Eve collection.

André Eve has no idea how many roses he has in his garden. If numbers were important to him, he would probably have taken up growing vegetables like his father. Anyway, such is their density that they are impossible to count. André plans to retire from full-time management of the nursery shortly, to become a consultant and to spend more time just living with and enjoying his roses.

*T*his grassed walk is one of the few open spaces among the roses in André Eve's garden behind his house in Pithiviers, which he started planting up in 1980. A visit to this garden is a rose experience to be savoured.

187

The many petalled – and richly fragrant – flowers of the old Hybrid Perpetual 'Souvenir d'Alphonse Lavallée' combine favourably with the soft blue of delphiniums here.

This garden must be seen to be believed. It is open in June and July. Another garden being created around the offices of Les Roses Anciennes de André Eve, Pithiviers-le-Vieil, will be worth a visit in rose seasons of the future.

GALLICA ROSE

'COMPLICATA'

No ONE knows from whence this rose came. It is usually listed as a Gallica, but both its growth habit and its flowers indicate that it clearly has the genes of other species in its make-up – *Rosa macrantha* in particular. I have also seen *R. canina* put forward as a possible progenitor. It is certainly too vigorous to be wholly Gallica, attaining a height, given support, of up to twelve to fifteen feet, especially if allowed to grow to its heart's content. I prefer it as a shrub, with an occasional pruning to keep it in shape, when it can be quite spectacular in early June each year.

Its flowers are large (four inches across) and single; their clear, almost shocking pink pales to soft pink in the centre, which then gives way to bright yellow stamens. They are sweetly scented and produced very freely all along long, arching branches. Foliage is crisp, profuse and mid- to dark green. The plant is not over-thorny and very healthy, tolerating even the poorest of soils. It makes a good informal hedge and, because of its tolerance of shade, will also do well as a woodland plant, looking especially effective in groups of five or more.

EGLINGHAM HALL
EGLINGHAM,
NORTHUMBERLAND, ENGLAND

THE PRETTY VILLAGE OF EGLINGHAM SITS IN ISOLATION about ten miles off the Great North Road, twenty or so miles from Alnwick, in hill-farming Northumbrian countryside.

The Hall is located on the edge of the village, hidden from the road by a stand of mature trees – mostly oak and ash, with a yew here and there to add to its density. The main drive to the house sweeps around through these trees, which were evidently planted as a shelter from the cold north, for the southern aspect of the house looks out on open spacious lawns, undulating pastures and distant hills. Immediately in front of the house and interrupting the view to the south-east is one of the largest and most glorious wych elms I have ever seen.

Part of the house and farm have been on this site at least since the sixteenth century, and there is documentary evidence that Oliver Cromwell stayed here during the Civil War. In 1704 the house was considerably enlarged using a local stone which has mellowed with time to a warm grey colour. Although an impressive, sizeable country house, Eglingham Hall is the hub of a working farm of about 200 acres of grazing for sheep and cattle. The present owner, April Potts, has been here for nearly twenty years, having taken over the family farm from her mother, Juliet Bewicke; the Bewicke family has owned this little piece of the North of England since the turn of the century, and it was her grandmother who laid the foundations for the gardens as they are today. Previously April grew her roses in North Wales and when she moved back to her old home she brought with her quite a few of her favourites to add to those already here.

April is very much a 'hands-on' person with a love for gardening. It soon became clear that she would not be able to maintain the formal gardens in quite the well-manicured fashion of former days – farming, especially sheep and cattle, being a full-time occupation – so she set about turning this formality into a fairly relaxed style of garden without altering the structural layout. Her philosophy is, 'If you do it

*E*glingham Hall is here seen from the vantage point of the Victorian wrought-iron gate at the back of the terraced rose garden. Oliver Cromwell once stayed in the hall during one of his visits to Northumberland.

HYBRID RUGOSA

'ROSERAIE DE L'HAY'

Raised in France in 1901, this is perhaps the most famous of all the Rugosa roses, and deservedly so, for it is capable of a wide range of uses in all sorts of different gardens. It is most often seen as a specimen shrub, developing into a dense bush up to twelve feet high and eight feet wide without too much attention – just light pruning each year to keep it tidy. Its other common use is as a hedge, when, again, it knits into a dense, impenetrable barrier, particularly effective as a boundary hedge. Mix it with others of its type, such as 'Blanc Double de Coubert' and 'Scabrosa', to make a decorative partition within the garden.

All the Rugosas are healthy and therefore ideal subjects for gardens such as Eglingham where there is no time for the finer points of rose husbandry such as spraying. All Rugosas, too, are scented and although some may have a stronger scent than 'Roseraie de l'Hay', none has such an original one, for its flowers have the distinct aroma of cloves. Unlike *Rosa rugosa* and some of its hybrids which set large hips, this variety is sterile and seldom, if ever, produces any fruit. This is a disappointment to some gardeners, but to me the sheer quantity of crimson-purple double flowers, opening from long, pointed buds, is enough.

yourself without gardeners, it is easier to let it "happen".' The only concessions she makes to regularity are the paths that intersect the various borders and terraces. As a young girl, April spent a lot of time with an old gardener employed by the family while he worked; this Mr Brown had a saying which has stuck in her mind: 'The paths make the garden and the edges make the paths.'

The family believe that Gertrude Jekyll, who had family connections in Northumberland, may have advised April's grandmother on the initial layout. Little evidence for this remains today; while Jekyll might have planted roses, she would have used them differently. Besides the large numbers of roses, other plants figure fairly prominently in this garden – herbs, perennials and low-growing shrubs forming the ground cover necessary to keep weeds to a minimum, especially the dreaded ground elder which always seems to thrive in old garden soils such as this.

The part of the garden now devoted to roses covers approximately three-quarters of an acre and slopes naturally upwards to the west from the house. When originally laid out, the half farthest away was terraced into three tiers, each held in place by drystone walls which harbour, by accident or design, an assortment of easy-going rockery-type plants. Especially prevalent on the highest and driest of the three walls are ferns in variety. The boundary at the back of this part of the garden is a tall, ancient stone wall partly covered with climbing plants.

Access from the house end of the garden to the top tier of the terrace is possible by paths on either side overhung with shrubs and roses, but the most tempting route climbs a series of stone steps leading upwards through the middle of the garden to a wrought iron gate in the wall which, in turn, leads to a vegetable garden. It is tempting because you have to squeeze through a profusion of dense shrub roses encroaching on and over these steps, terrace by terrace, as you ascend.

I have yet to mention a rose by name! I should perhaps tell you that I visited this garden in mid-July and, even then, the shrub roses had not reached their peak; the harsher climate of the north makes them approximately two weeks later than I am used to farther south. Even the early-flowering varieties such as *Rosa pimpinellifolia* and its hybrids were only just going over. It was a lovely soft pink, double form of Scotch Rose that I came upon first beside the front door – which is on the east side and shaded from the sun by a tall yew hedge – proving how useful such roses are in difficult situations. Here they are clipped annually to form dense, tidy mounds beside the wall. Victorian catalogues listed large numbers of these accommodating little roses in an assortment of colours. Most of them are now lost, but from time to time rarities crop up here and there, in almost all cases impossible to name.

Emerging from above assorted shrubs along the south wall of the house is an extremely good example of the coppery-orange Noisette climber 'Alister Stella Gray'. A little farther, on the sixteenth-century part of the house, is a pink single climber or shrub rose I have seen in the distant past but have yet to identify.

To the left of the main rose garden, a series of rustic arches supports some interesting climbers and ramblers. Striking among these is a fine example of 'Paul's Himalayan Musk'. The Wichuraiana types were not yet in flower at the time of my visit, but I recognized good examples of 'American Pillar' and 'Dorothy Perkins'. The Hybrid Multifloras were, however, in bloom and there was a particularly fine specimen of the soft pink scented 'Blush Rambler'.

April is interested in sheepdog trials as well as gardening and farming and she and her dogs more than hold their own in this highly competitive sport. She is also an

ardent fan of Elvis Presley, to whose memory a little part of her garden is dedicated. Its centrepiece is a stone urn surrounded by yet more of the double pink Scotch Roses, the charming and very floriferous clear pink Moss 'James Mitchell' and the Hybrid Musk 'Felicia'. By mistake 'William Lobb', a deep greyish-purple Moss, was planted next to this rose and they are growing in close embrace – proving, I think, that it is difficult to get it wrong when blending the older varieties.

Here and there among the roses and alongside the paths in the lower part of the garden you find remnants of the old formal layout in the form of box hedging and topiary birds sculptured on top of ancient yew hedges. Behind one section of box edging is a large bed of 'Rosa Mundi', the famous striped Gallica – its charm enhanced here by the fact that several plants have reverted back to the clear deep pinkish-red of its parent, *Rosa gallica officinalis*. 'Rosa Mundi' appears randomly elsewhere throughout the gardens. Another Gallica in evidence in this area is April's favourite rose of all, the delicious, beautifully shaped and superbly scented 'Empress Josephine' (*R. × francofurtana*).

Moss roses are obvious favourites, judging by the number to be found scattered throughout the garden. There are several more examples of those varieties already mentioned, together with a fine specimen of the Red Moss, 'Henri Martin'. Although Moss roses flower just once each year, they are excellent value; besides the fragrant flowers, the moss on the stems and receptacles is also often scented.

April Potts believes in letting the garden 'happen'. The only concession to regularity is her belief in a saying that she learned from an old gardener when she was a child: 'The paths make the garden, and the edges make the paths.' The roses here are Rugosa 'Roseraie de l'Hay'.

*L*ots *of ferns flourish alongside the old roses on the terraces of this lovely garden. The pink rose here behind 'Roseraie de l'Hay' is the continuous-flowering 'Felicia', but April Potts's real preference is for the old non-remontant varieties* (facing page)*.

Several vantage points allow this rose garden to be seen as a whole. When I saw it in July the balance of differing shades of green foliage to coloured plants and flowering roses seemed somehow to be just right. It is refreshing to find someone who loves, as April does, summer-flowering varieties, for we are now in an age where continuity of flower, irrespective of beauty of form, appears to be the main criterion for choosing roses. Not that April's preference for the non-repeats has stifled her choice of varieties, for quite a few twice-blooming and continuous-flowering shrub roses are strategically placed throughout the grounds. The most obvious when I was there were the stalwart Rugosa 'Roseraie de l'Hay', with its rich crimson-purple clove-scented flowers and abundant healthy green foliage, and the many-petalled, deep pink, heavily perfumed Hybrid Perpetual 'Baronne Prévost' planted by grandmother many years earlier. Two others that caught my attention were another Hybrid Perpetual, the lovely purple, fully double 'Reine des Violettes', and the showy 'Mme Isaac Pereire' with its large, blowzy, heavily fragrant flowers of deep mauvy-pink. Two more important roses must be mentioned. The almost thornless Alba 'Mme Legras de St Germain' is one of the few whites, while several plants of 'Blush Damask' have been allowed to grow into large shrubby mounds producing masses of medium-sized, fully double, scented blush-pink flowers in high summer.

Those who believe in weed-free, orderly gardening would not feel at home at Eglingham Hall. Very little pruning is done. If any rose shows signs of needing spraying too often, it is shown the door, and all are sustained by nature's pure fertilizer – good old well-rotted farmyard muck.

Hill farming these days calls for long hours of hard work, as I discovered when I tried my hand at rounding up the sheep with April, and running the business side is no sinecure, either. I feel privileged to have been allowed a glimpse of this garden, for it is not open to the public; in fact, it is essentially private. It provides for its gardener, in her own words, 'My own world – my own space.'

GALLICA ROSE

'EMPRESS JOSEPHINE'

*T*HE ORIGIN of this lovely Gallica is not known. It is actually a hybrid between *Rosa gallica* (or, more likely, a variety of Gallica) and *R. pendulina*. It was at first grown and distributed as *R. × francofurtana*, so that name strictly has precedence, and only later named 'Empress Josephine' in her memory. A Redouté print labelled *R. turbinata* clearly depicts this rose, so it may well have been known and grown by Josephine.

Gallicas were undoubtedly known to the Romans and Greeks in Classical times and several varieties were around during the Middle Ages, but it was not until the middle of the seventeenth century – when the Dutch started to grow seedlings from naturally pollinated

seeds – that they really took off as a family. During the succeeding two centuries or so, thousands were developed. French nurserymen in the early 1800s listed over 1,200 and the empress herself had some 167 in her collection at Malmaison at the time of her divorce from Napoleon in 1809.

As a rose, 'Empress Josephine' is exquisite in form and delightful in habit. It is fragrant and very free-flowering. A particularly endearing feature is its softly textured greyish-green foliage. It is almost thornless and grows to no more than a graceful four feet or so in good soil. Its only fault is that it very much dislikes wet weather, reacting by failing to open up its flowers. This is April Potts' favourite rose.

BEHIND THE POND
EAST HAMPTON, LONG ISLAND, NEW YORK, USA

'I HAVE ALWAYS WANTED TO BE A LANDSCAPER,' CONFIDED Lee Radziwill as we walked together around her seven-acre garden beside the Atlantic ocean. It is plain that she already is one: her garden is full of interesting and unusual features – as well as lots of roses and other genera. Gardening is 'a life-long passion' she has shared over the past six years with her husband, film producer Herbert Ross, and together they have gradually fashioned this magnificent setting into a delightful environment in which to relax, with lots of greenery, lots of shapes and plenty of colour. This is quite an achievement in the harsh climate of Long Island with its extremes of heat and cold, where the best plans are sometimes rudely disrupted by weather. Once Lee Radziwill lived and gardened in the English Cotswolds and there she learned much about plants and their foibles. 'While many of the same plants will grow here too,' she says, 'they often behave very differently and so present me with quite a challenge.'

The generously proportioned house stands on the highest point, roughly in the centre of the site, with gradual slopes to the east down across sprawling expanses of lawn scattered with trees. Prominent among the evergreens are some especially elegant specimens of *Cryptomeria japonica* grown as tall standards, with their trunks bare. On the other side the land falls gradually away to the dunes by the sea, some 200 yards away.

You enter the estate by a long drive which curves southwards around the edge of the garden and then sweeps up towards the house. First impressions are of spaciousness and maturity, the spaciousness from the well-tended lawns; the maturity, at least initially, from an avenue of identical cone-shaped clipped beech trees, six on either side, each one twenty feet or more high and at least ten feet wide, all dense with foliage almost to the ground. Mature they may be, but they were actually planted here less than two years ago – remarkable plantsmanship and most effective landscaping.

The Hybrid Rugosa 'Red Grootendorst' growing happily close to the ocean is one of several Rugosas to be found among the many roses in Lee Radziwill's and Herbert Ross's garden at East Hampton.

Gardening has been a life-long passion for Lee Radziwill. Here the white Polyantha rose 'Clotilde Soupert' and the more modern procumbent rose 'Swany' grow alongside the swimming pool in her spacious seaside garden (facing page).

BOURBON ROSE

'SOUVENIR DE LA MALMAISON'

I KNOW SEVERAL people who consider this Bourbon rose one of the finest of its type ever produced. If it were a little better inclined to tolerate wet weather, I too would place it higher up on my list of favourites. In the bud stage there is no clue to the beauty of the flower which is about to unfold. It has many petals, each perfectly overlaid on the other to form a flat, sometimes quartered, flower about four inches across, in a most beautiful face-powder-pink. Deliciously scented, they are produced in clusters of three to five.

It was named after the château where the Empress Josephine grew her famous rose collection, but it is doubtful if she ever set eyes on this rose, although it was probably raised earlier than its designated date of 1843.

It reaches a height of about three feet in good soils and will usually grow a little wider than tall. Slightly inclined to mildew, it enjoys being mollycoddled. Its foliage is greyish-green and it has few thorns on similar-coloured wood. There is an excellent climbing form dating back to 1893. 'Souvenir de la Malmaison' does particularly well under glass in Britain and those who live in warmer climates should never be without it somewhere in their garden.

The car park to the south of the house is cleverly concealed from all directions with plantings of mixed shrubs, including roses, and small trees. Rugosas do well in these harsher climates, so it was no surprise that the first roses I came upon were several of these, growing at the entrance to a steep pathway, the slope broken intermittently with steps, which leads down past a swimming pool towards the shore. Although there are other Rugosas in this area, three varieties in particular stand out – 'Blanc Double de Coubert', the not so well-known but equally floriferous 'Sir Thomas Lipton', also white, and the red 'F.J. Grootendorst', which produces delightfully fimbriated little double flowers rather like Dianthus in dense clusters all over the bushes from June to November. This also has pink and white forms. What the 'Grootendorst' roses lack in finesse they amply make up for in durability.

As the pathway zigzags on down towards the sea, it becomes apparent that the land here has been terraced, partly as a defence against extra-high tides, but also to enable the gardens to extend farther down the slope.

Several roses are to be found at the various levels, the first a substantial group of the delightful little white Polyantha 'Clotilde Soupert', the second the much more modern but equally pleasing 'White Meidiland', serving as an excellent ground coverer, and the third the lovely large-flowered Polyantha 'Gruss an Aachen', a peachy-cream variety doing itself great credit in this difficult, if sheltered, situation. Nearer to the sea, on the dunes themselves, the garden gives way to nature's own

flora such as the white-flowered beach plum and hundreds of wild blue lupins. Also scattered here and there and almost thriving, despite the famished sand, are many plants of the common pink Rugosa. One particular plant forming a wide bushy mound stands out in perfect symmetry against the background of blue ocean when seen as part of the wider view from the terrace.

The roomy, modern house is very much an extension of the garden, handsome plants in stylish pots everywhere and espalier-trained pear trees on the south wall of the semi-enclosed patio adding to the prevailing atmosphere of unpretentious quiet opulence. On the south side of the patio a conservatory hosts a unique monoculture of passion flowers (*Passiflora caerulea*), twelve in all, growing in large special Lee-Radziwill-designed dark green wooden planters with their vines trained on tall fretted pyramids topped with finials. Quite apart from the relaxing nature of this study in green, grey and white, I found their shadows and reflections on the polished marble floors hauntingly beautiful. Passion flowers are one of Lee Radziwill's favourite flowers, bringing to mind, she said, visions of the semi-precious stones peridot and amethyst quivering and sparkling as they would have done when set in eighteenth-century costume jewellery.

Serving to accentuate the importance of shapes and forms in the landscape of this garden are the clipped box and yew trees growing all along the narrow terrace which makes up the west side of the house. Some are in the ground, others in large

Just visible through the limbs of a tree is the Rose Garden. It is dense with roses of all sorts and surrounded by a well-groomed yew hedge of a height that enables the roses to be seen from without as well as from within.

The modern climbing rose 'Alchymist' climbs up into an established tree in Behind the Pond's garden; an unusual role for this variety but one with which it can easily cope (facing page).

pots, none pretentious, none elaborate, all no more than waist high, but, as a feature, most effective.

The Rose Garden slopes down on the southern side of the large eastern lawn. Except for the entrance at the top end, it is completely surrounded by a well-trimmed, wide yew hedge about three feet high, to enable the roses to be seen from without as well as from within. Its pleasingly simple design has two paths running the entire length making three clearly defined beds, each crammed full of shrub roses. At intervals along the centre of each of the two outer beds are pillars support-ing a climbing or rambling rose. Except that pastel shades predominate, there is no particular colour theme. Among the climbers and ramblers are several white varieties, from the modern climbing 'Iceberg' which flowers so freely all summer through to the much older but equally free-flowering climbing Tea rose 'Sombreuil'. The hybrid Setigera 'Long John Silver', a beautiful rose with lovely light green foliage, is also very hardy, doing well on Long Island. So does the vigorous 'Seagull'; it flowers only once each summer, but produces an excellent crop of hips in autumn.

Both old and newer varieties of shrub roses grow together in all three borders, with the emphasis very much on a long flowering season. Two of the older varieties in evidence are the pure white Damask 'Mme Hardy' and 'Souvenir de la Malmaison', both highly scented and arguably among the world's most beautiful roses. Of the more recently introduced roses, two are conspicuous, both pink – the once-flowering but ever-lovely 'Constance Spry' and the continuous-flowering, shapely 'Heritage'. Apart from the Floribunda 'Iceberg', which is used to maximize the flowering season, several Hybrid Musks are also doing sterling service, in particular the bright pink 'Felicia' and the soft blush-white 'Penelope'.

Although I encounter the same varieties in many gardens, I never cease to be surprised at how many different ways there are of growing them. Lee Radziwill grows them massed together as I have seen nowhere else. It is most effective, contrasting strongly with the open landscape of the rest of this delectable garden.

HYBRID SETIGERA

'LONG JOHN SILVER'

AMERICAN THROUGH and through, this rose was bred by Horvath in 1934 during a period when, in search of hardiness and health, he used the American native species *Rosa setigera* and the Hybrid Tea 'Sunburst' to produce this distinctive climber with fully double, old-fashioned-looking, scented flowers of pure white. Another rose raised by this breeder is a yellow called 'Jean Lafitte', which is apparently very good.

Quite apart from its beautiful flowers, 'Long John Silver's' other attributes include remontancy and lovely bright green foliage. It is vigorous, not over-thorny and seems not to be

bothered by any diseases. It is probably best grown on a structure such as a pergola, arch or tripod, for its long, thick, arching branches are easily trained in all directions.

Earlier breeders also worked successfully with *R. setigera*. In the USA Feast produced in the mid-nineteenth century 'Baltimore Belle' and 'Queen of the Prairie', and at the same time in Hungary Geschwind bred the lovely 'Erinnerung an Brod'. I believe there is great scope for some ambitious young hybridizer to explore the possibilities of crossing *R. setigera* with some of our modern hybrids.

PLUMPTON PLACE
LEWES, EAST SUSSEX, ENGLAND

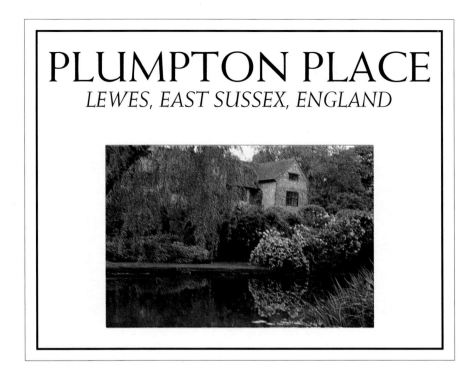

I FIRST MET GERD PERKINS IN THE AUTUMN OF 1992. SHE HAD asked me to help her design her Secret Garden of Roses at Plumpton Place. From letters and telephone conversations, I knew that she was a warm person and a strong character. She knew exactly what she wanted by way of design; one letter said, 'I do not like formality, I do not like over-designed gardens and I am not a slave to fashion in any shape or form and that includes plants (I hate all that grey).' She was also precise about the atmosphere she wished to achieve: ' . . . a romantic rose garden, rustic, lots of scent, billowing, cascading, Edwardian – Gertrude Jekyll etc, etc.' My input would be very much on the technical side, helping her choose specific varieties.

I arrived at Plumpton just before dinner, rather later than planned, and assumed that I would not see the garden until the next day, but there was a most beautiful hunter's moon that night and Gerd invited me to walk around the garden with her after the other dinner guests had departed. I felt privileged in that hour or so to be allowed to share her passion for Plumpton Place and, in particular, her gardens. This beautiful property had been in her family's possession for only a few years, but she had already stamped her influence everywhere – mostly in the form of roses. She had achieved this in spite of spending less than four months of the year here for, being married to an American businessman, she spent much of her time in California. No doubt the ambience of the place that evening was enhanced for me by the moonlight, the reflections of the house and its landscape in the lakes that form a major part of the gardens and Gerd's endearing cultured Norwegian–American accent.

Plumpton Place is a small to medium, well-proportioned listed Tudor house sitting discreetly on the edge of the South Downs just north of the historic town of Lewes and about ten miles from Brighton. It was restored at the turn of the century by Lutyens and again sensitively renovated in the mid 1980s by Gerd and her husband Tom as their English home.

Plumpton Place, seen here across the moat, is a listed Tudor house restored at the turn of the century by Lutyens. The present gardens are the creation of the late Gerd Perkins. On the banks of the moat are a mixture of ramblers and scramblers including 'Francis E. Lester', 'Veilchenblau' and 'Kiftsgate'.

'*Francis E. Lester*', *closest to the camera,* '*Veilchenblau*' *and* '*Kiftsgate*' *tumble towards the moat at Plumpton Place, Sussex. Later in the year the flowers will be replaced by a mass of tiny orange hips.*

The house stands on an island formed on one side by a narrow moat fed by springs high up in the downs and on the other by a sizeable lake divided by a weir to take into account the natural fall of the land. In all Plumpton consists of about sixty-five acres.

To reach the gardens on the island around the house you walk through a gatehouse into a small courtyard garden consisting of two small, well-kept lawns bordered by an array of brightly coloured plants. This is in no way strident, but might be best described as a 'flame' garden, for there is not a pastel shade in sight. Two or three cut-leaved acers and one or two berberis stand out as shrubs among densely planted lower-growing herbaceous plants such as potentilla, the brighter hostas and red hot pokers (*Kniphofia*), all cleverly combined to form the basis of these borders. On the walls are such plants as the ornamental vine, *Vitis* 'Brant' and Virginia creeper (*Parthenocissus quinquefolia*). Not many roses are in evidence here, few in this colour range appealing to Gerd. However, several plants of *Rosa chinensis* 'Mutabilis' are used to effect. This rose can never decide whether it is a bush or a climber; here its indecisiveness fulfils the role of both border plant and wall coverer. Its colour is variable from soft peachy-pink to coppery-red, often with all colours together in the same large cluster of five-petalled flowers.

From this colourful little entrance garden you will move across a long, narrow wooden bridge high above the steeply banked moat to a much quieter, more

expansive area. On both sides numerous varieties of rambler and scrambler roses have been planted into the banks of the moat. Two in particular stand out – 'Francis E. Lester' with masses of white-flushed-pink single flowers and *R. helenae* with large trusses of small creamy-white scented flowers. Both of these roses are always well foliated and give good value in the autumn with coloured foliage and hips.

Planted in the lawns on either side of the short drive leading to the front door are some superb examples of mop-headed standard Portugal laurels (*Prunus lusitanica*). Scattered about on the paved area in front of the house is a variety of plants growing and thriving in terracotta pots, including a few roses. I am continually surprised at how few roses I find growing in containers. Roses make good pot plants and I believe more should be grown in this way. All that is necessary is a good soil-based compost – say three parts soil, two parts peat or coconut fibre and one part gritty sand, good drainage in the bottom of the container and a good balanced base fertilizer high in potash. The container should hold more than a gallon or so of soil. The variety doing well in a container at Plumpton is the Hybrid Musk 'Ballerina' with its masses of small pink single flowers, one of the most free-flowering of all the Hybrid Musks.

The walls at the front of the house face west and are adorned with a wide variety of climbing plants such as clematis and many roses, notably the ubiquitous 'New Dawn' showing off to effect. On either side of the front door is planted a wonderful specimen of *Clerodendrum bungei*.

The walls of Plumpton Place are adorned with a wide variety of climbing plants. Here clematis in variety provide the background to 'Kathleen Ferrier' and the softer pink 'Felicia'.

201

'Macrantha Raubritter' can always be relied upon to give a good display and several are to be found in the gardens at Plumpton Place. Here it 'flops' over a wall into the plumes of goat's beard (Aruncus dioicus) (facing page).

Around to the northern side of the house a terrace furnished with rustic tables and seating overlooks the lake. Planted here, most effectively, are two different Rugosa hybrids. The sometimes temperamental 'Mrs Anthony Waterer', a deep red, is doing well in this position, but a shapely example of the purple 'Hansa' is doing even better. They were placed here deliberately for the strength and quality of their fragrance. From this point balustrading runs back from the terrace high above the moat and returns towards the bridge. In front of this Gerd planted a three-foot-wide border with mixed old-fashioned roses on the north side and Hybrid Musks along the west side, an open area with ample sun. Outstanding among the Old Roses is the soft pink Centifolia 'Fantin-Latour', strategically placed to waft its perfume as you pass it on your way to the terrace. Eye-catching among the Hybrid Musks is 'Felicia', a healthy, reliable, tidy-growing variety. Judicious pruning contains the Old Roses to well below eye-level to maintain the views.

Back across the bridge, the walk through the dappled shade of a mixture of interesting small trees is rewarded by the sight of a magnificent specimen of the scented 'Sanders' White' growing along the length of the west wall of an ancient Sussex barn. A Wichuraiana rambler, 'Sanders' White' is flexible and easy to train.

Walk from this barn in a southerly direction, and the house comes back into view through young trees almost as a backdrop to hanging gardens across the water: all along the terrace, unseen from above, are planted shrubs and roses. The most noticeable is 'Macrantha Raubritter', tumbling almost to the moat. 'Raubritter' is naturally procumbent, producing masses of cupped, bright clear pink, scented flowers in mid-summer. At either end of the hanging gardens is a large specimen of weeping willow, each almost as tall as the house, their branches drooping gracefully as only weeping willows can practically into the water. From here the grounds naturally slope to the east from the house and, to accommodate the differing levels, the lake is split by a weir. The noise from the tumbling water adds a busyness to this open area of the grounds. Assorted waterfowl swim around, constantly rippling the reflections of the house and gardens with their wake.

WHEN SEEN at its best, this rose will convince even the most ardent rejectors of non-remontant roses that it should be growing in their gardens, for it has to be one of the most beautiful of shrubs.

The exquisite many-petalled form of its blush-pink flowers is pure Centifolia-like, but in other respects this rose is not easy to classify. Its leaves are not as coarse as those of most Centifolias; their colour is more grey-green, and the whole plant is not as thorny.

Its origins are a mystery. There appears to be no reference to a rose introduced especially for the French

CENTIFOLIA ROSE

'FANTIN-LATOUR'

artist whose name it bears. My belief is that it acquired its name after Fantin-Latour's death because it resembles roses painted by him. I have heard one suggestion that it was once an unnamed understock, but I cannot agree; it is far too refined and aristocratic for such a role. In any case, it does not root easily enough from cuttings to be a cost-effective understock.

As a garden rose it is simplicity itself to grow. Just find a spot where it can do its own thing and let it get on with it, no matter what the soil type. Dead-heading each year will suffice for pruning. If planted against a wall, it will attain a height of at least ten feet.

HYBRID MUSK

'FELICIA'

Although a few Hybrid Musks were introduced in the 1930s by a man named Bentall, most were raised between 1913 and 1928 by the Revd Joseph Pemberton, for whom Bentall worked as a gardener. 'Felicia', one of his last introductions and one of his best, dates from 1928. All the Hybrid Musks were way ahead of their time when introduced; in fact, they were at first classified as Hybrid Teas. 'Felicia' is scented and its shapely, fully double blooms are a mixture of rich pink and salmon. They are produced almost continuously from mid-June to October on a shrubby, relatively thornless, well-foliated plant with leathery greyish-green leaves.

'Pemberton's Musks', as they were called in his day, are mostly well disposed to good health and 'Felicia' is no exception. It grows in a fairly tidy fashion and if regularly dead-headed each summer and pruned fairly hard each spring makes an excellent dense specimen shrub to about three and a half feet. It is one of the best of its type for hedging and at Plumpton performs this role most effectively. When budded on to a stem, 'Felicia' becomes a very good standard rose. Because it seems to last well in water, it is a useful rose to have here and there in the garden for cutting for the house.

Clearly visible from the house, at the opposite end of the lake, is a cottage converted from an old mill. Beside it the water runs quickly through a sluice to a small pool and from thence into a stream to meander on through Sussex. This water feature has been cleverly landscaped with roses. In particular, two shapely plants of *Rosa helenae* grow on either side of the mill race over which you pass, via stepping stones placed just below water level, into the gardens of the cottage. Despite their distance from the main house and their diminutive size, the mill house gardens have not escaped the attentions of Gerd Perkins' landscaping skills. Here again, among lavender and other scented plants, roses dominate. In fact, at the rear of the cottage, an L-shaped border consists entirely of densely planted mixed shrub roses including Mosses, Gallicas, Centifolias, Hybrid Musks and some Austin roses. Purist landscapers, myself included perhaps, would never have mixed such a wide variety of types in such a relatively small space. Only a non-English mind could have conceived this and made it work as it has.

Soon after acquiring the house, Gerd planted beech hedges in an oval shape in an open part of the grounds. By 1992 these had grown to above head height to create an enclosure of about a quarter of an acre in which to plant a Secret Rose Garden. The layout inside is simple – just four pairs of wide curved beds following the contours of the hedges, planted up with roses of pastel shades only, except for a centrepiece of the red hybrid Gallica 'Scharlachglut'. Between each pair of the curved beds on

either side, pergolas built of rustic timber support white and pale pink rambler roses. Down the centre of each of the outer and wider beds are six tripods, each about eight feet high and supporting climbers and ramblers. The narrower, inner beds have rustic pillars seven feet tall, again adorned with climbers and ramblers. The beds themselves are made up of both old-fashioned varieties and modern shrub roses. Among the more unusual roses used to provide height on the tripods are the white Setigera hybrid 'Long John Silver', a fascinating rose which, along with 'City of York', the other white used here, should be more widely grown. Among the roses in the beds are the ever-flowering little Victorian Polypompon 'White Pet' and the much more modern, free-flowering, medium-sized variety 'Jacqueline du Pré'. All the roses were planted in the spring of 1993 and by the summer of 1994 Gerd had made up her mind which ones she really liked from those I had selected for her.

During dinner at that first meeting two years earlier I had learned from her friends that Gerd was bravely fighting cancer. The last time I saw Plumpton Place and Gerd Perkins was in early July 1994. Invited there to assist in a garden walk with a local Greenfingers Club, my wife and I stayed overnight and got to know and admire this remarkable lady a little more. At the end of August we heard the sad news that she had passed away while back home in America. Her gardens live on and her husband Tom Perkins has allowed us to publish this piece as a celebration of her love of gardening and roses.

Rambling roses make ideal ground cover in semi-shade positions. Here purple 'Veilchenblau' and white 'Seagull' cohabit most agreeably in a shady spot in the woodland part of Plumpton Place.

Gerd Perkins commissioned a Secret Garden just before she died. It is full of her favourite roses, among them 'Astra Desmond', seen here, a medium-growing rambler used as a pillar rose (facing page).

INDEX

207

BIBLIOGRAPHY

The following books were referred to by the author in the course of this book.

American Rose Society, *Modern Roses 7*, 1969, *Modern Roses 9*, 1986
Austin, D., *The Heritage of Roses*, London 1988
Austin's Rose Catalogue, Wolverhampton 1995
Beales Rose Catalogue, Norwich 1995
Beales, A., *Old-Fashioned Roses*, London 1990
Beales, P., *Classic Roses*, London 1985
Beales, P., *Twentieth-century Roses*, London 1988
Beales, P., *Roses*, London 1992
Bean, W.J., *Trees and Shrubs Hardy in the British Isles*, London 1980
Bloom, Alan and Adrian, *Garden Plants*, London 1992
Dickerson, B.C., *The Old Rose Adviser*, USA 1992
Dobson, B., *Combined Rose List*, USA 1993

Druit, L. and M. Shoup, *Landscaping with Antique Roses*, USA 1992
Eve, André, *Rose Catalogue*, Paris 1995
Gibson, M., *Rose Gardens of England*, London 1988
Hilliers' Manual of Trees and Shrubs, Winchester 1990
Le Rougetel, H., *A Heritage of Roses*, London 1989
Notcutts' Book of Plants, Suffolk 1993
Russell, V., *Gardens of the Riviera*, London 1993
Scanniello S. and T. Bayard, *Roses of America*, New York 1990
Talbot, G., *Queen Elizabeth the Queen Mother*, London 1978
Thomas, G., *The Graham Stuart Thomas Rose Book*, London 1994
Also referred to were numerous pamphlets, leaflets and guidebooks about public gardens featured in this book.